W9-BWH-889

BANG!™

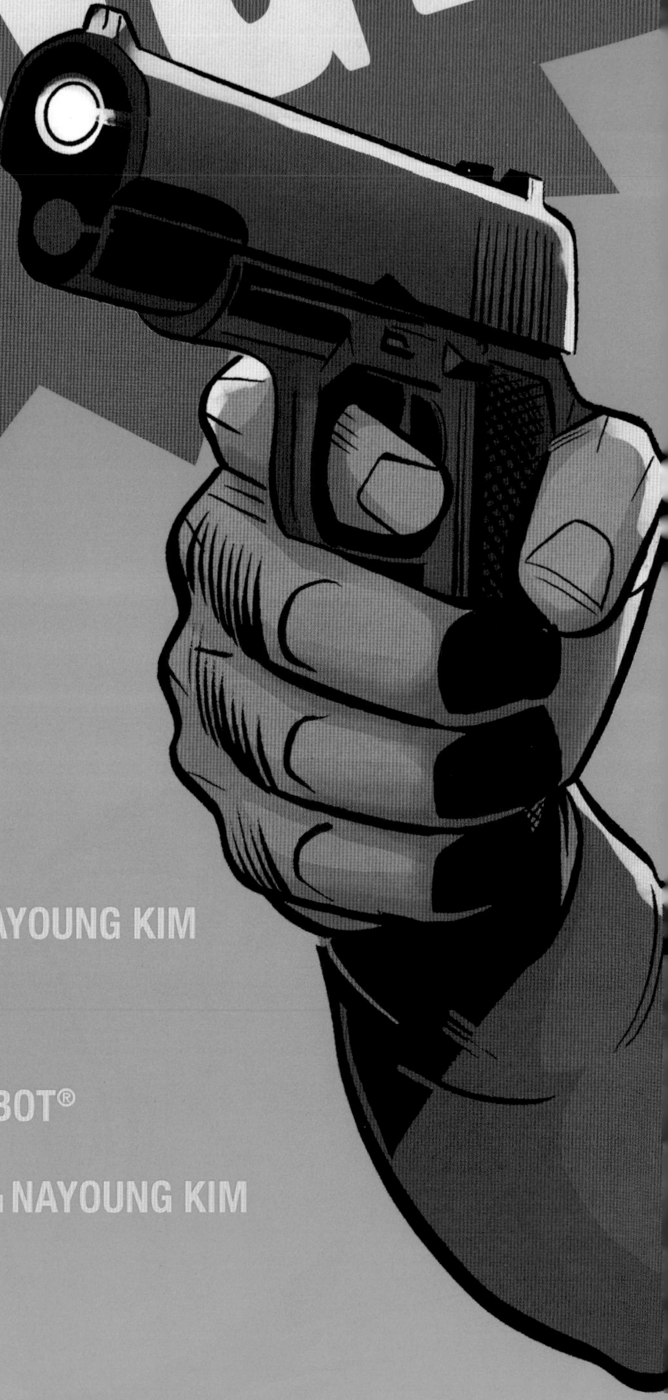

STORY BY

MATT KINDT

ART BY

WILFREDO TORRES

COLOR ART ISSUES #1–#3 BY

NAYOUNG KIM

COLOR ART ISSUE #4 BY

BILL CRABTREE WITH **NAYOUNG KIM**

COLOR ART ISSUE #5 BY

BILL CRABTREE

LETTERING BY

NATE PIEKOS OF **BLAMBOT®**

COVER ARTISTS

WILFREDO TORRES WITH **NAYOUNG KIM**

VARIANT COVERS BY

MATT KINDT

BANG! CREATED BY

MATT KINDT AND **WILFREDO TORRES**

DARK HORSE BOOKS

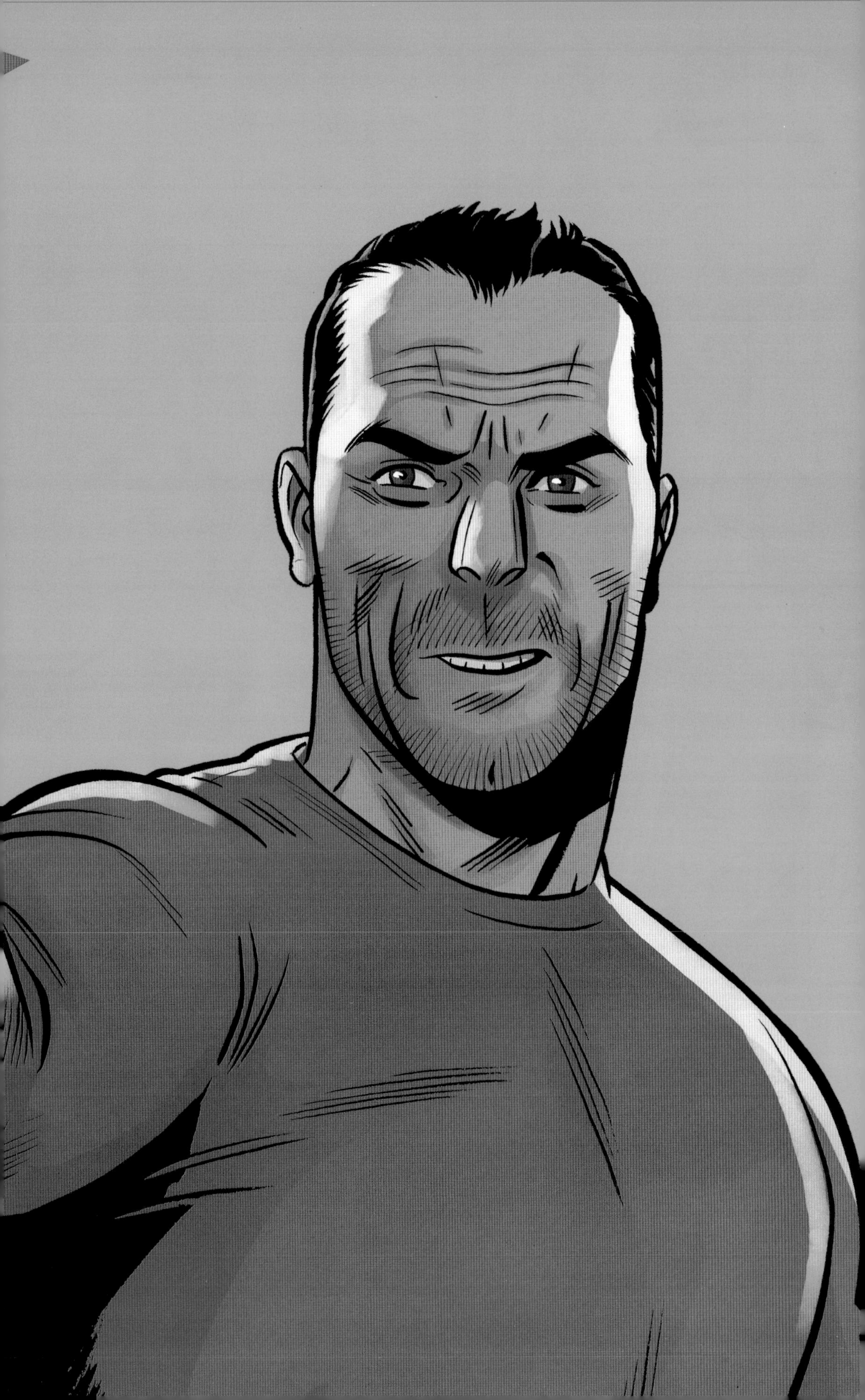

President and Publisher
MIKE RICHARDSON

Editor
DANIEL CHABON

Assistant Editor
CHUCK HOWITT

Designer
PATRICK SATTERFIELD

Digital Art Technician
ANN GRAY

Published by Dark Horse Books
A division of Dark Horse Comics LLC
10956 SE Main Street
Milwaukie, OR 97222

First edition: November 2020
Ebook ISBN: 978-1-50671-617-6
Trade paperback ISBN: 978-1-50671-616-9

10 9 8 7 6 5 4 3 2 1
Printed in China

Comic Shop Locator Service: comicshoplocator.com

BANG! Volume 1

BANG!™ © 2020 Matt Kindt and Wilfredo Torres. All rights reserved. Dark Horse Books® and the Dark Horse logo are registered trademarks of Dark Horse Comics LLC. All rights reserved. No portion of this publication may be reproduced or transmitted, in any form or by any means, without the express written permission of Dark Horse Comics LLC. Names, characters, places, and incidents featured in this publication either are the product of the author's imagination or are used fictitiously. Any resemblance to actual persons (living or dead), events, institutions, or locales, without satiric intent, is coincidental.

This volume collects BANG! #1–#5.

Library of Congress Cataloging-in-Publication Data

Names: Kindt, Matt, author. | Torres, Wilfredo (Comic book artist), artist.
   | Kim, Nayoung (Comic book artist), colourist. | Piekos, Nate, letterer.

Title: Bang! / story by Matt Kindt ; art by Wilfredo Torres ; color art by
   Nayoung Kim ; lettering by Nate Piekos of Blambot.
Description: Milwaukie, OR : Dark Horse Comics, 2020. | Summary: "Collects
   the complete Dark Horse Comics series BANG! #1-#5, along with all covers
   and bonus material"-- Provided by publisher.
Identifiers: LCCN 2020019761 (print) | LCCN 2020019762 (ebook) | ISBN
   9781506716169 (trade paperback) | ISBN 9781506716176 (ebook)
Subjects: LCSH: Comic books, strips, etc.
Classification: LCC PN6728.B268 K56 2020 (print) | LCC PN6728.B268
   (ebook) | DDC 741.5/973--dc23
LC record available at https://lccn.loc.gov/2020019761
LC ebook record available at https://lccn.loc.gov/2020019762

NEIL HANKERSON Executive Vice President TOM WEDDLE Chief Financial Officer RANDY STRADLEY Vice President of Publishing NICK McWHORTER Chief Business Development Officer DALE LaFOUNTAIN Chief Information Officer MATT PARKINSON Vice President of Marketing VANESSA TODD-HOLMES Vice President of Production and Scheduling MARK BERNARDI Vice President of Book Trade and Digital Sales KEN LIZZI General Counsel DAVE MARSHALL Editor in Chief DAVEY ESTRADA Editorial Director CHRIS WARNER Senior Books Editor CARY GRAZZINI Director of Specialty Projects LIA RIBACCHI Art Director MATT DRYER Director of Digital Art and Prepress MICHAEL GOMBOS Senior Director of Licensed Publications KARI YADRO Director of Custom Programs KARI TORSON Director of International Licensing SEAN BRICE Director of Trade Sales

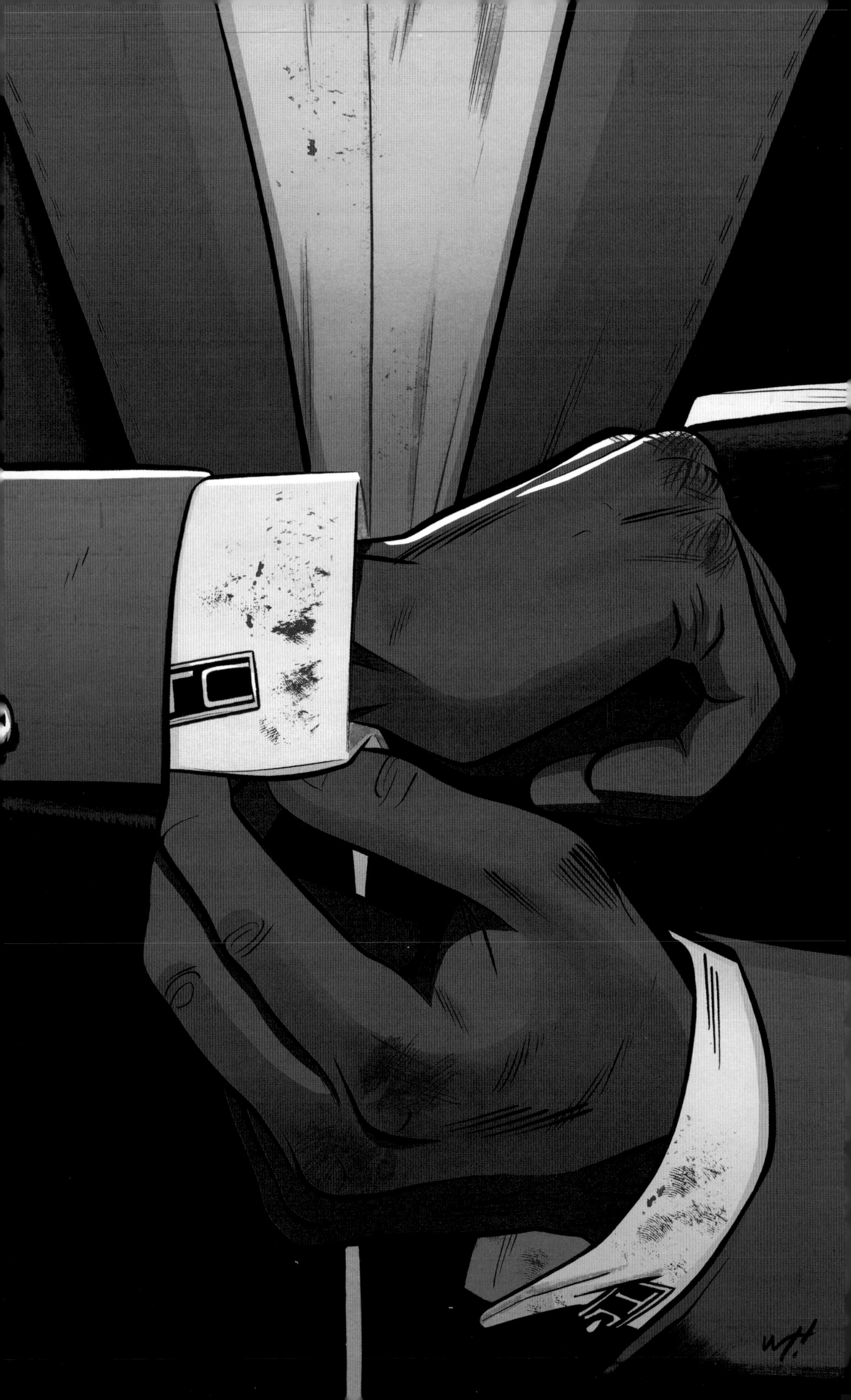

"You can't come with me, Fanny. It's against regulations."

Thomas Cord pulls her close to him even as his words push her away. The tropical humidity hangs dense in the air. The extra layer of moisture on Fanny's skin is slick in his hands as he squeezes her arms. Her blouse hangs loose over her tense, lithe body. He feels her ragged breath as her breasts press against his chest.

"I've come this far, Thomas Cord. I'm not going to let you leave me now. Not after all we've been through."

"It's the nature of my work, Fanny. I told you. I have a mission to accomplish. A mission bigger than you and I."

"If I didn't know better, I'd think you got close to me because you were bored," Fanny complains with an air of finality as she turns away from him.

"I could say the same thing, my dear," Cord replies. "What are the chances of a creature as beautiful as you being held captive out here in the jungles of Brazil?"

Fanny turns back to Cord, smiling again. "It's fate. You and I. These rebels kidnapped me weeks ago. They held me ransom. They treated me like a plaything. I can't imagine what would have happened if you hadn't destroyed their camp and rescued me."

Cord's eyes narrow, measuring Fanny as she saunters back toward him. "I don't believe in fate."

Fanny slides her hands under Cord's shirt as she looks into his dark, reptilian eyes. "I can give you something to believe in, Thomas."

Cord holds her at a distance. He knows it's wrong. And he has a lot of work to do. *The Eighteen Stigmata of Philip Verge* is still missing, and if he doesn't rescue it from the clutches of Goldmaze it could mean the end of the entire South American continent. But Fanny's golden skin glistens provocatively in the afternoon sun.

He had to hand it to her. She knew every button to push. Her bronze hair. Her red blouse blowing loose in the wind, hinting at the intrigues she held in reserve. It was triggering memories of every woman he'd ever loved. She seemed to be the living embodiment of all of them. that was crazy. Fanny was just a victim. A hostage.

There is no such thing as fate . . . is there?

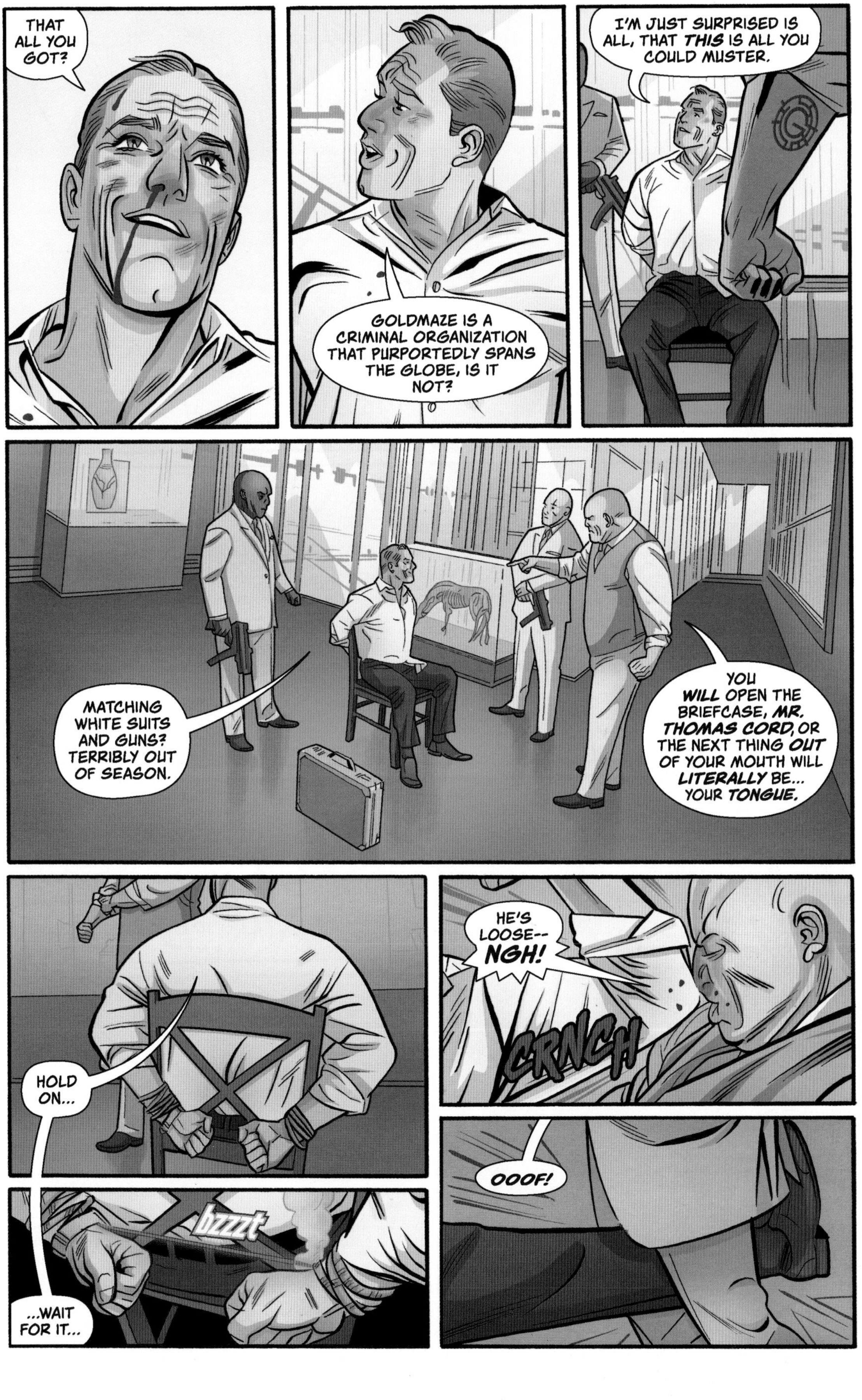
THAT ALL YOU GOT?
GOLDMAZE IS A CRIMINAL ORGANIZATION THAT PURPORTEDLY SPANS THE GLOBE, IS IT NOT?
I'M JUST SURPRISED IS ALL, THAT THIS IS ALL YOU COULD MUSTER.
MATCHING WHITE SUITS AND GUNS? TERRIBLY OUT OF SEASON.
YOU WILL OPEN THE BRIEFCASE, MR. THOMAS CORD, OR THE NEXT THING OUT OF YOUR MOUTH WILL LITERALLY BE... YOUR TONGUE.
HOLD ON...
bzzzt
...WAIT FOR IT...
HE'S LOOSE-- NGH!
CRNCH
OOOF!

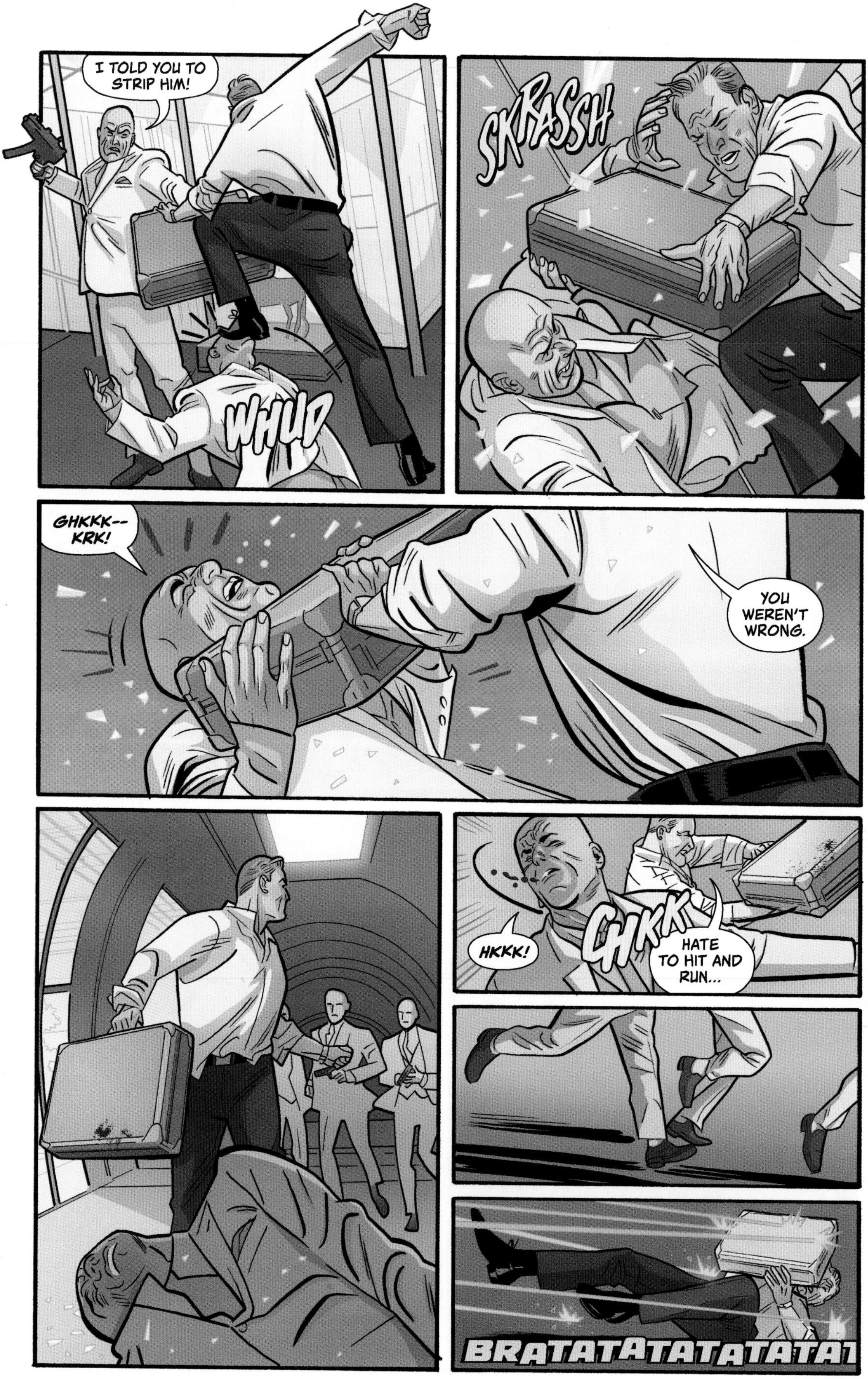
I TOLD YOU TO STRIP HIM!
WHUD
SKRASSH
GHKKK-- KRK!
YOU WEREN'T WRONG.
HKKK!
GHKK
HATE TO HIT AND RUN...
BRATATATATATATATAT

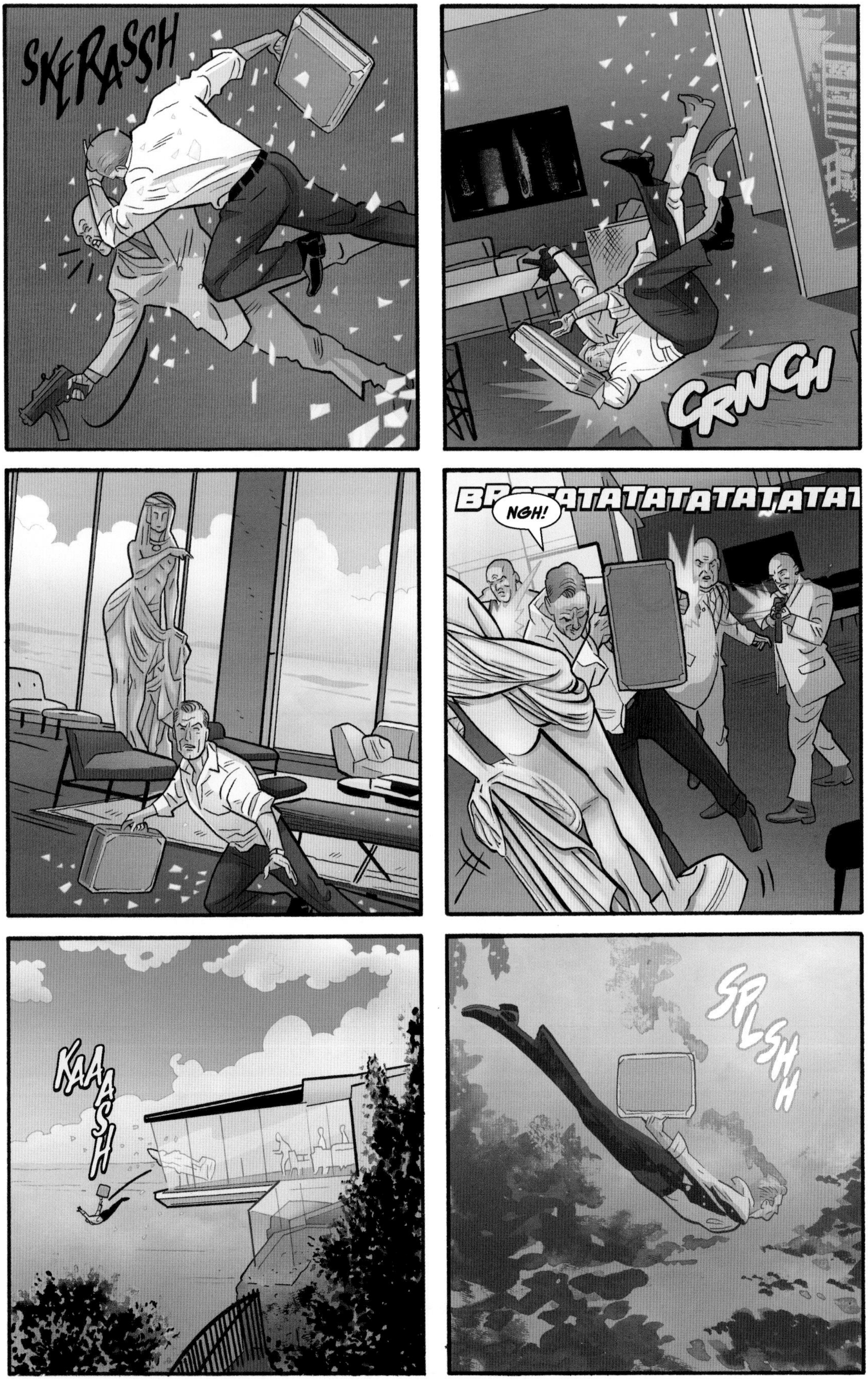
SKERASSH
CRNCH
BRATATATATATATATATAT
NGH!
KAAASH
SPLSHH

:SIGH:

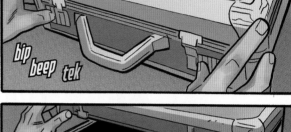

bip beep tek

FSSH

THE 18 STIGMATA OF
PHILIP VERGE

HALFWAY ACROSS THE WORLD, FIFTY GOLDMAZE AGENTS: K.I.A., TWO WRECKED HELICOPTERS, AND A COLLAPSED BUILDING...ALL FOR...A PAPER-BACK?

NOTHING COMES EASY...

YOU KNOW THAT'S NOT TRUE.

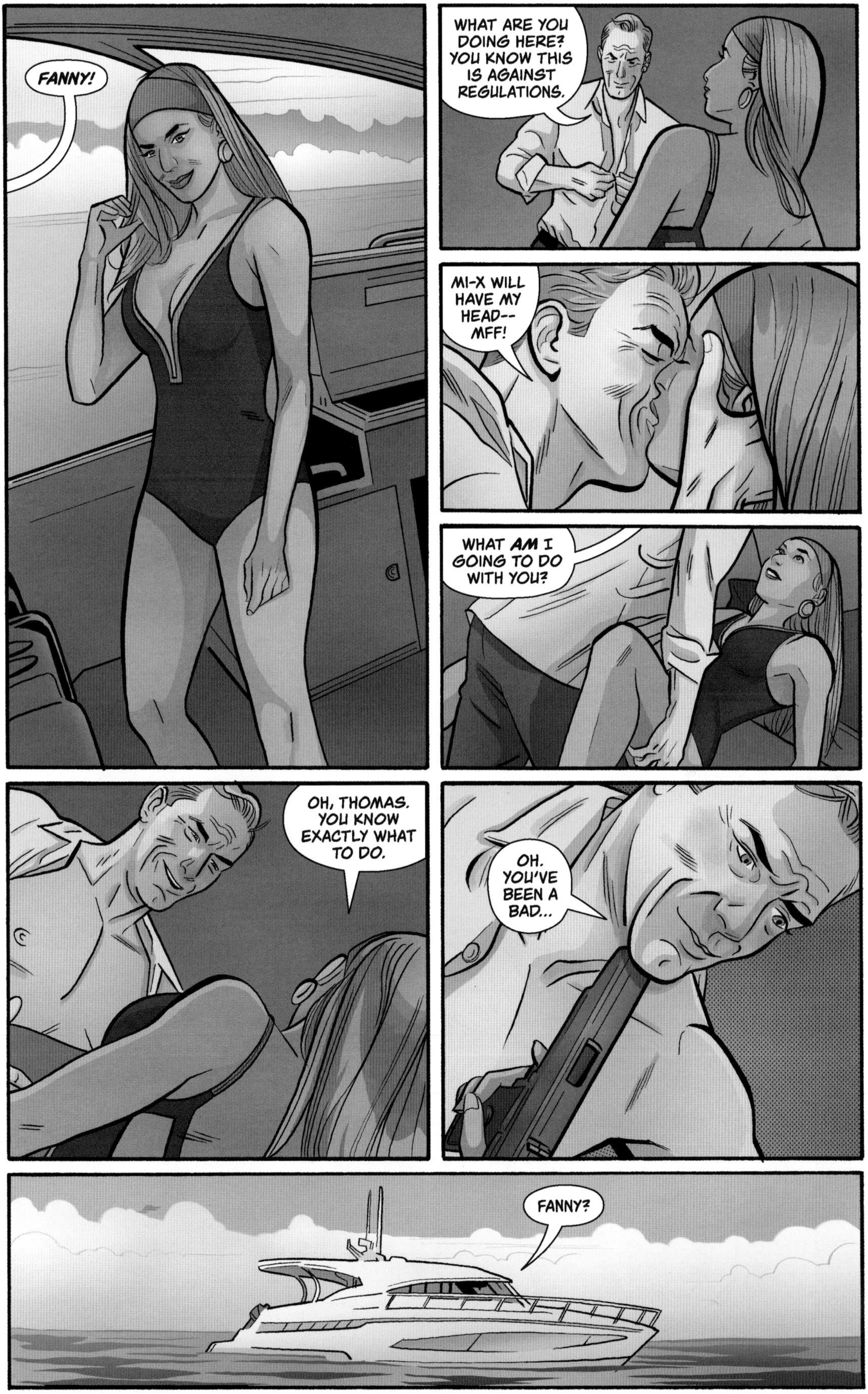
FANNY!
WHAT ARE YOU DOING HERE? YOU KNOW THIS IS AGAINST REGULATIONS.
MI-X WILL HAVE MY HEAD-- MFF!
WHAT *AM* I GOING TO DO WITH YOU?
OH, THOMAS. YOU KNOW EXACTLY WHAT TO DO.
OH. YOU'VE BEEN A BAD...
FANNY?

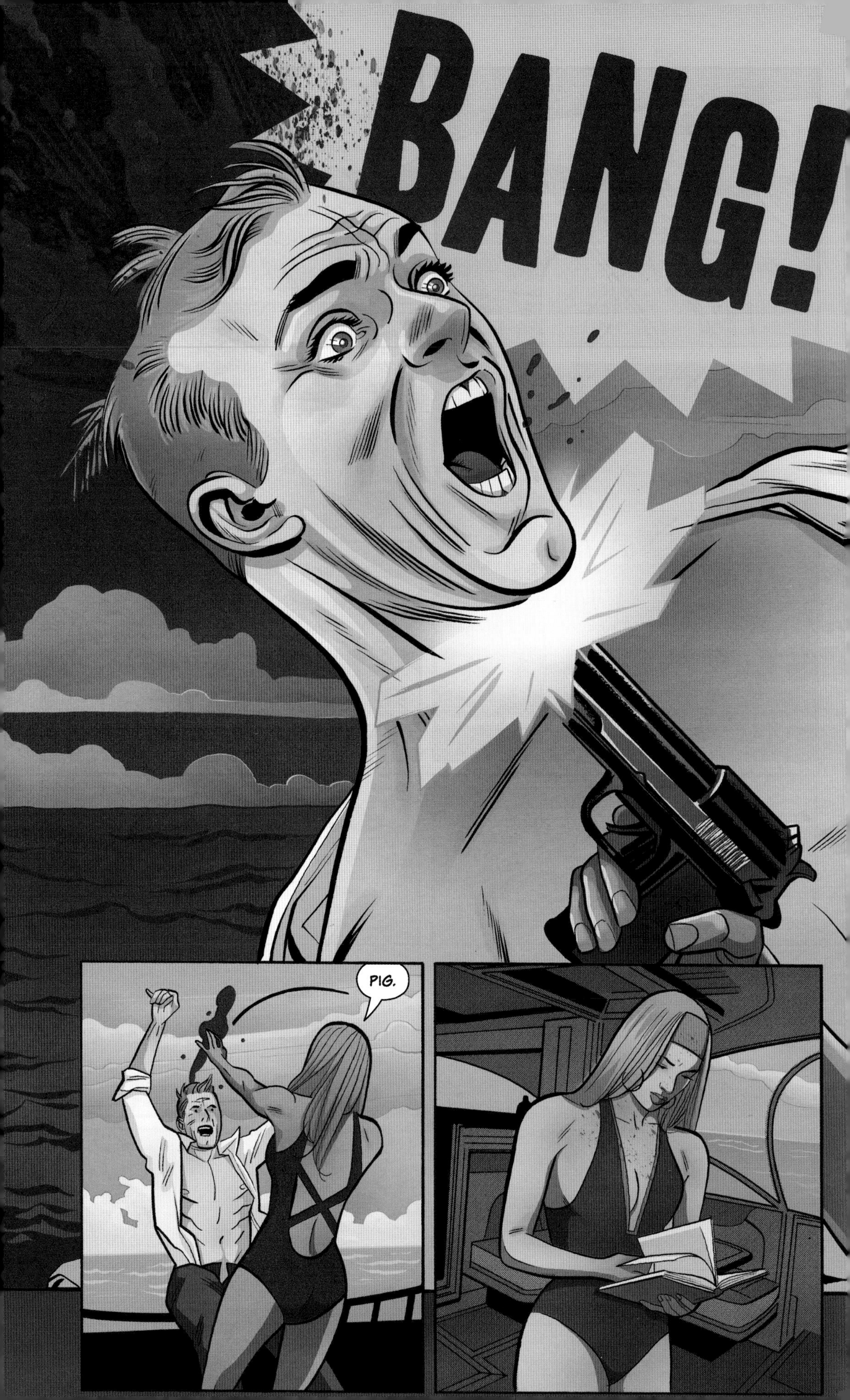
BANG!
PIG.

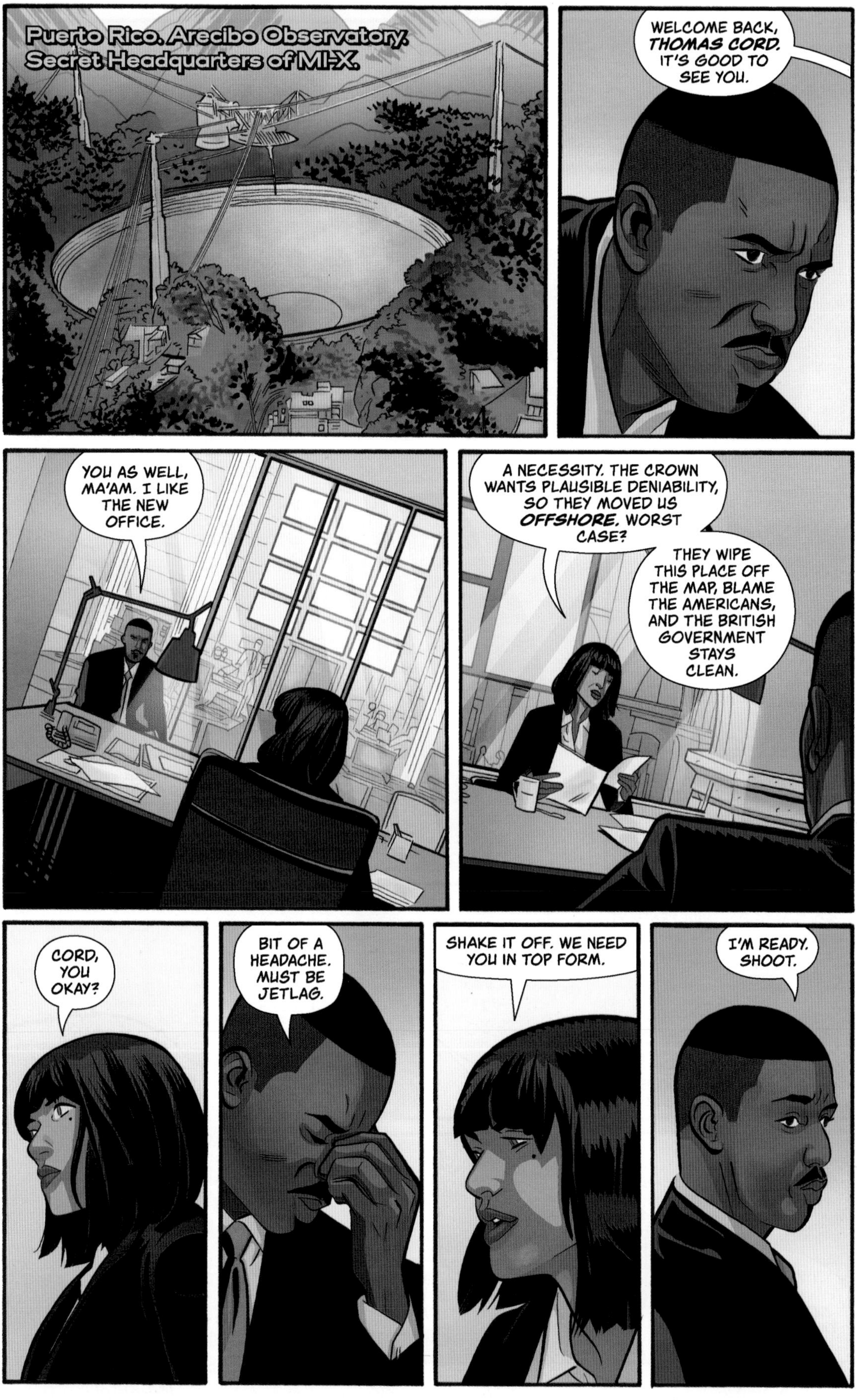
Puerto Rico. Arecibo Observatory.
Secret Headquarters of MI-X.
WELCOME BACK, THOMAS CORD. IT'S GOOD TO SEE YOU.
YOU AS WELL, MA'AM. I LIKE THE NEW OFFICE.
A NECESSITY. THE CROWN WANTS PLAUSIBLE DENIABILITY, SO THEY MOVED US OFFSHORE. WORST CASE?
THEY WIPE THIS PLACE OFF THE MAP, BLAME THE AMERICANS, AND THE BRITISH GOVERNMENT STAYS CLEAN.
CORD, YOU OKAY?
BIT OF A HEADACHE. MUST BE JETLAG.
SHAKE IT OFF. WE NEED YOU IN TOP FORM.
I'M READY. SHOOT.

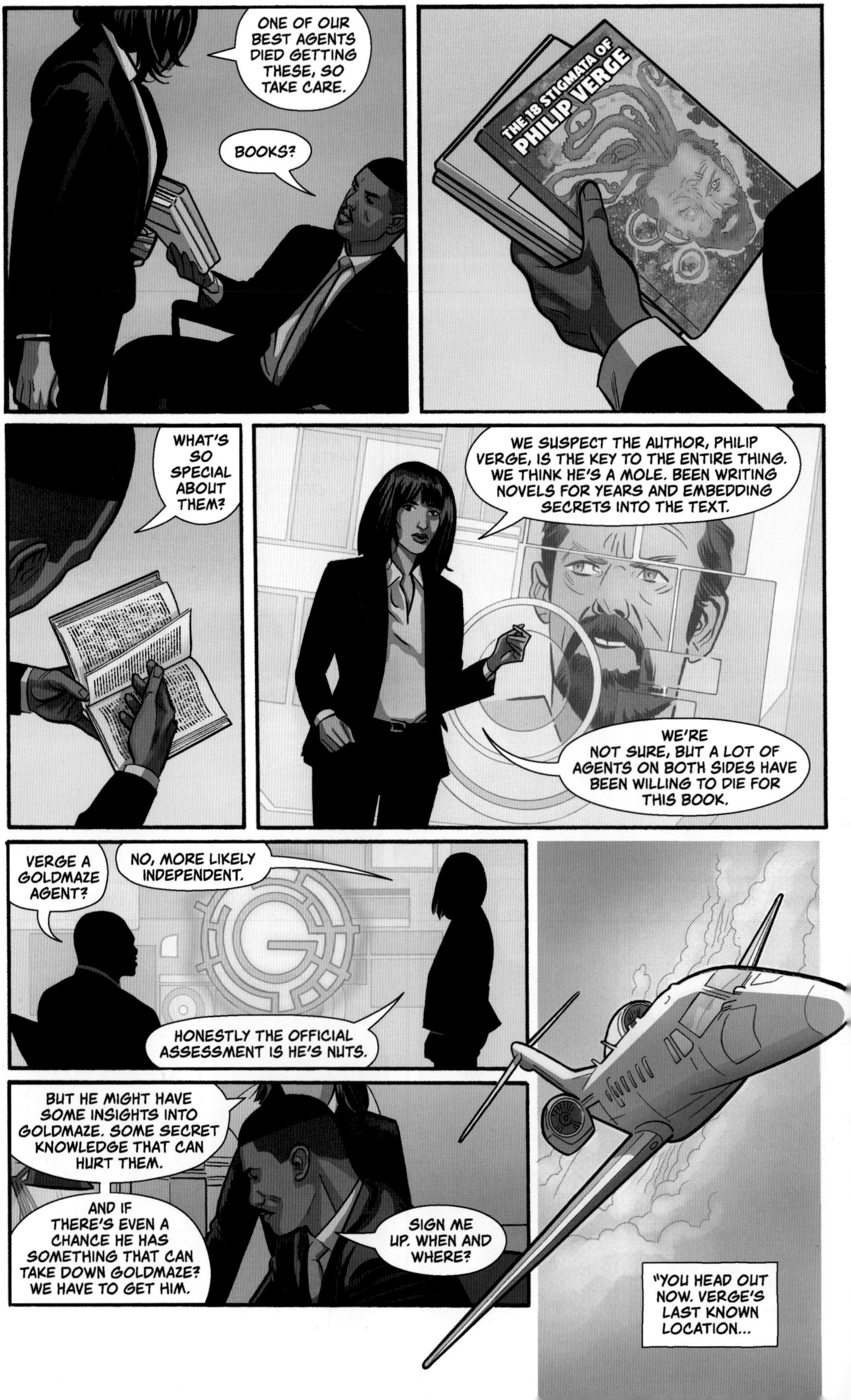
ONE OF OUR BEST AGENTS DIED GETTING THESE, SO TAKE CARE.
BOOKS?
THE 18 STIGMATA OF PHILIP VERGE
WHAT'S SO SPECIAL ABOUT THEM?
WE SUSPECT THE AUTHOR, PHILIP VERGE, IS THE KEY TO THE ENTIRE THING. WE THINK HE'S A MOLE. BEEN WRITING NOVELS FOR YEARS AND EMBEDDING SECRETS INTO THE TEXT.
WE'RE NOT SURE, BUT A LOT OF AGENTS ON BOTH SIDES HAVE BEEN WILLING TO DIE FOR THIS BOOK.
VERGE A GOLDMAZE AGENT?
NO, MORE LIKELY INDEPENDENT.
HONESTLY THE OFFICIAL ASSESSMENT IS HE'S NUTS.
BUT HE MIGHT HAVE SOME INSIGHTS INTO GOLDMAZE. SOME SECRET KNOWLEDGE THAT CAN HURT THEM.
AND IF THERE'S EVEN A CHANCE HE HAS SOMETHING THAT CAN TAKE DOWN GOLDMAZE? WE HAVE TO GET HIM.
SIGN ME UP. WHEN AND WHERE?
"YOU HEAD OUT NOW. VERGE'S LAST KNOWN LOCATION...

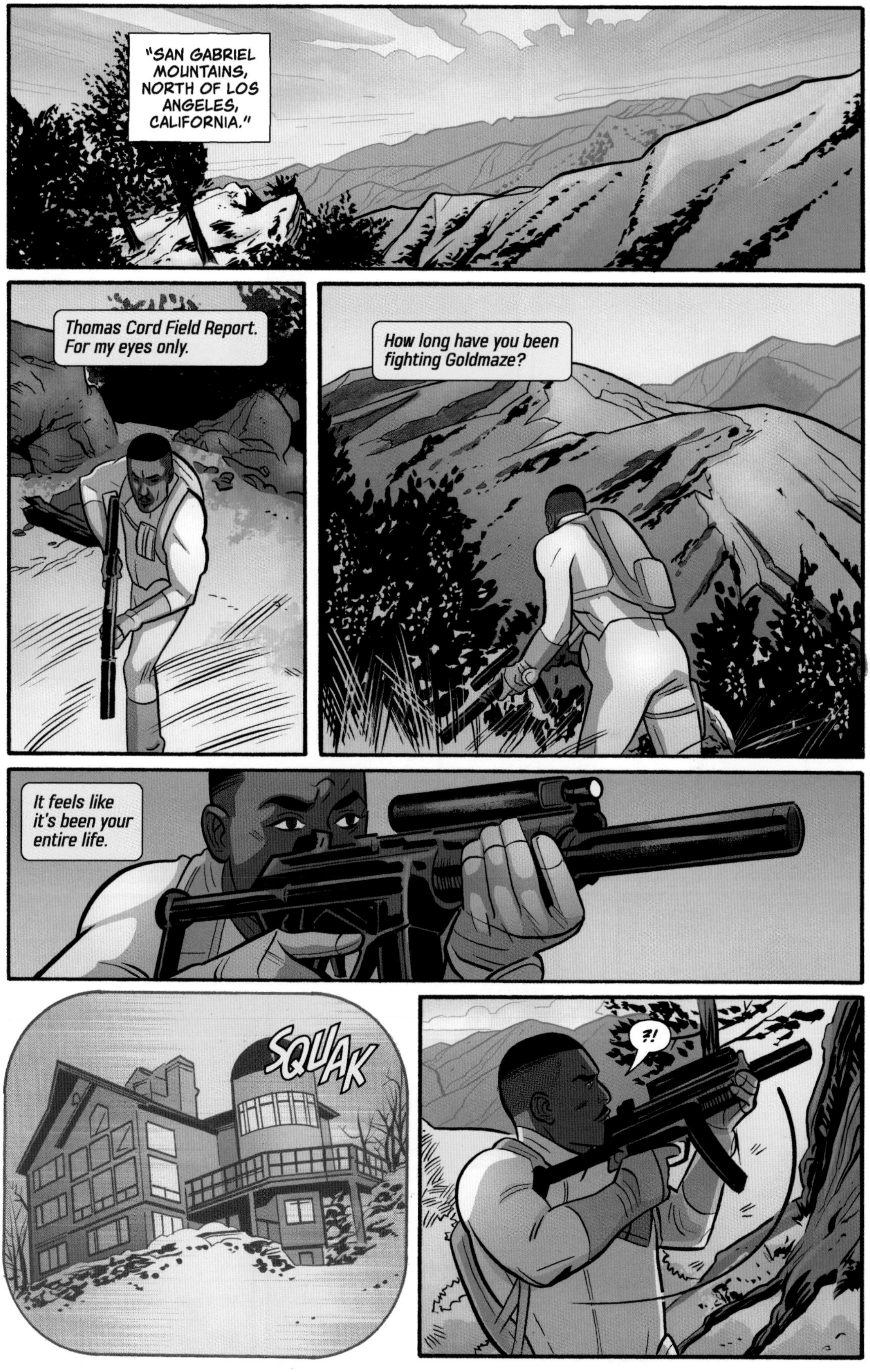
"SAN GABRIEL MOUNTAINS, NORTH OF LOS ANGELES, CALIFORNIA."
Thomas Cord Field Report. For my eyes only.
How long have you been fighting Goldmaze?
It feels like it's been your entire life.
SQUAK
?!

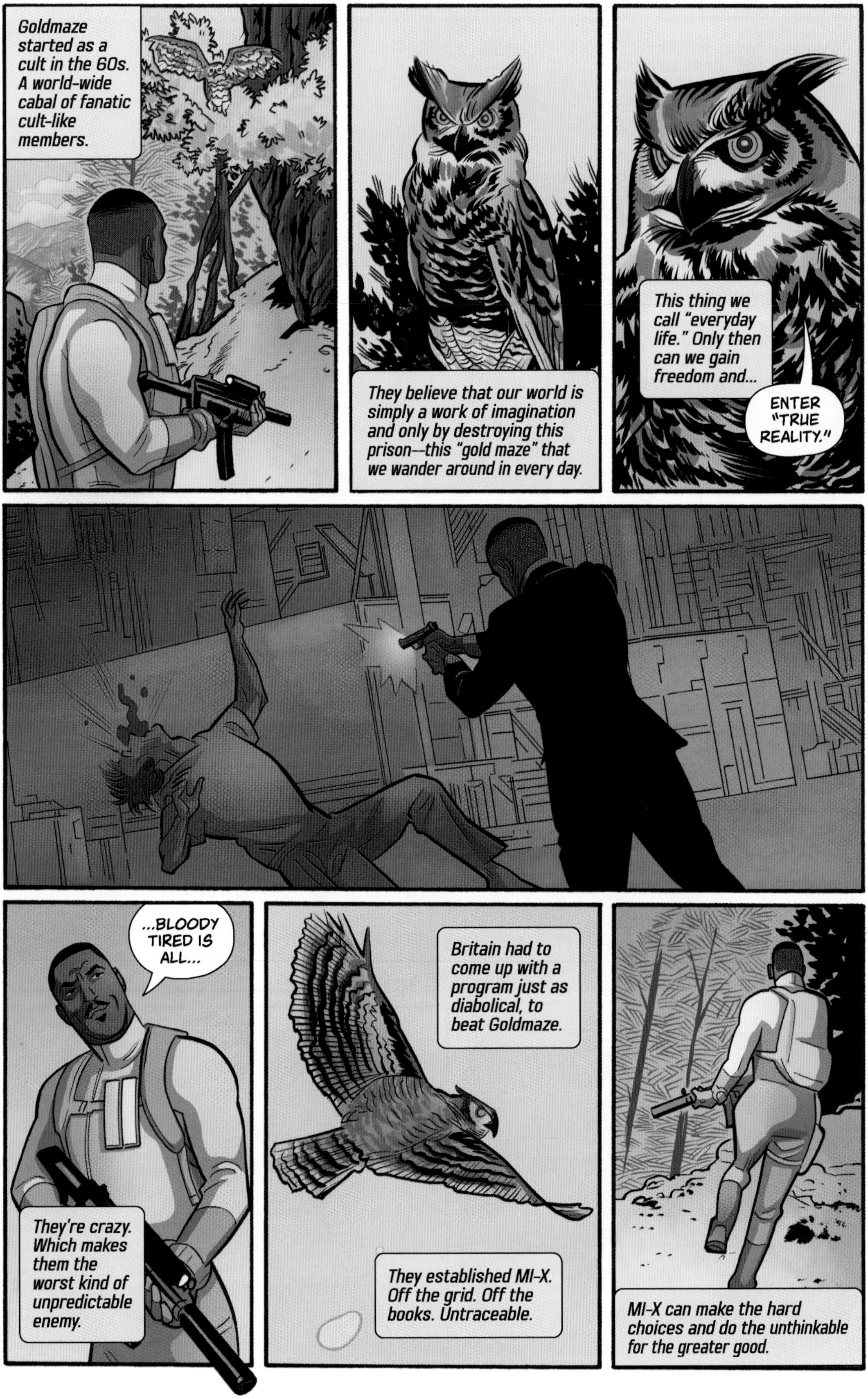
Goldmaze started as a cult in the 60s. A world-wide cabal of fanatic cult-like members.
They believe that our world is simply a work of imagination and only by destroying this prison—this "gold maze" that we wander around in every day.
This thing we call "everyday life." Only then can we gain freedom and...
ENTER "TRUE REALITY."
...BLOODY TIRED IS ALL...
They're crazy. Which makes them the worst kind of unpredictable enemy.
Britain had to come up with a program just as diabolical, to beat Goldmaze.
They established MI-X. Off the grid. Off the books. Untraceable.
MI-X can make the hard choices and do the unthinkable for the greater good.

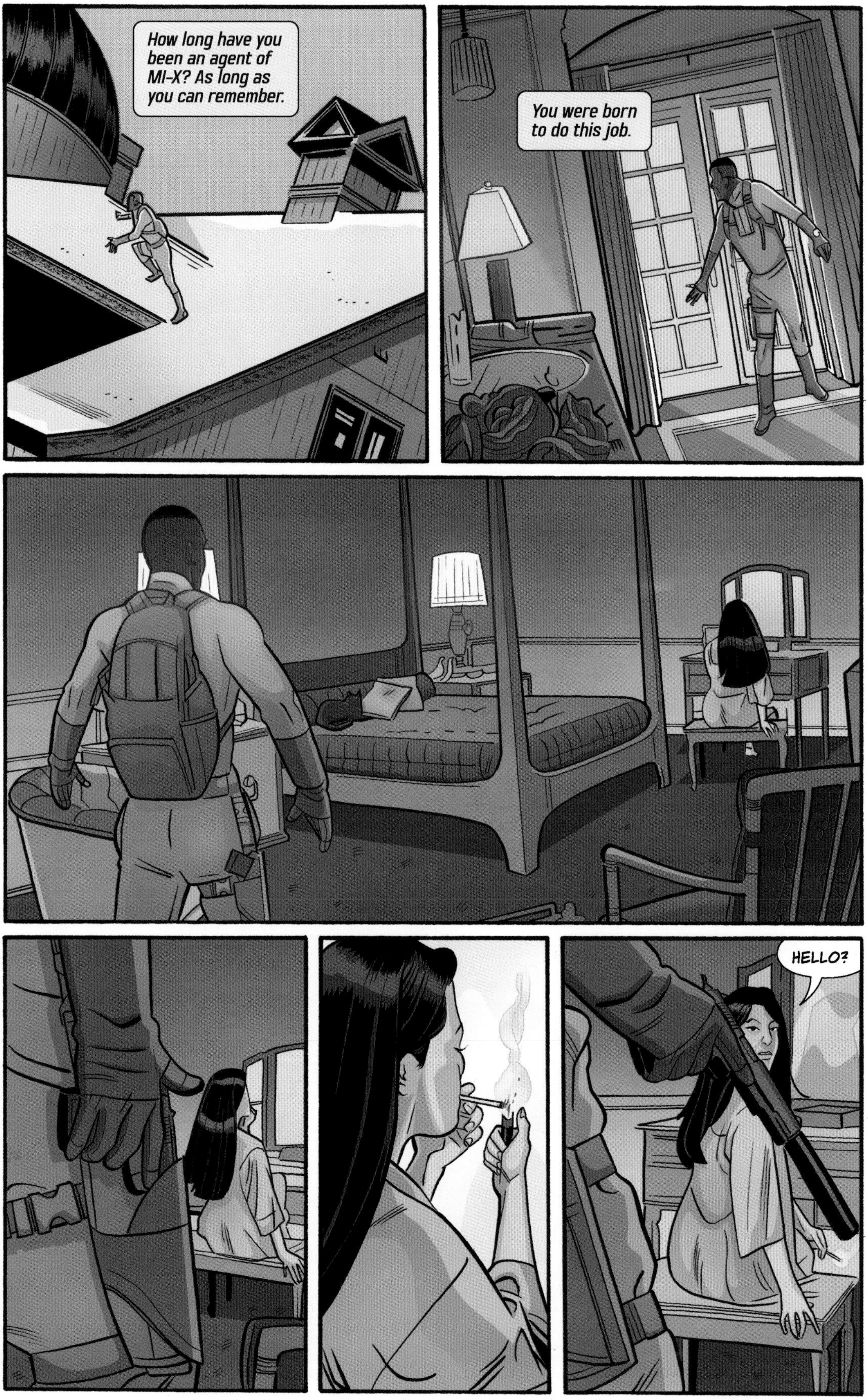
How long have you been an agent of MI-X? As long as you can remember.
You were born to do this job.
HELLO?

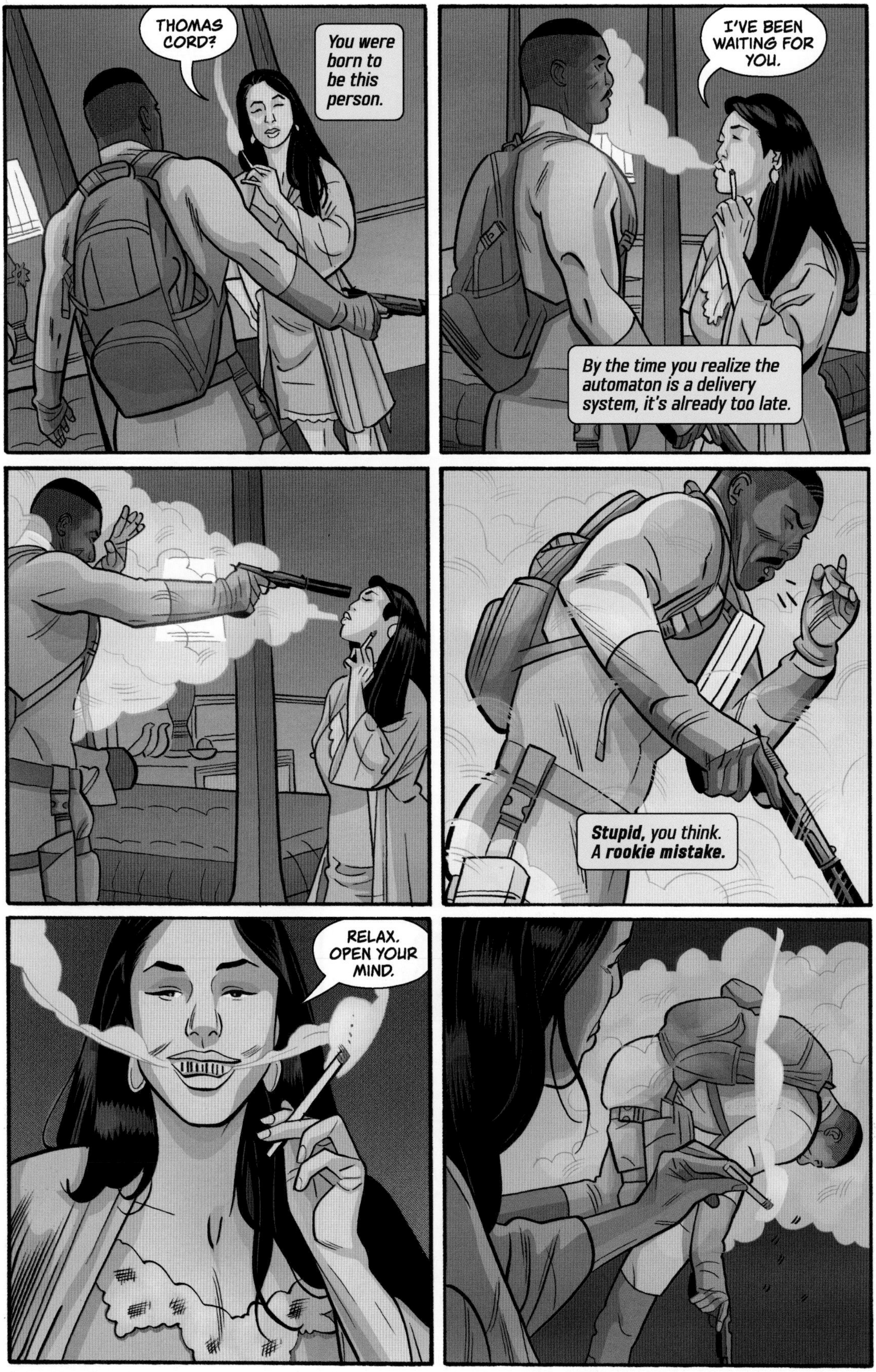
THOMAS CORD?
You were born to be this person.
I'VE BEEN WAITING FOR YOU.
By the time you realize the automaton is a delivery system, it's already too late.
Stupid, you think. A rookie mistake.
RELAX. OPEN YOUR MIND.

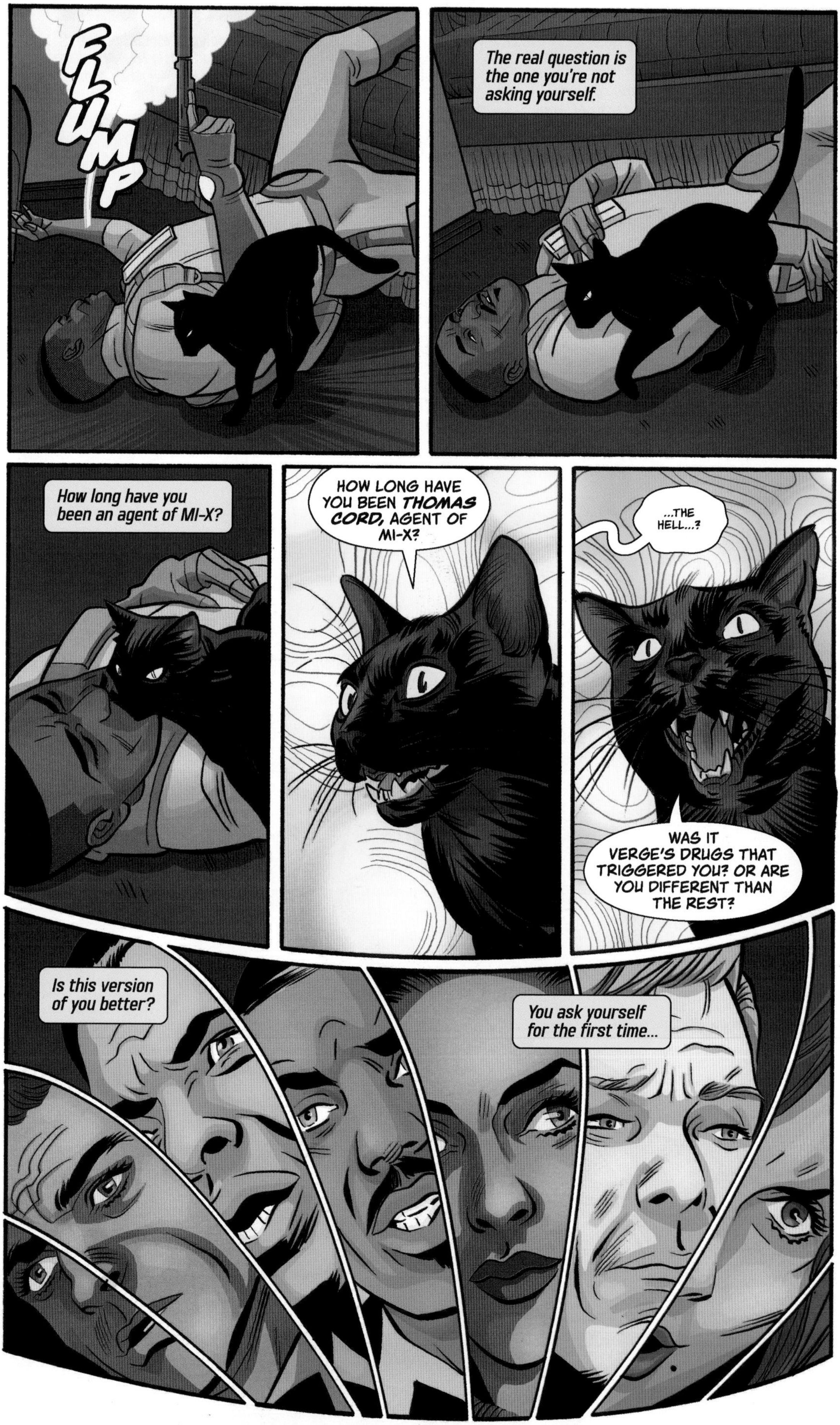
FLUMP
The real question is the one you're not asking yourself.
How long have you been an agent of MI-X?
HOW LONG HAVE YOU BEEN THOMAS CORD, AGENT OF MI-X?
...THE HELL...?
WAS IT VERGE'S DRUGS THAT TRIGGERED YOU? OR ARE YOU DIFFERENT THAN THE REST?
Is this version of you better?
You ask yourself for the first time...

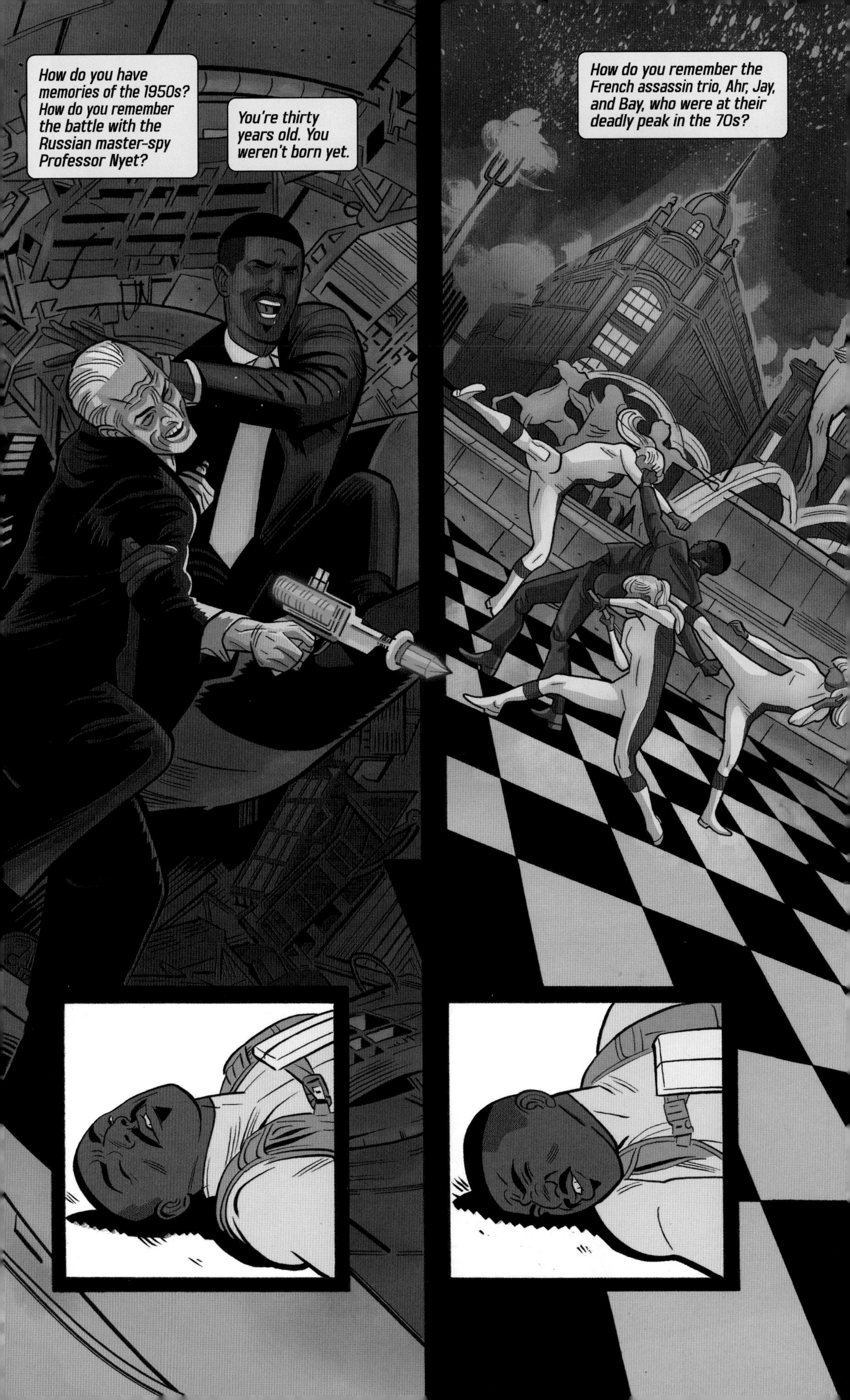
How do you have memories of the 1950s? How do you remember the battle with the Russian master-spy Professor Nyet?
You're thirty years old. You weren't born yet.
How do you remember the French assassin trio, Ahr, Jay, and Bay, who were at their deadly peak in the 70s?

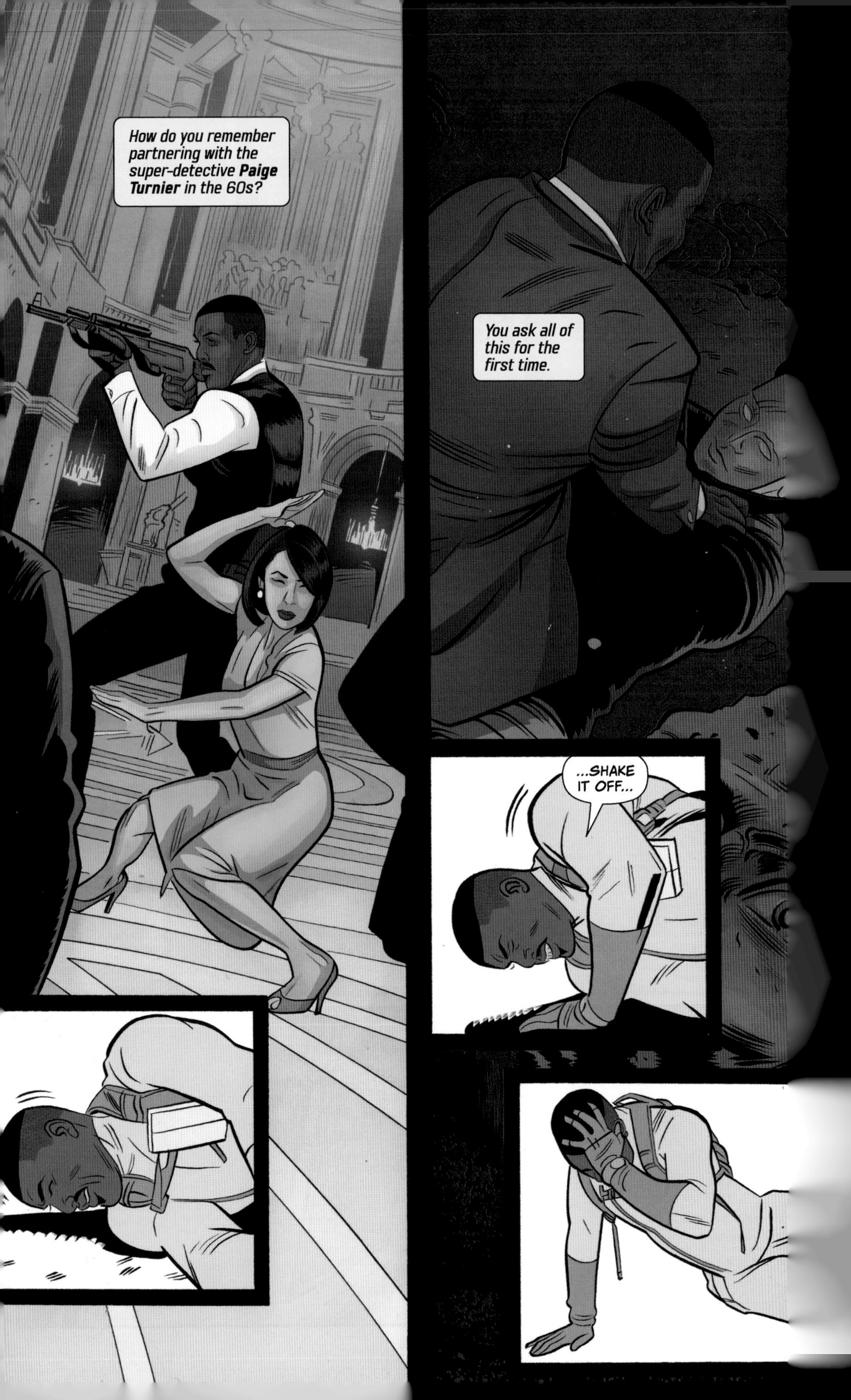
How do you remember partnering with the super-detective **Paige Turnier** in the 60s?
You ask all of this for the first time.
...SHAKE IT OFF...

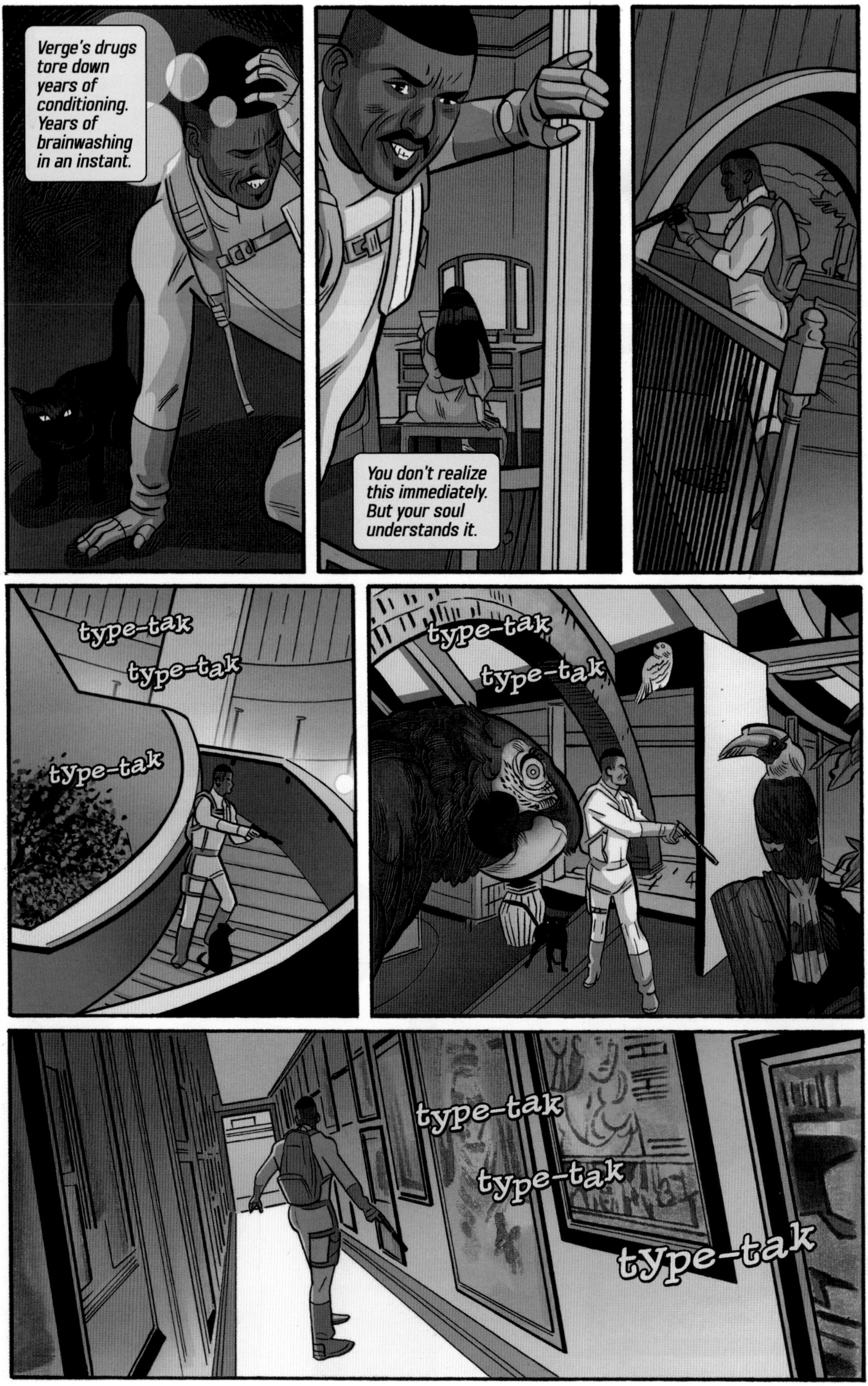
Verge's drugs tore down years of conditioning. Years of brainwashing in an instant.
You don't realize this immediately. But your soul understands it.
type-tak
type-tak
type-tak
type-tak
type-tak
type-tak
type-tak
type-tak

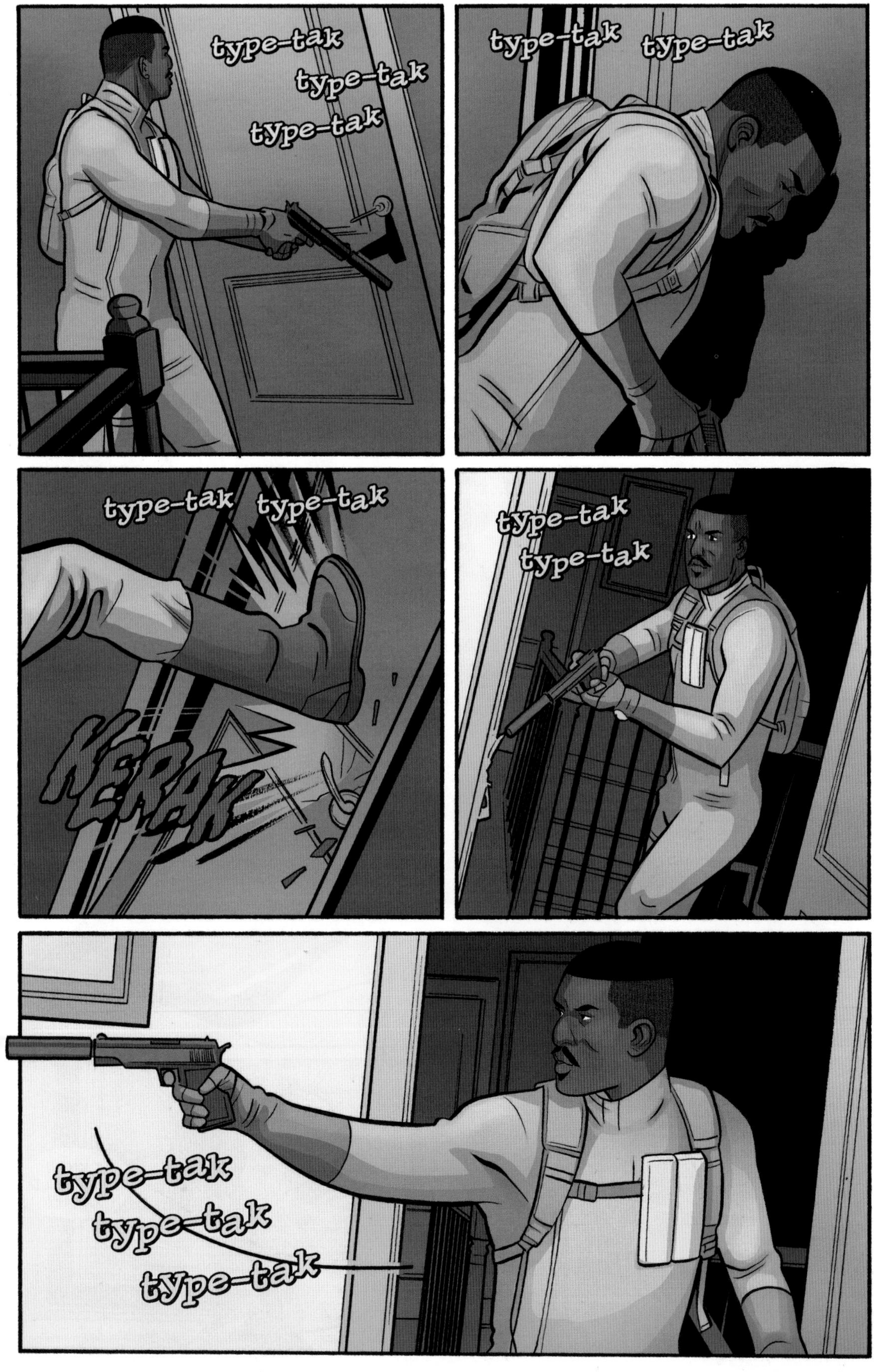

type-tak
type-tak
type-tak
type-tak
type-tak
type-tak
type-tak
KERAK
type-tak
type-tak
type-tak
type-tak
type-tak

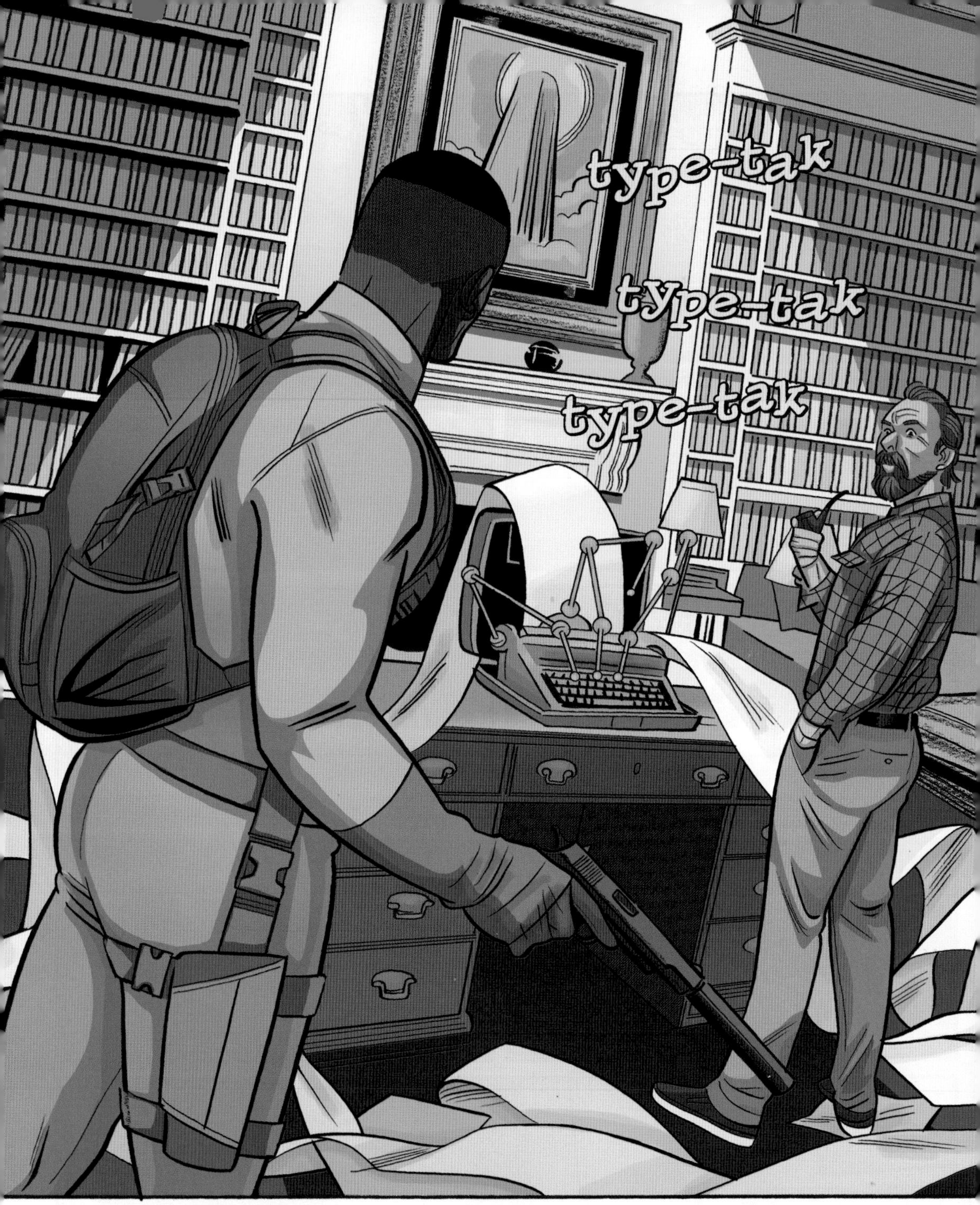
type-tak
type-tak
type-tak
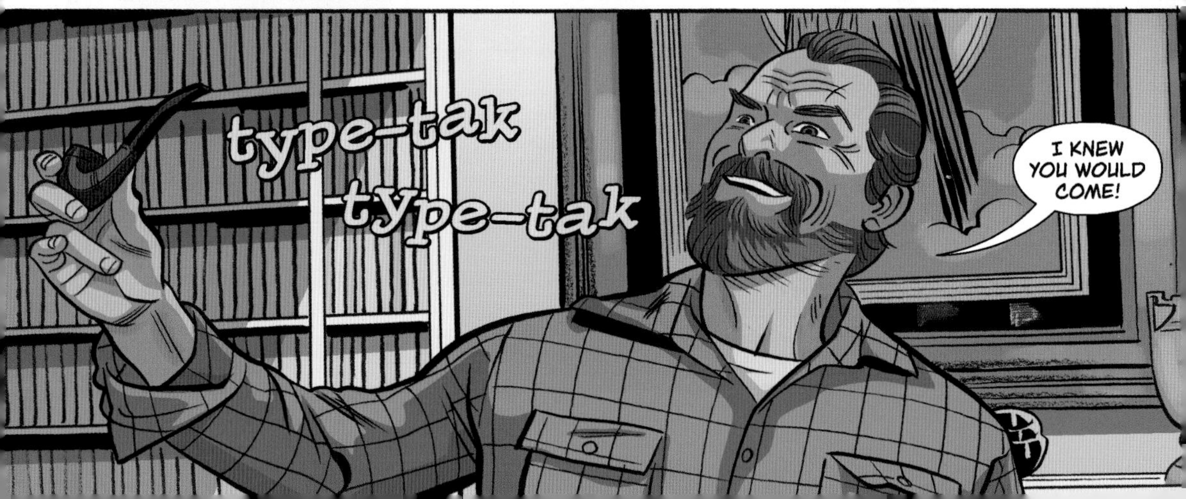
type-tak
type-tak
I KNEW YOU WOULD COME!

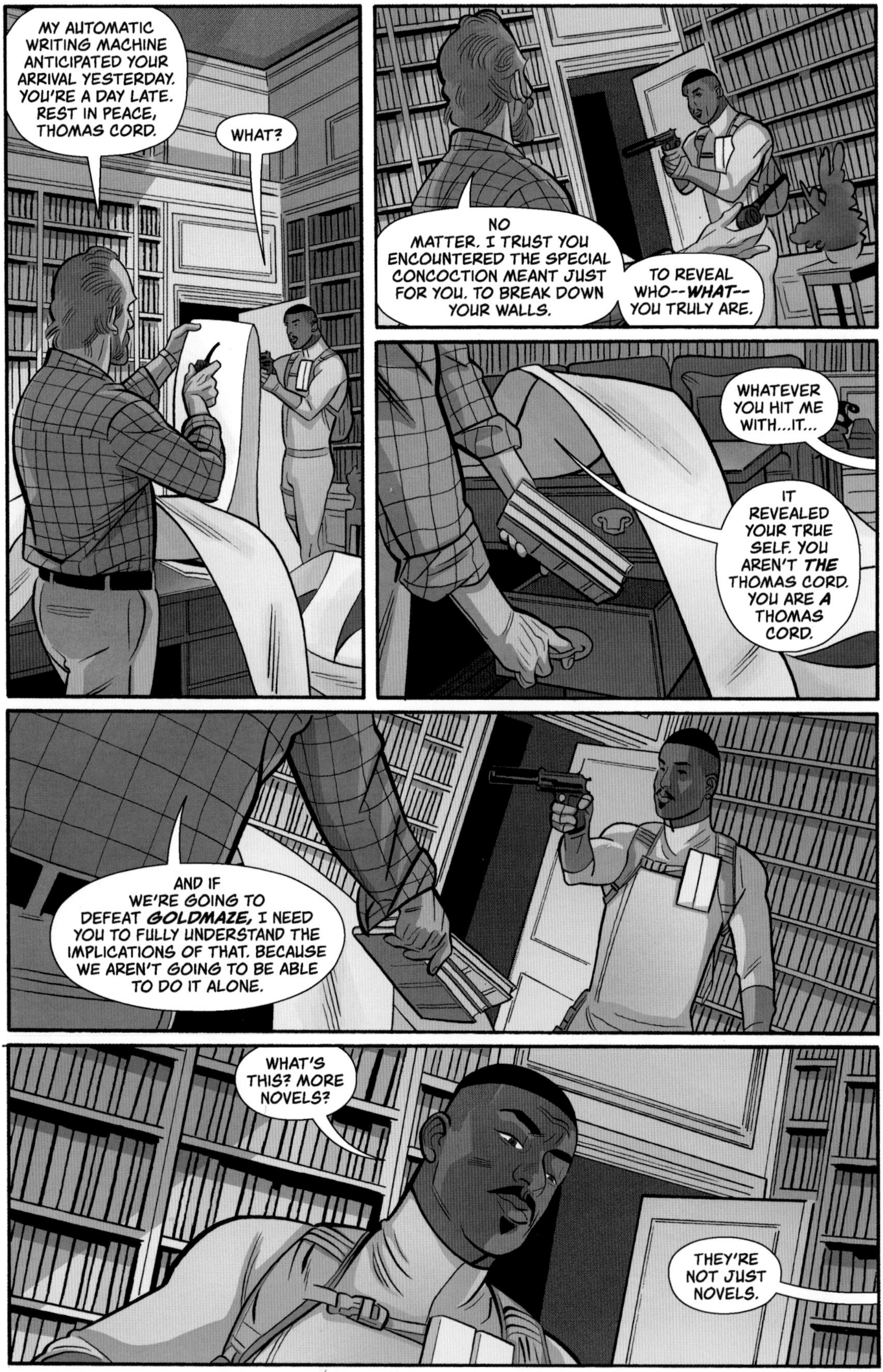
MY AUTOMATIC WRITING MACHINE ANTICIPATED YOUR ARRIVAL YESTERDAY. YOU'RE A DAY LATE. REST IN PEACE, THOMAS CORD.
WHAT?
NO MATTER. I TRUST YOU ENCOUNTERED THE SPECIAL CONCOCTION MEANT JUST FOR YOU. TO BREAK DOWN YOUR WALLS.
TO REVEAL WHO--*WHAT*--YOU TRULY ARE.
WHATEVER YOU HIT ME WITH...IT...
IT REVEALED YOUR TRUE SELF. YOU AREN'T *THE* THOMAS CORD. YOU ARE *A* THOMAS CORD.
AND IF WE'RE GOING TO DEFEAT *GOLDMAZE,* I NEED YOU TO FULLY UNDERSTAND THE IMPLICATIONS OF THAT. BECAUSE WE AREN'T GOING TO BE ABLE TO DO IT ALONE.
WHAT'S THIS? MORE NOVELS?
THEY'RE NOT JUST NOVELS.

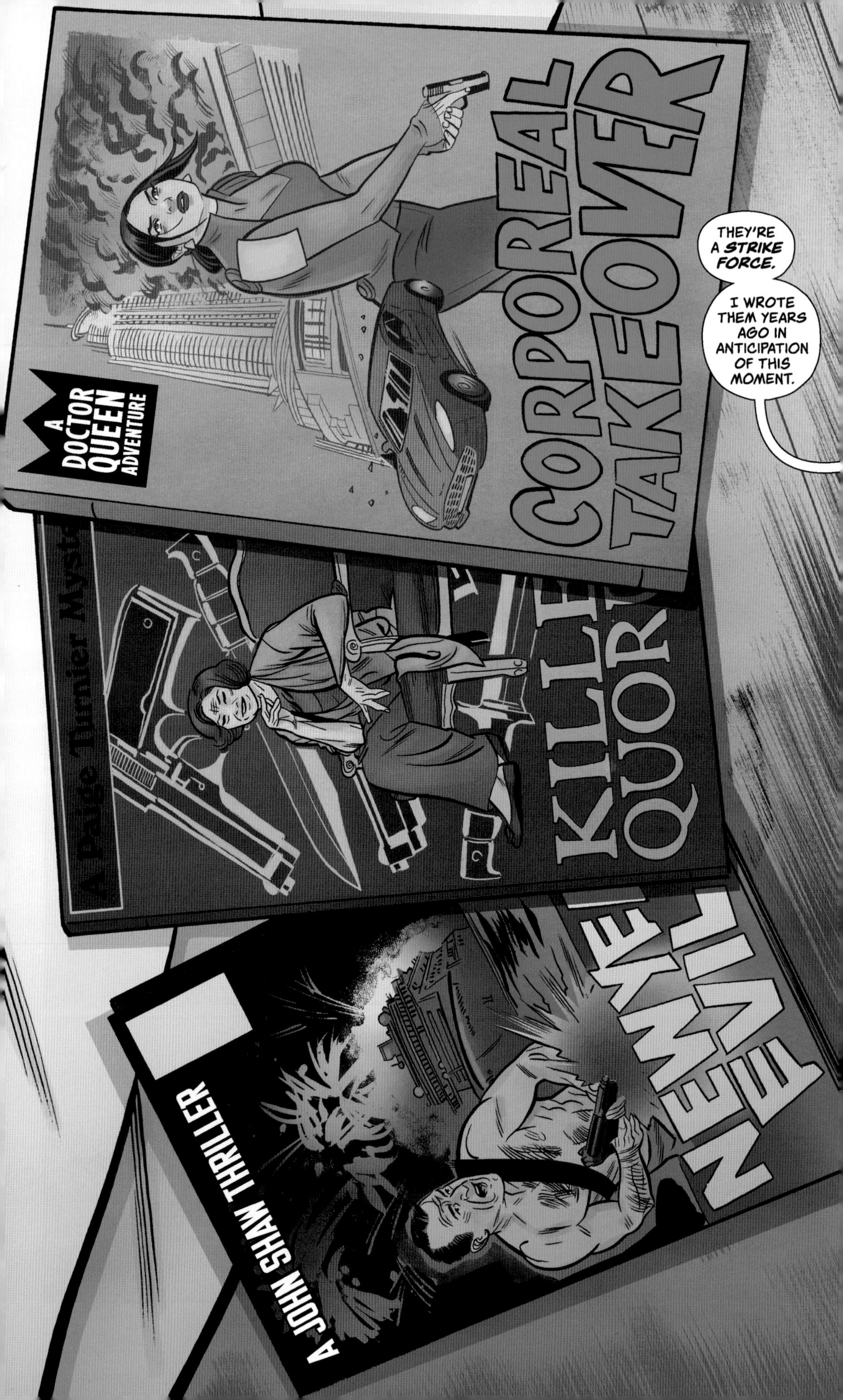
A DOCTOR QUEEN ADVENTURE
CORPOREAL TAKEOVER
A JOHN SHAW THRILLER
THEY'RE A *STRIKE FORCE.*
I WROTE THEM YEARS AGO IN ANTICIPATION OF THIS MOMENT.

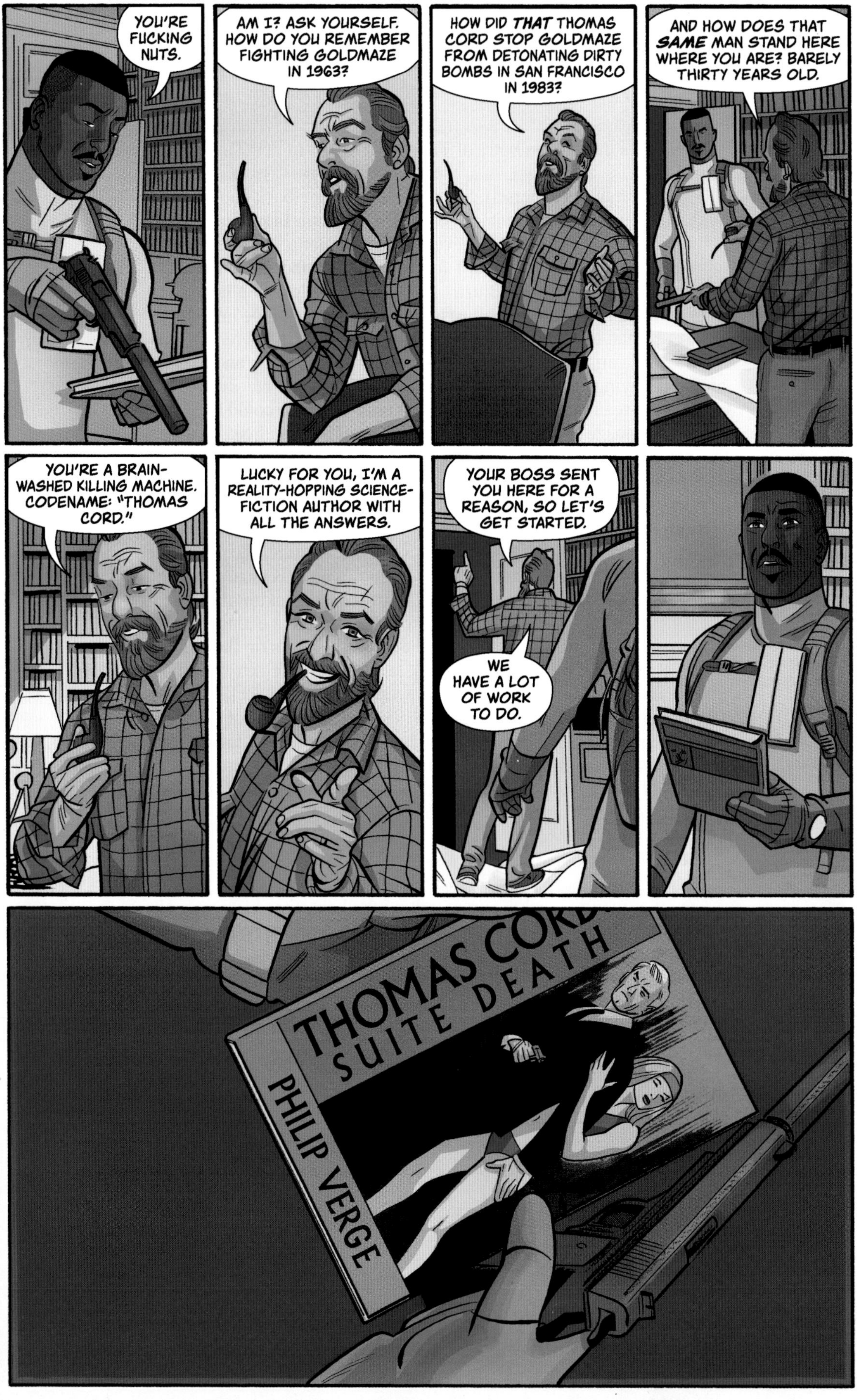

YOU'RE FUCKING NUTS.
AM I? ASK YOURSELF. HOW DO YOU REMEMBER FIGHTING GOLDMAZE IN 1963?
HOW DID THAT THOMAS CORD STOP GOLDMAZE FROM DETONATING DIRTY BOMBS IN SAN FRANCISCO IN 1983?
AND HOW DOES THAT SAME MAN STAND HERE WHERE YOU ARE? BARELY THIRTY YEARS OLD.
YOU'RE A BRAIN-WASHED KILLING MACHINE. CODENAME: "THOMAS CORD."
LUCKY FOR YOU, I'M A REALITY-HOPPING SCIENCE-FICTION AUTHOR WITH ALL THE ANSWERS.
YOUR BOSS SENT YOU HERE FOR A REASON, SO LET'S GET STARTED.
WE HAVE A LOT OF WORK TO DO.
THOMAS CORD
SUITE DEATH
PHILIP VERGE

Fanny pushes the lifeless body of Thomas Cord off of her. The job was finally done.

"Pig," she mutters to herself. She picks up the paperback book and absent-mindedly flips through its pages. Her bronze hair blows in the wind as the cool sea air dries her honeyed skin. How long had she been an agent of Goldmaze? It was hard for her to remember now. So many years ago in the jungles of Brazil. Thirteen years old and a hostage of rebel separatists looking for an easy ransom. Years of rape and torture was all she had to look forward to. Until Goldmaze. Until Frederick Jason-Michael came into her life. She owed them everything, and she was intent on paying them back. But she also believed in the cause. This world? This reality? It was a prison. And only when we could break out of this gold maze . . . this prison of walls would we be free. What did Thomas Cord know of reality? He was nothing but a weapon wielded by his hooded masters. A misogynistic, unfeeling killing machine. No longer would she have to put up with his rough, hungry hands. His sense of entitlement. His—

Fanny is broken from her reverie by a noise. Carefully, she places the book back into the suitcase and locks it. Fanny's heart is racing. She did hear something. Was it a splash? Did Cord have a backup plan? He'd told her that it was just him. He was a rogue super agent acting alone.

Fanny walks to the back of the yacht carefully. She's on the balls of her feet, ready to fight. A sharp pain and a bolt of electricity shoot through the back of her head, and Fanny crumples to the deck.

Over her stand three MI-X agents in black wetsuits. One of them had gotten the jump on Fanny and brought his submachine gun down across the back of her head. She was unconscious but not dead. Orders were orders, and MI-X wanted Fanny alive. But every one of the MI-X agents wanted to kill her. She'd gotten one of their best.

Thomas Cord was dead.

One of the black-clad agents kneels over Cord to confirm his death.

"H-he's gone."

The other men in black begin searching the boat. One of them grabs the suitcase while the others bind Fanny's arms behind her back and zip her into an extraction bag.

"It's going to be a steady diet of pentothal and torture for her."

One of the black-clad agents begins placing explosives on the yacht while the others load Fanny onto the small stealth dinghy moored to the yacht.

"Time's up. Let's blow it and go."

The agents jump quietly into their dinghy and push away f yacht. The motor of their boat hums quietly as they make distan look at each other quietly. Each with the solemn feeling that com losing one of your own in the field. Behind them the yacht explo a ball of flame.

Thomas Cord was dead. But he would return.

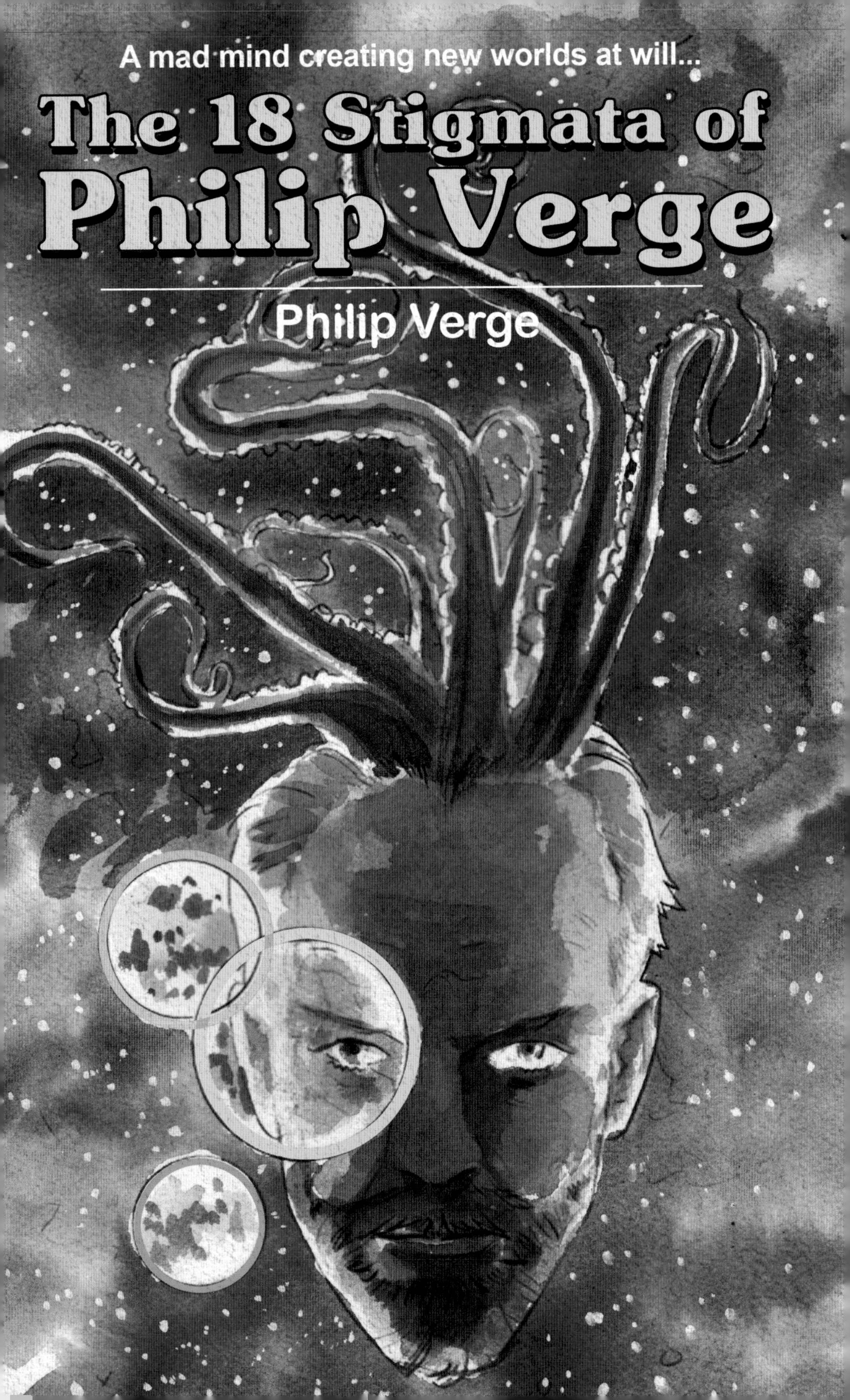
A mad mind creating new worlds at will...
The 18 Stigmata of Philip Verge
Philip Verge

BANG!

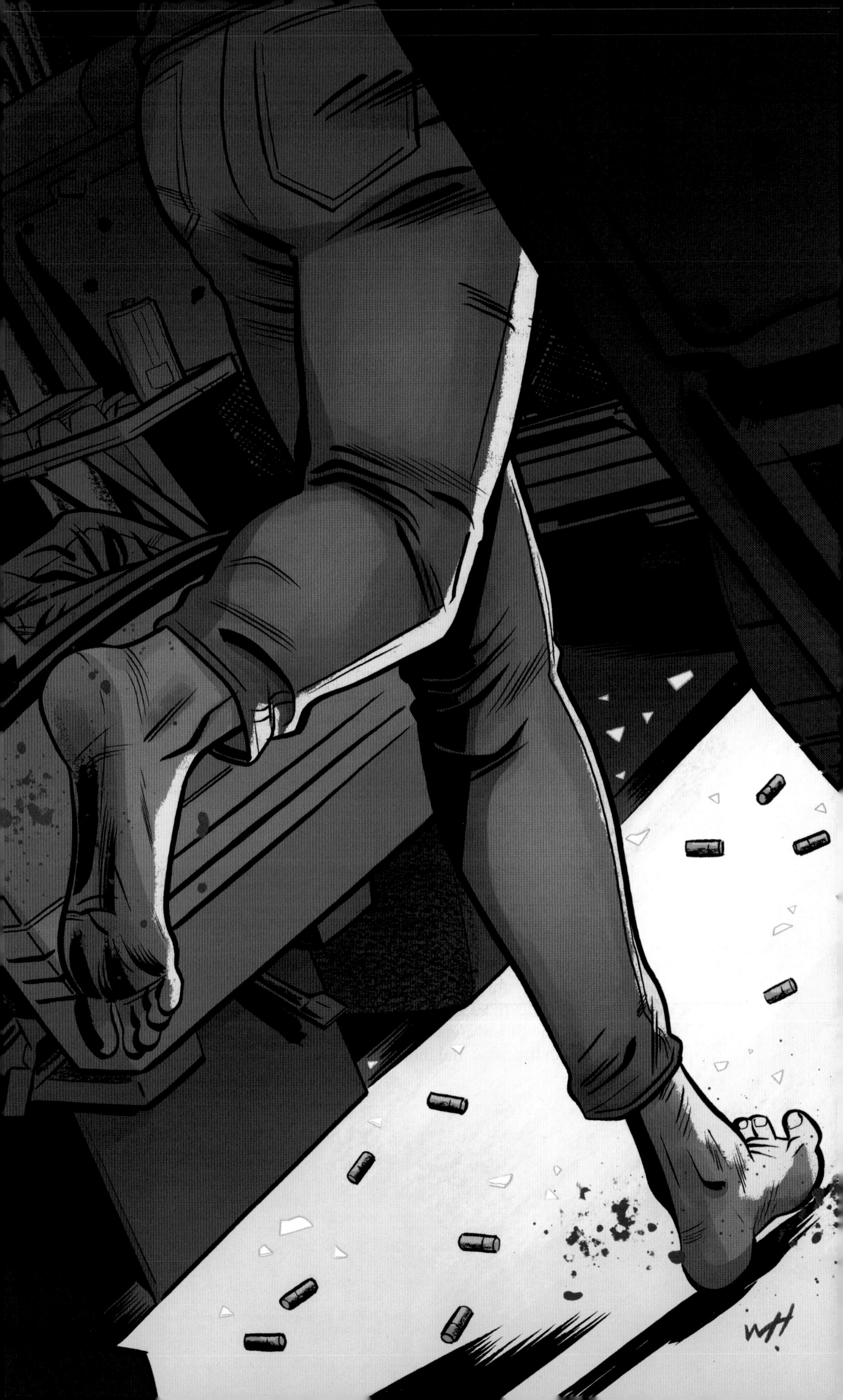

John Shaw cautiously cracks open the door of his modest one-bedroom apartment. He lives on the sixth floor, and the elevator is always broken, but the FedEx delivery girl that now stands at the door with his package is never out of breath. She never complains. It's always the same girl. Long dark hair. Hat pulled down. Smiling. The FedEx girl. No. Not a girl. A woman. He's just getting old. Had she smiled at him, or was he just a lonely, old, washed-up detective desperate for any kind of human interaction that didn't involve inflicting pain? Before he can answer that question, she hands him his package and is gone, down the stairs, and he is alone. Again.

Shaw sits at the small kitchen table in his small one-bedroom apartment and stares at the package. The package. The package had changed his life. When had it first showed up? Not long after his divorce. When it seemed he still might have a chance of putting his marriage and his life back together. But the package had changed everything. He opens the lid. A new shipment. Row after row of small inhalers.

He's given up examining the package for clues. It's shipped from an overseas address that is a shell company of countless shell companies. A maze of LLCs and corporations. He's done his due diligence. Whoever was supplying him with these drugs does not want to be found.

He'd had the chemical inhalers analyzed by an old friend at the police lab that still owed him a favor. The drugs were complex—like nothing that exists. They take effect immediately, and their effects last nearly an hour. But what about the side effects? Shaw is convinced they are addictive. He is constantly thinking about them. Always ready to use it. But chemically? They're not habit forming. What was habit forming was the endorphins that they sparked in him.

One vial enhanced his senses. He could see, hear, smell, and touch with near superhuman ability. He could actually hear heartbeats.

Another vial would give him the strength of one hundred men. That one he had to be careful with. He could put his fist through a man's chest (and had).

And the third? Intellect. Whenever he inhaled that one, he could feel the neurons firing in his head—waking up parts of his mind that he'd never been aware of before. He could see all the pieces fit together. Life made sense. That was the hardest one to come down from. It was like momentarily having the awareness of a god and then suddenly crashing back to Earth with the mind and thoughts of an animal.

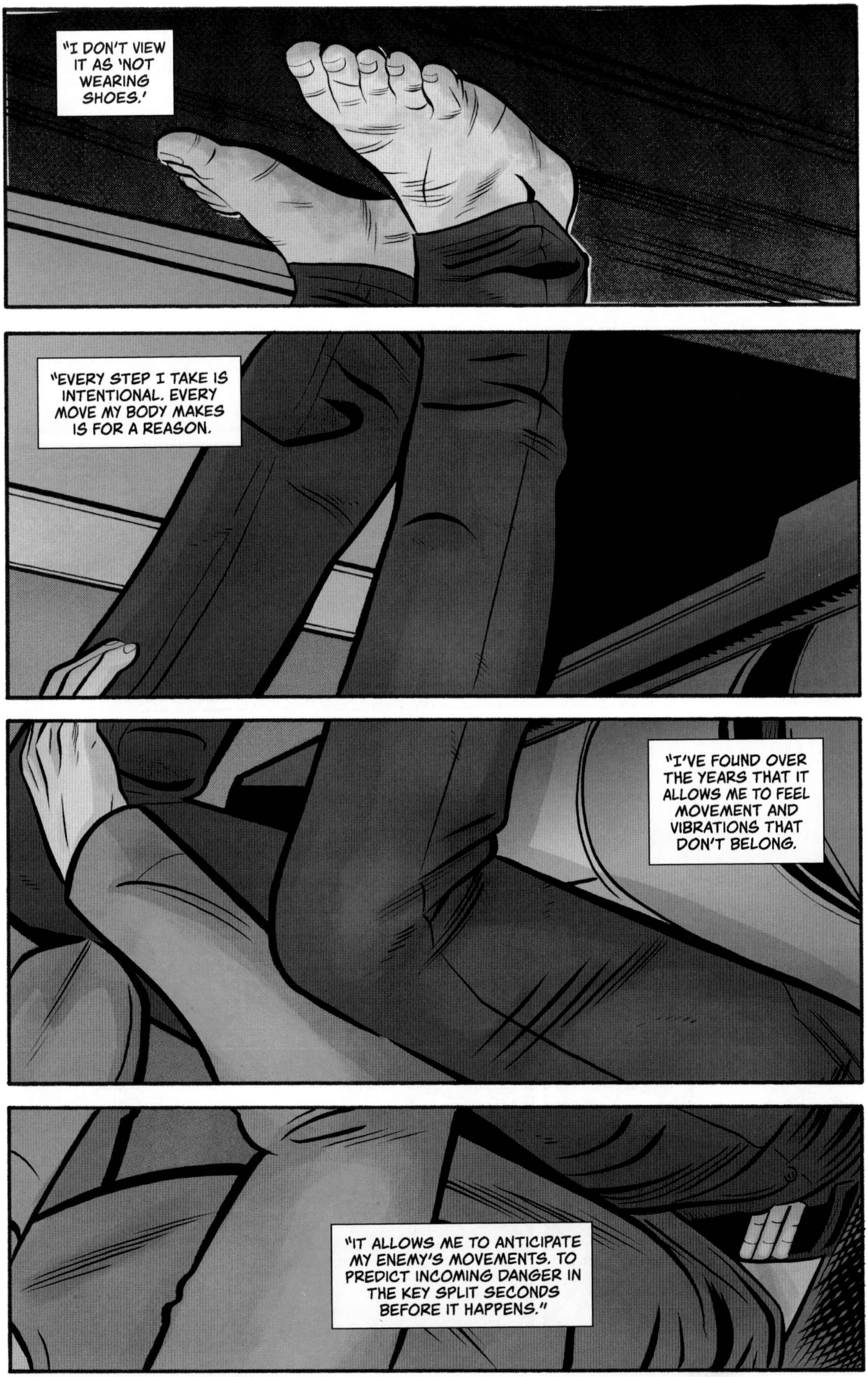
"I DON'T VIEW IT AS 'NOT WEARING SHOES.'
"EVERY STEP I TAKE IS INTENTIONAL. EVERY MOVE MY BODY MAKES IS FOR A REASON.
"I'VE FOUND OVER THE YEARS THAT IT ALLOWS ME TO FEEL MOVEMENT AND VIBRATIONS THAT DON'T BELONG.
"IT ALLOWS ME TO ANTICIPATE MY ENEMY'S MOVEMENTS. TO PREDICT INCOMING DANGER IN THE KEY SPLIT SECONDS BEFORE IT HAPPENS."

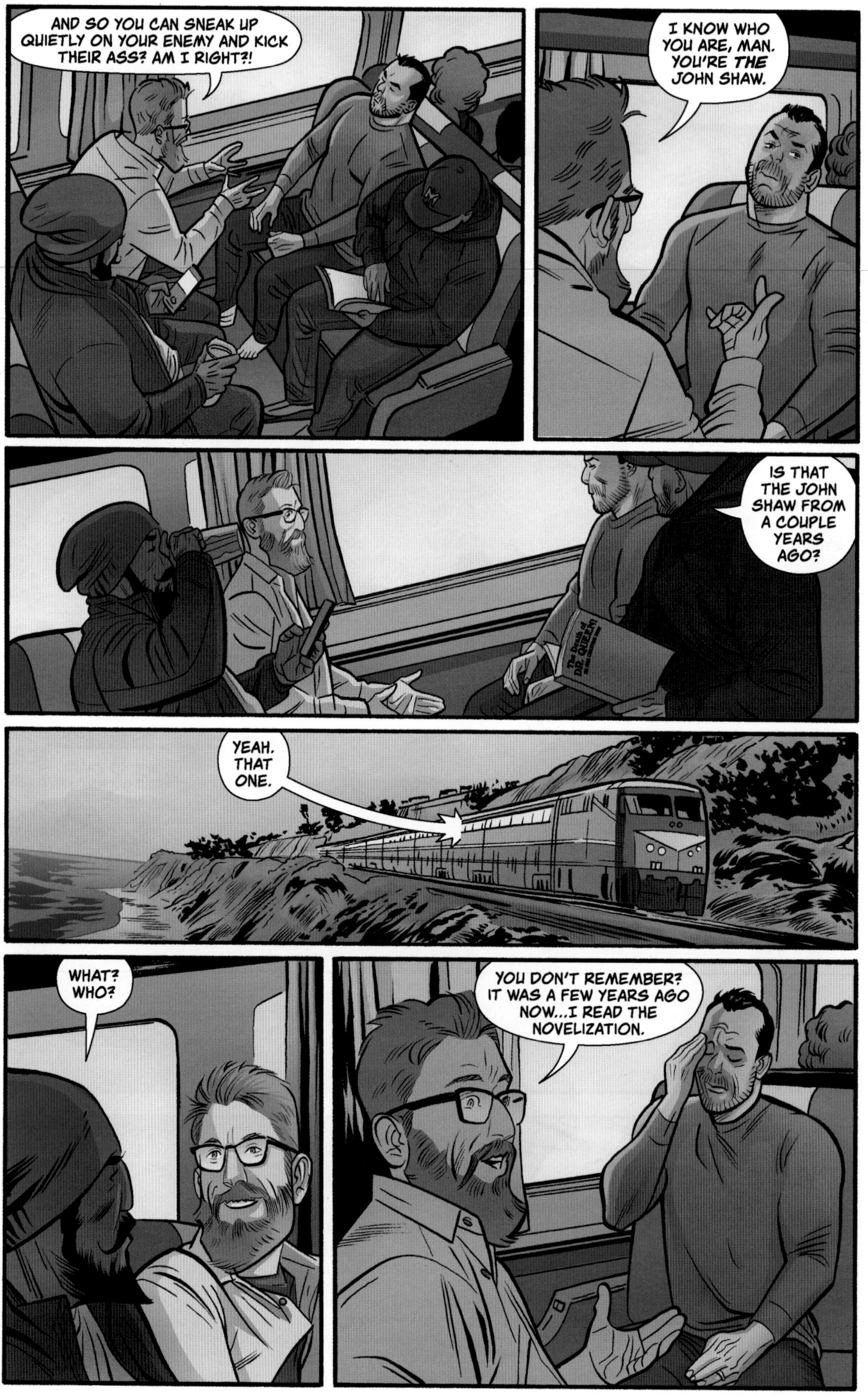
AND SO YOU CAN SNEAK UP QUIETLY ON YOUR ENEMY AND KICK THEIR ASS? AM I RIGHT?!
I KNOW WHO YOU ARE, MAN. YOU'RE *THE* JOHN SHAW.
IS THAT THE JOHN SHAW FROM A COUPLE YEARS AGO?
YEAH. THAT ONE.
WHAT? WHO?
YOU DON'T REMEMBER? IT WAS A FEW YEARS AGO NOW...I READ THE NOVELIZATION.

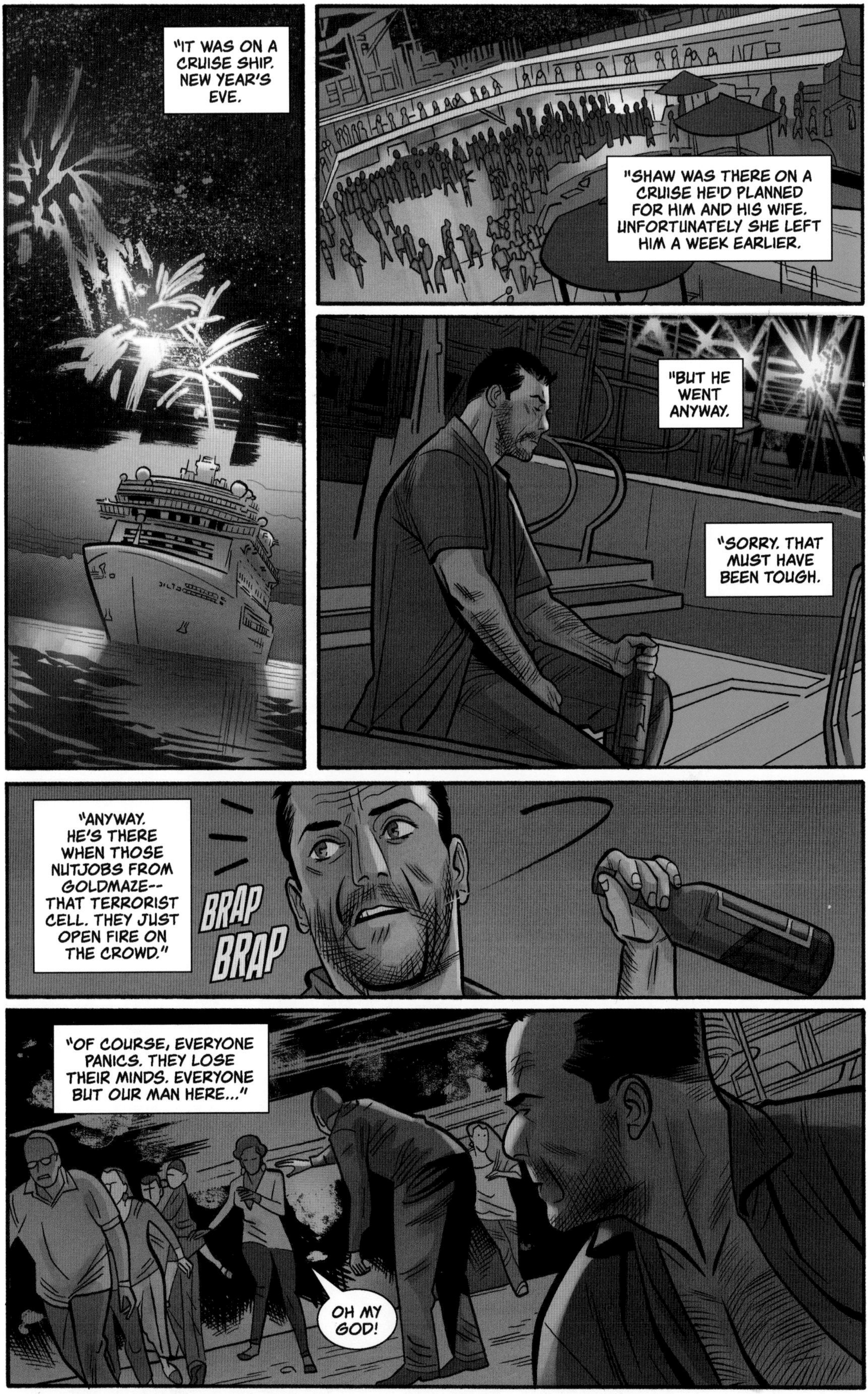
"IT WAS ON A CRUISE SHIP. NEW YEAR'S EVE.
"SHAW WAS THERE ON A CRUISE HE'D PLANNED FOR HIM AND HIS WIFE. UNFORTUNATELY SHE LEFT HIM A WEEK EARLIER.
"BUT HE WENT ANYWAY.
"SORRY. THAT MUST HAVE BEEN TOUGH.
"ANYWAY. HE'S THERE WHEN THOSE NUTJOBS FROM GOLDMAZE-- THAT TERRORIST CELL. THEY JUST OPEN FIRE ON THE CROWD."
BRAP
BRAP
"OF COURSE, EVERYONE PANICS. THEY LOSE THEIR MINDS. EVERYONE BUT OUR MAN HERE..."
OH MY GOD!

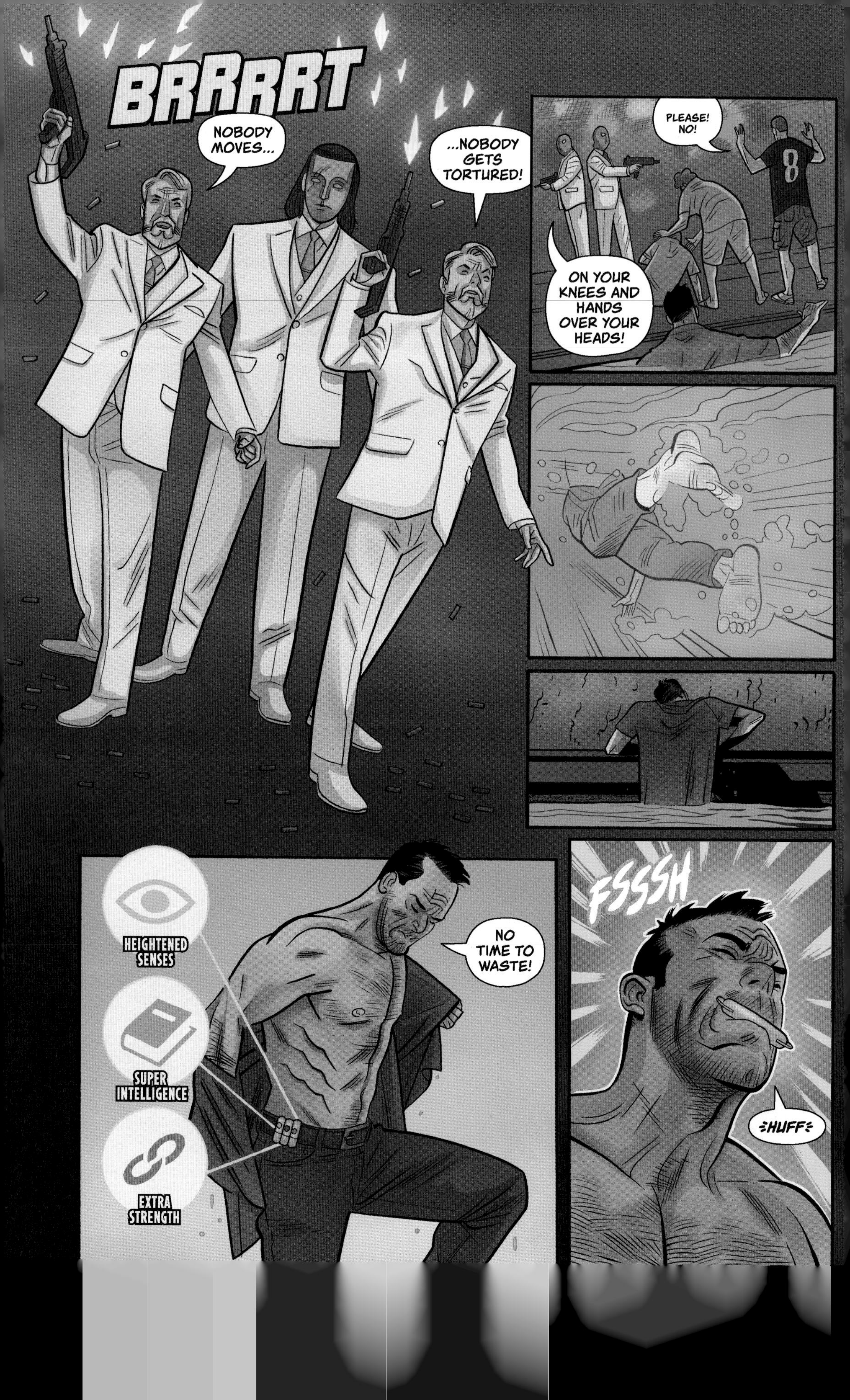
BRRRRT
NOBODY MOVES...
...NOBODY GETS TORTURED!
PLEASE! NO!
8
ON YOUR KNEES AND HANDS OVER YOUR HEADS!
HEIGHTENED SENSES
SUPER INTELLIGENCE
EXTRA STRENGTH
NO TIME TO WASTE!
FSSSH
HUFF

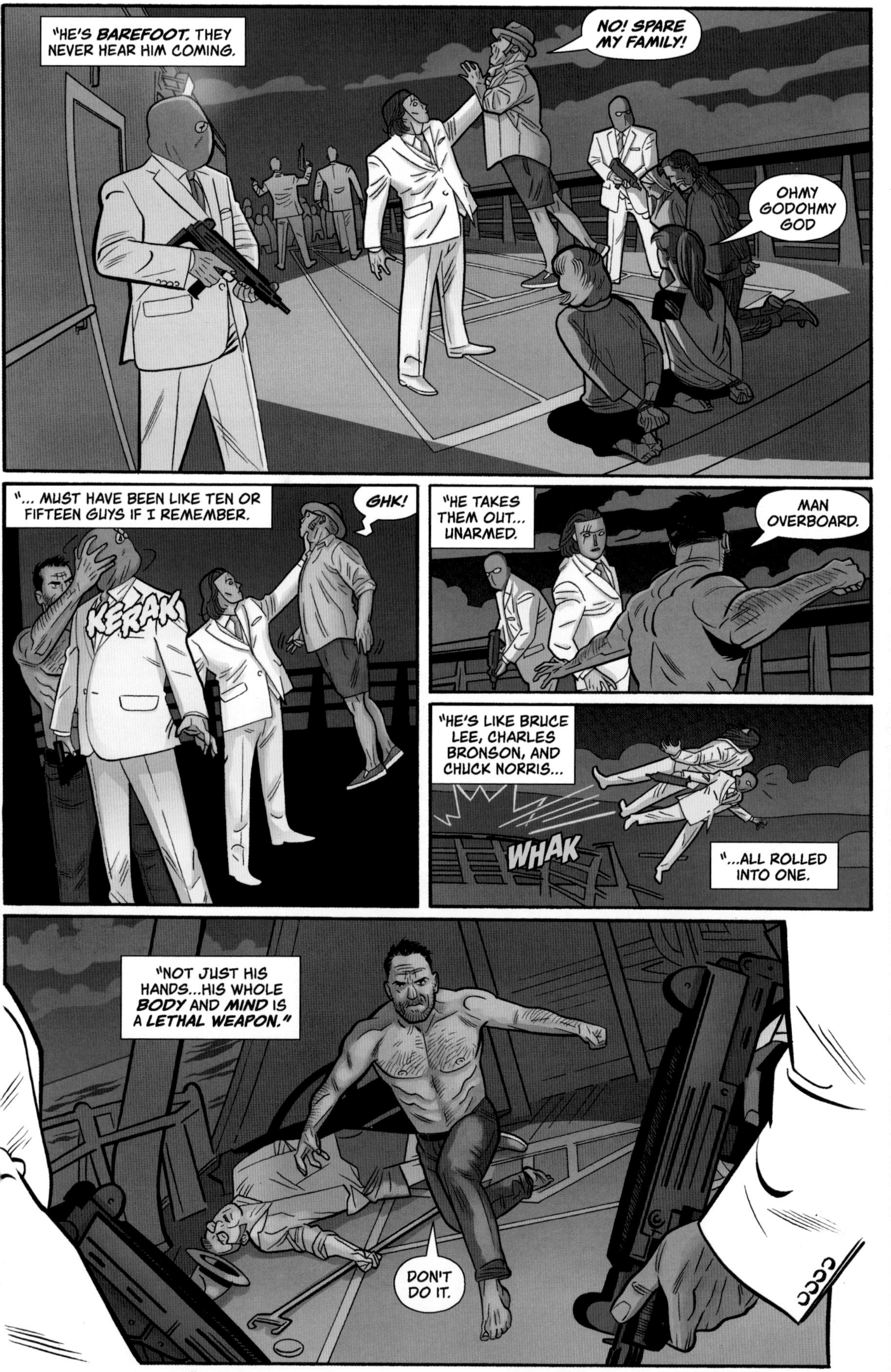

"HE'S BAREFOOT. THEY NEVER HEAR HIM COMING.
NO! SPARE MY FAMILY!
OHMY GODOHMY GOD
"... MUST HAVE BEEN LIKE TEN OR FIFTEEN GUYS IF I REMEMBER.
GHK!
KERAK
"HE TAKES THEM OUT... UNARMED.
MAN OVERBOARD.
"HE'S LIKE BRUCE LEE, CHARLES BRONSON, AND CHUCK NORRIS...
WHAK
"...ALL ROLLED INTO ONE.
"NOT JUST HIS HANDS...HIS WHOLE BODY AND MIND IS A LETHAL WEAPON."
DON'T DO IT.

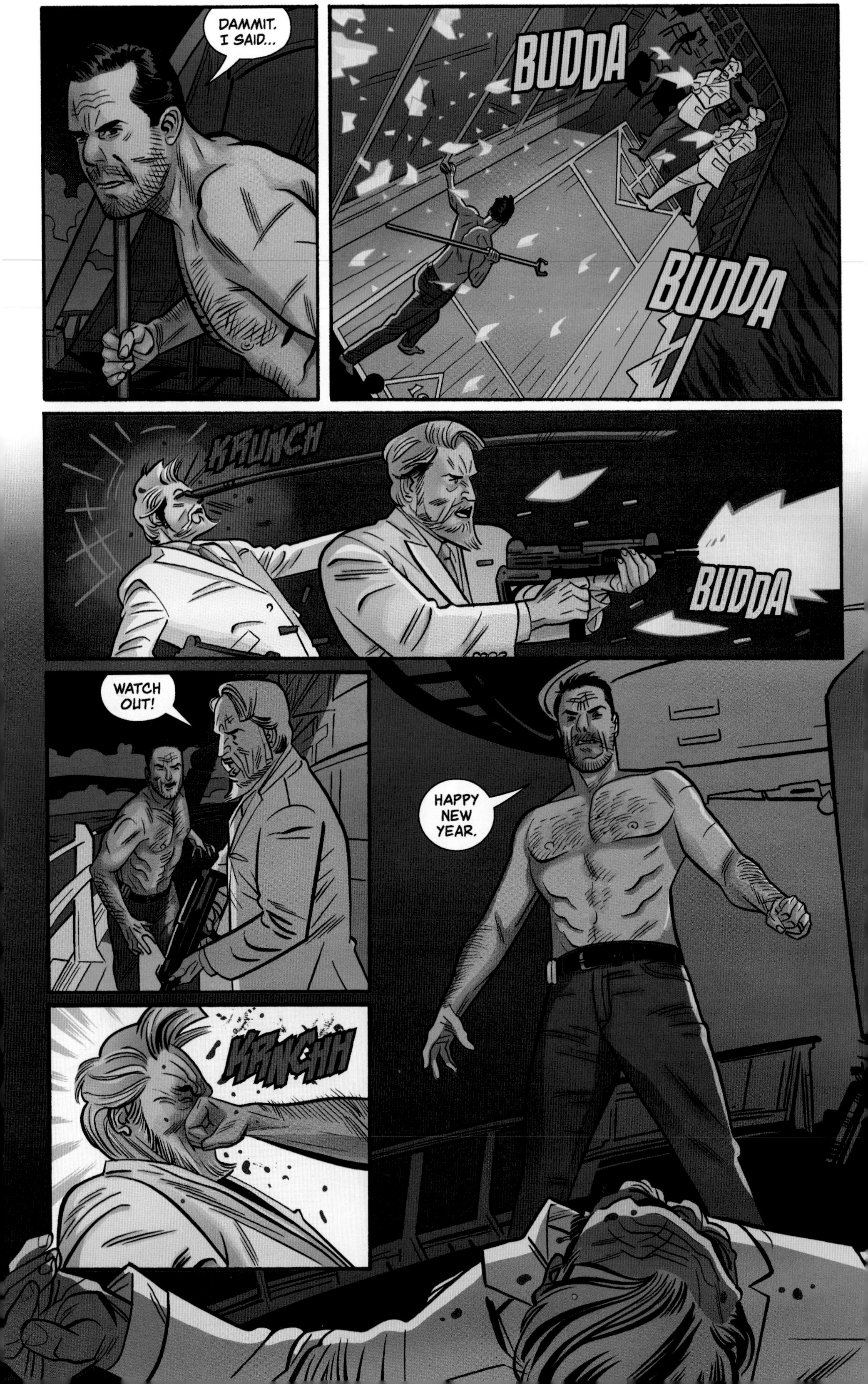
DAMMIT. I SAID...
BUDDA
BUDDA
KRUNCH
BUDDA
WATCH OUT!
HAPPY NEW YEAR.
KRNCHH

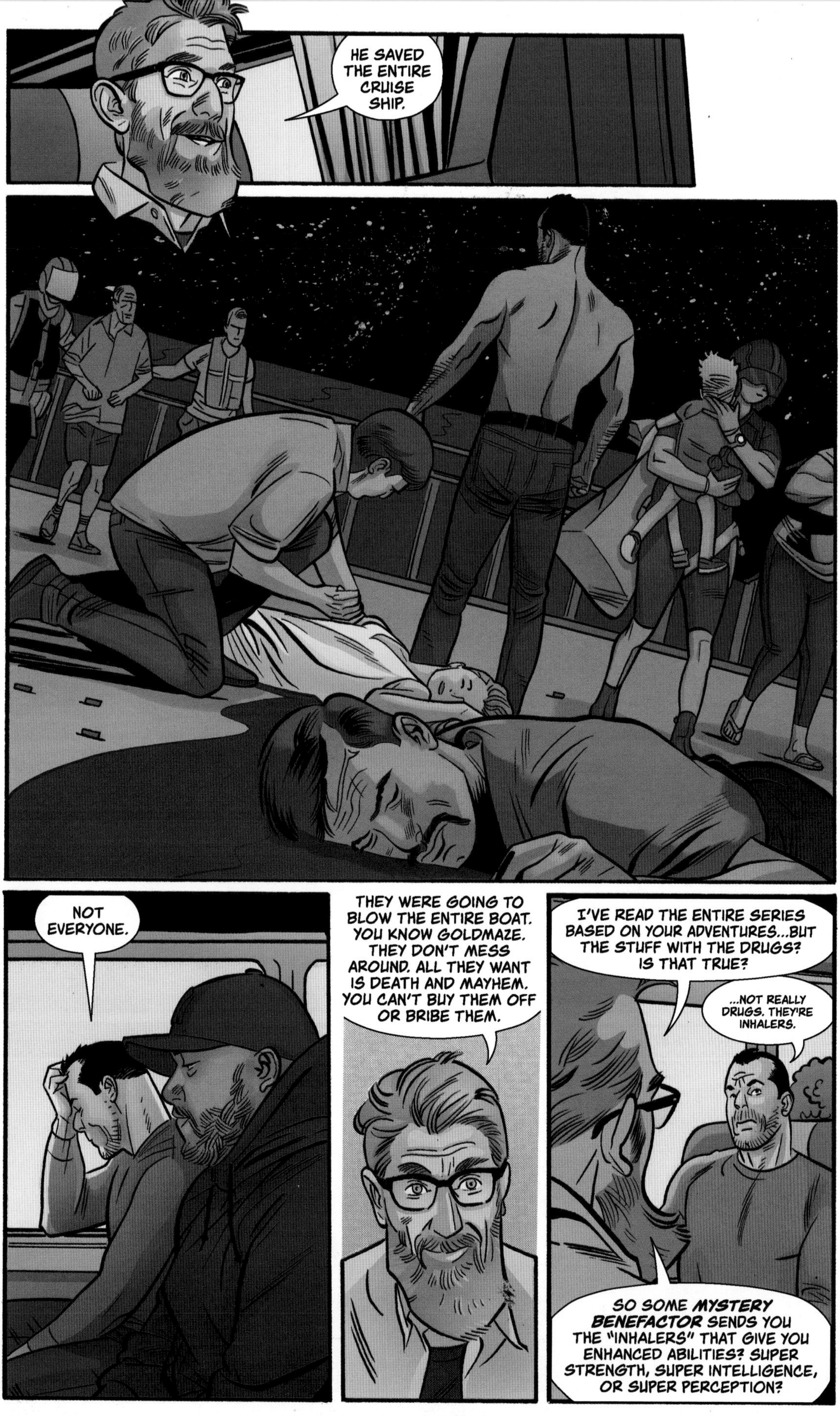
HE SAVED THE ENTIRE CRUISE SHIP.
NOT EVERYONE.
THEY WERE GOING TO BLOW THE ENTIRE BOAT. YOU KNOW GOLDMAZE. THEY DON'T MESS AROUND. ALL THEY WANT IS DEATH AND MAYHEM. YOU CAN'T BUY THEM OFF OR BRIBE THEM.
I'VE READ THE ENTIRE SERIES BASED ON YOUR ADVENTURES...BUT THE STUFF WITH THE DRUGS? IS THAT TRUE?
...NOT REALLY DRUGS. THEY'RE INHALERS.
SO SOME MYSTERY BENEFACTOR SENDS YOU THE "INHALERS" THAT GIVE YOU ENHANCED ABILITIES? SUPER STRENGTH, SUPER INTELLIGENCE, OR SUPER PERCEPTION?

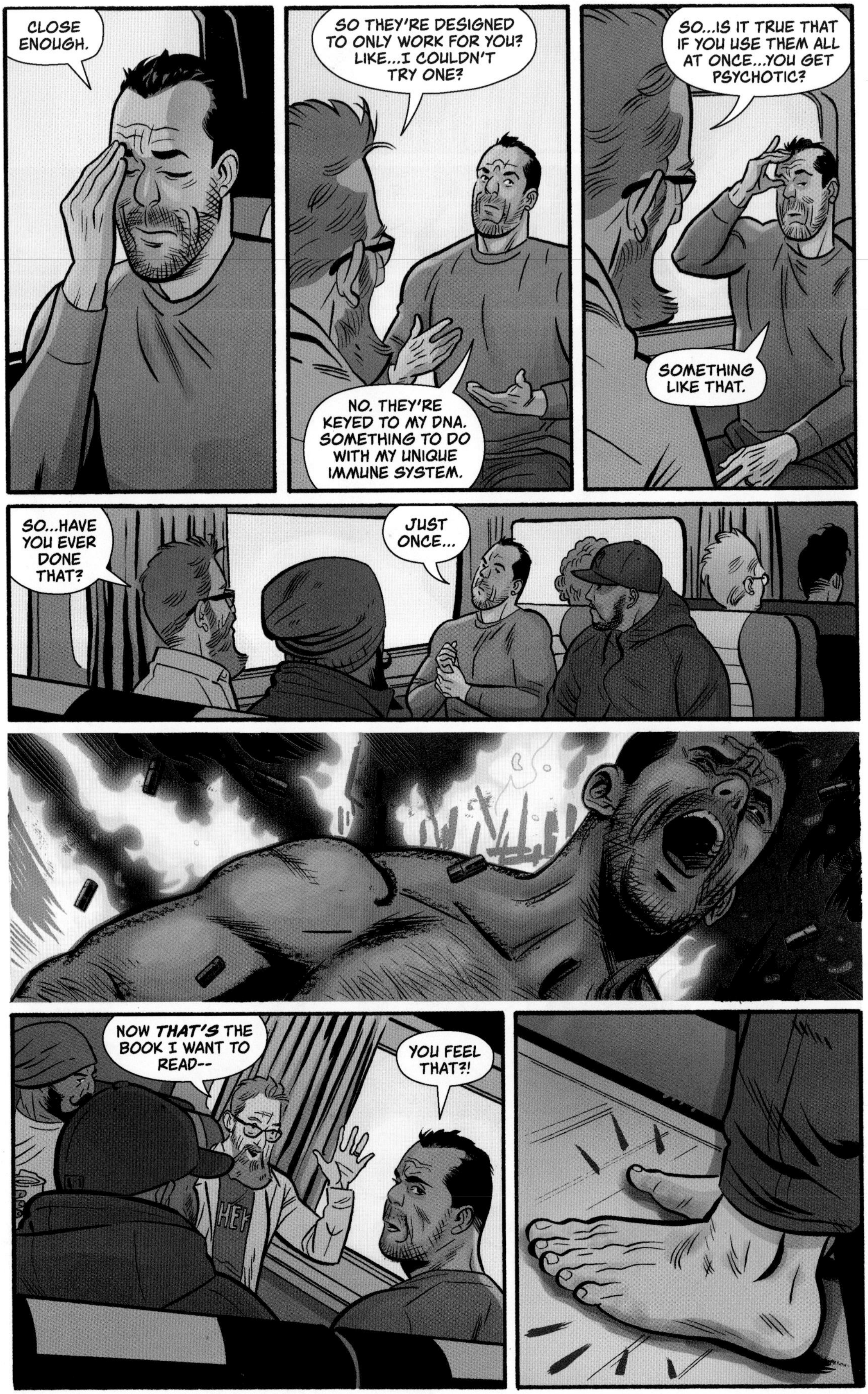
CLOSE ENOUGH.
SO THEY'RE DESIGNED TO ONLY WORK FOR YOU? LIKE...I COULDN'T TRY ONE?
NO. THEY'RE KEYED TO MY DNA. SOMETHING TO DO WITH MY UNIQUE IMMUNE SYSTEM.
SO...IS IT TRUE THAT IF YOU USE THEM ALL AT ONCE...YOU GET PSYCHOTIC?
SOMETHING LIKE THAT.
SO...HAVE YOU EVER DONE THAT?
JUST ONCE...
NOW *THAT'S* THE BOOK I WANT TO READ--
YOU FEEL THAT?!

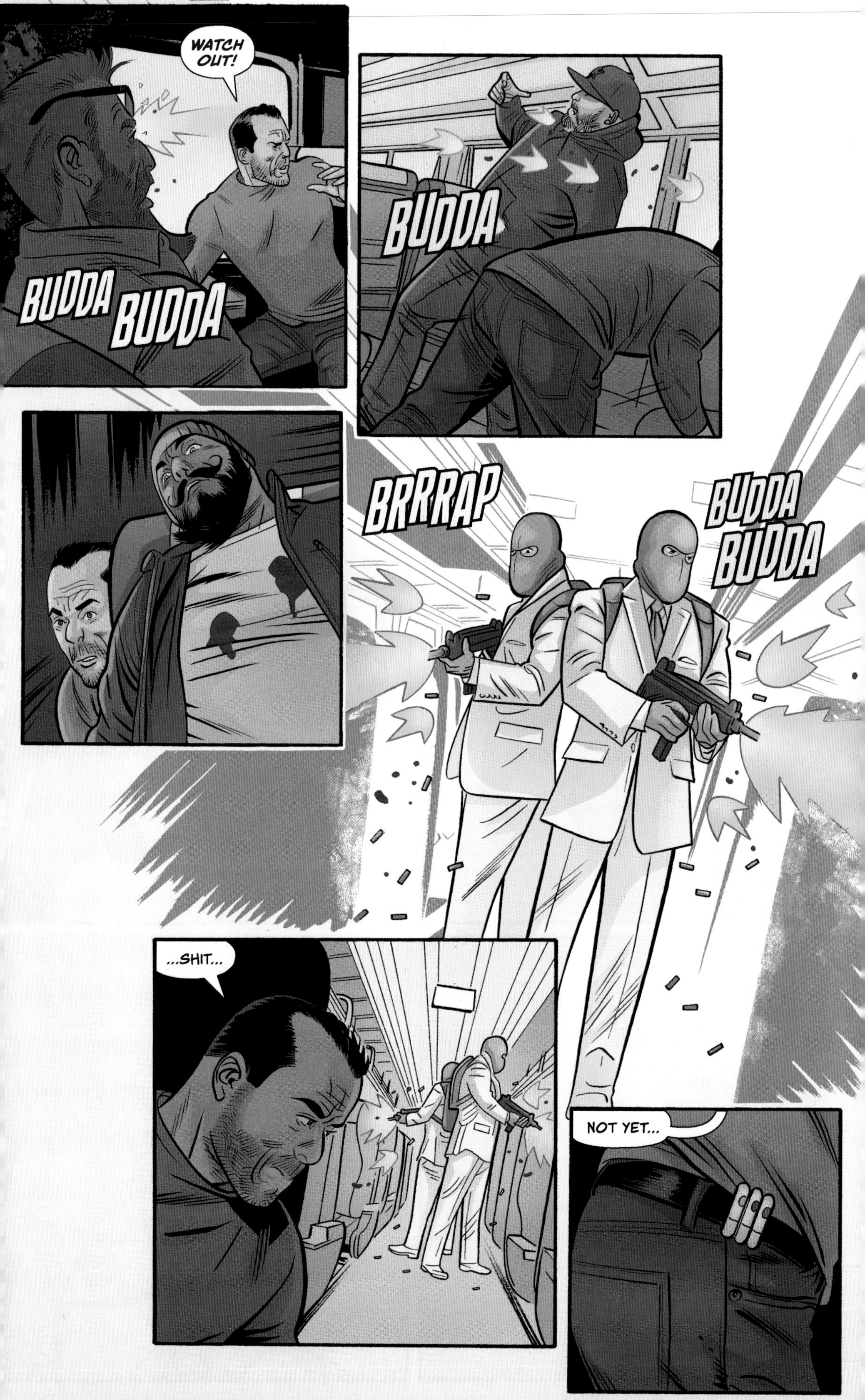

WATCH OUT!
BUDDA BUDDA
BUDDA
BRRRAP
BUDDA BUDDA
...SHIT...
NOT YET...

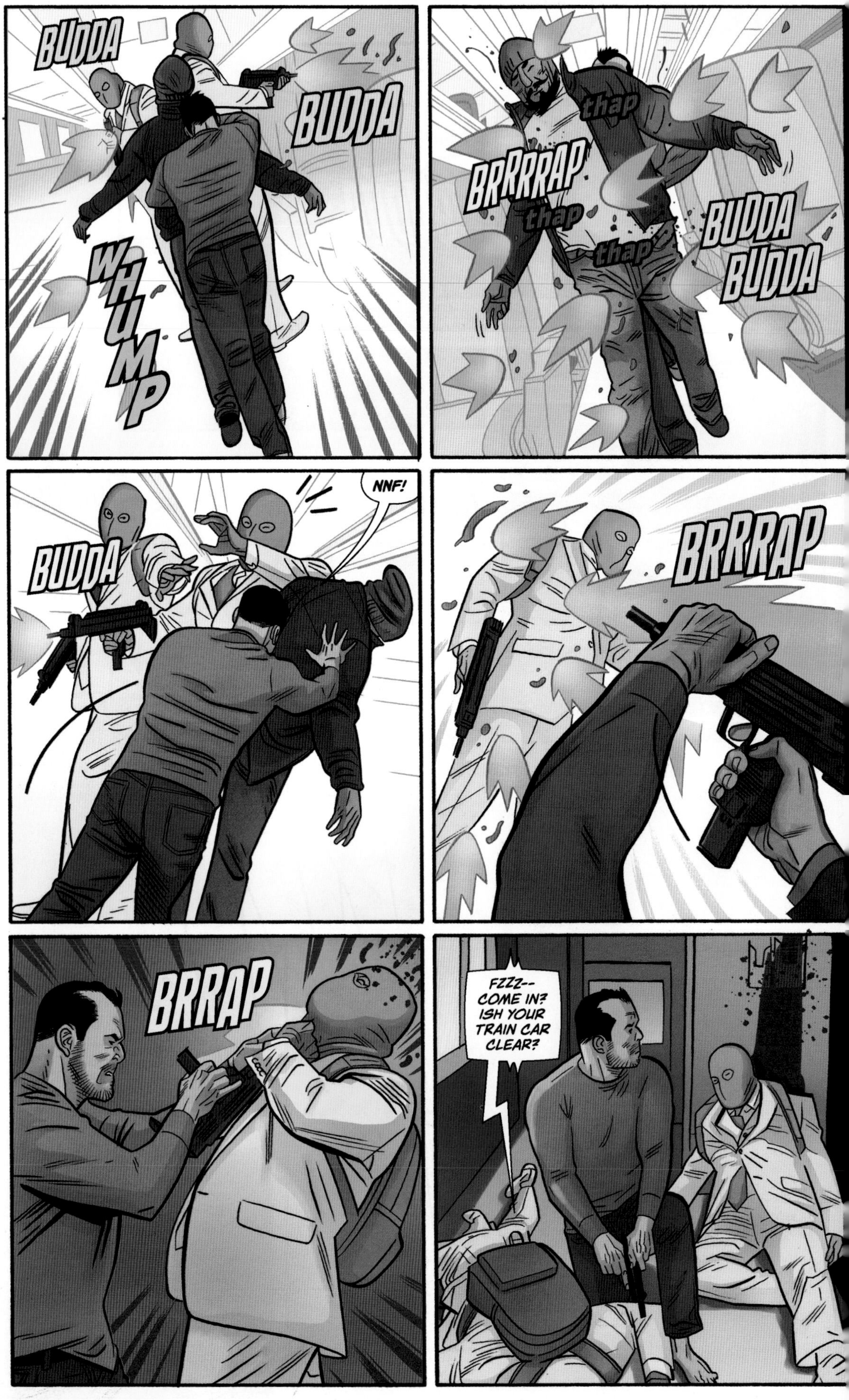
BUDDA
BUDDA
WHUMP
BRRRRAP
thap
thap
thap
BUDDA
BUDDA
BUDDA
NNF!
BRRRAP
BRRAP
FZZZ-- COME IN? ISH YOUR TRAIN CAR CLEAR?

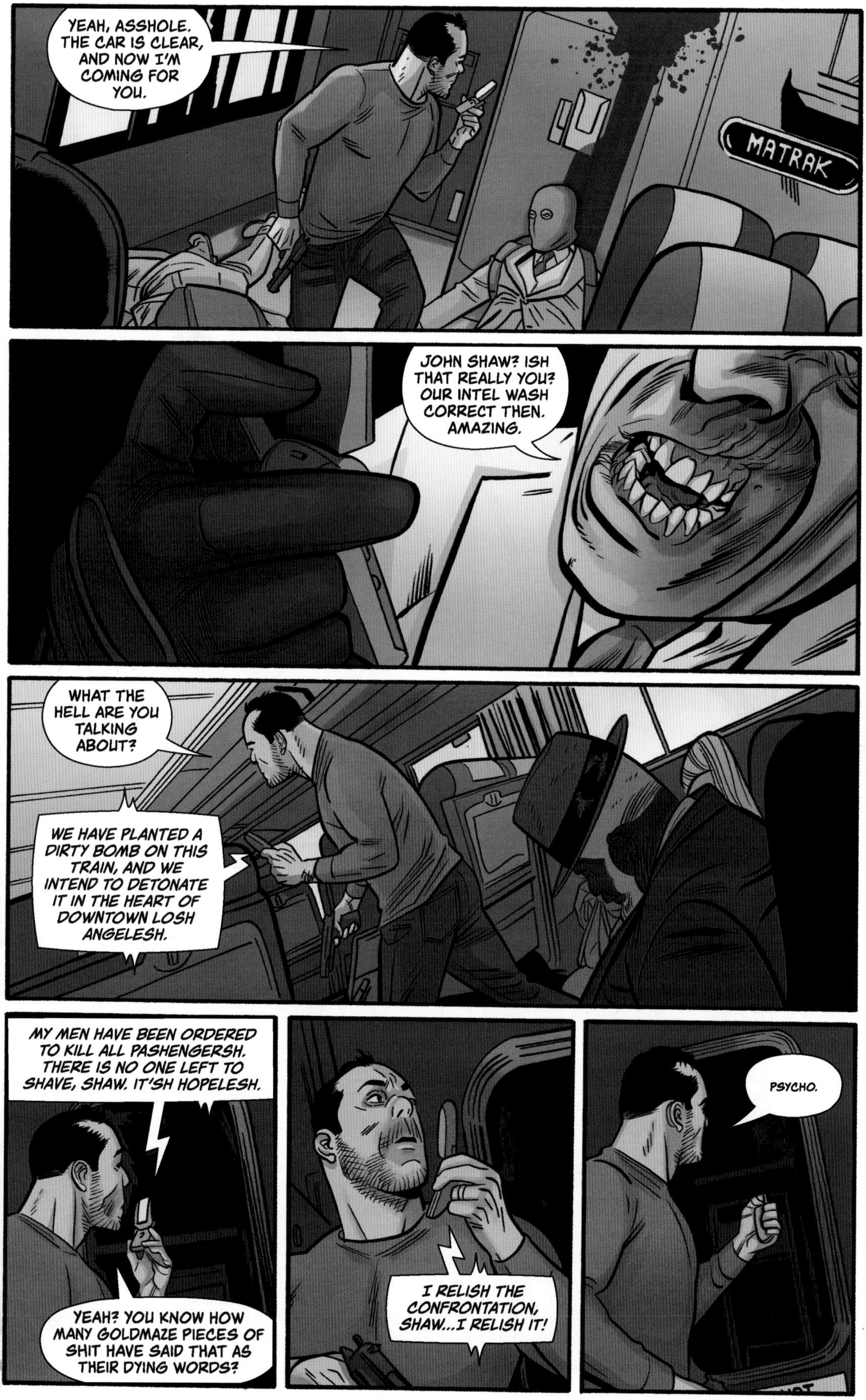
YEAH, ASSHOLE. THE CAR IS CLEAR, AND NOW I'M COMING FOR YOU.
MATRAK
JOHN SHAW? ISH THAT REALLY YOU? OUR INTEL WASH CORRECT THEN. AMAZING.
WHAT THE HELL ARE YOU TALKING ABOUT?
WE HAVE PLANTED A DIRTY BOMB ON THIS TRAIN, AND WE INTEND TO DETONATE IT IN THE HEART OF DOWNTOWN LOSH ANGELESH.
MY MEN HAVE BEEN ORDERED TO KILL ALL PASHENGERSH. THERE IS NO ONE LEFT TO SHAVE, SHAW. IT'SH HOPELESH.
YEAH? YOU KNOW HOW MANY GOLDMAZE PIECES OF SHIT HAVE SAID THAT AS THEIR DYING WORDS?
I RELISH THE CONFRONTATION, SHAW...I RELISH IT!
PSYCHO.

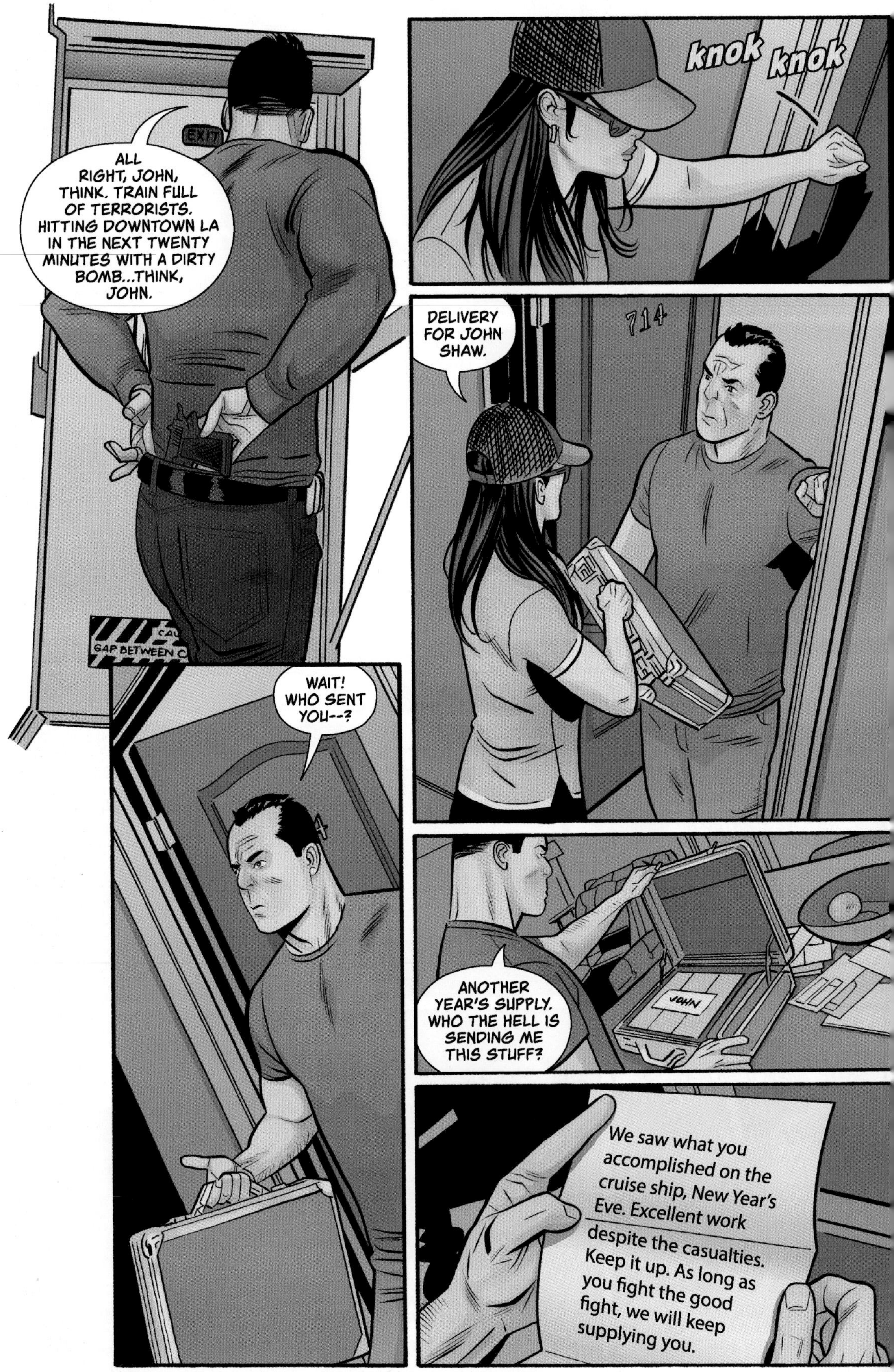
EXIT
ALL RIGHT, JOHN, THINK. TRAIN FULL OF TERRORISTS. HITTING DOWNTOWN LA IN THE NEXT TWENTY MINUTES WITH A DIRTY BOMB...THINK, JOHN.
knok knok
714
DELIVERY FOR JOHN SHAW.
WAIT! WHO SENT YOU--?
ANOTHER YEAR'S SUPPLY. WHO THE HELL IS SENDING ME THIS STUFF?
JOHN
We saw what you accomplished on the cruise ship, New Year's Eve. Excellent work despite the casualties. Keep it up. As long as you fight the good fight, we will keep supplying you.

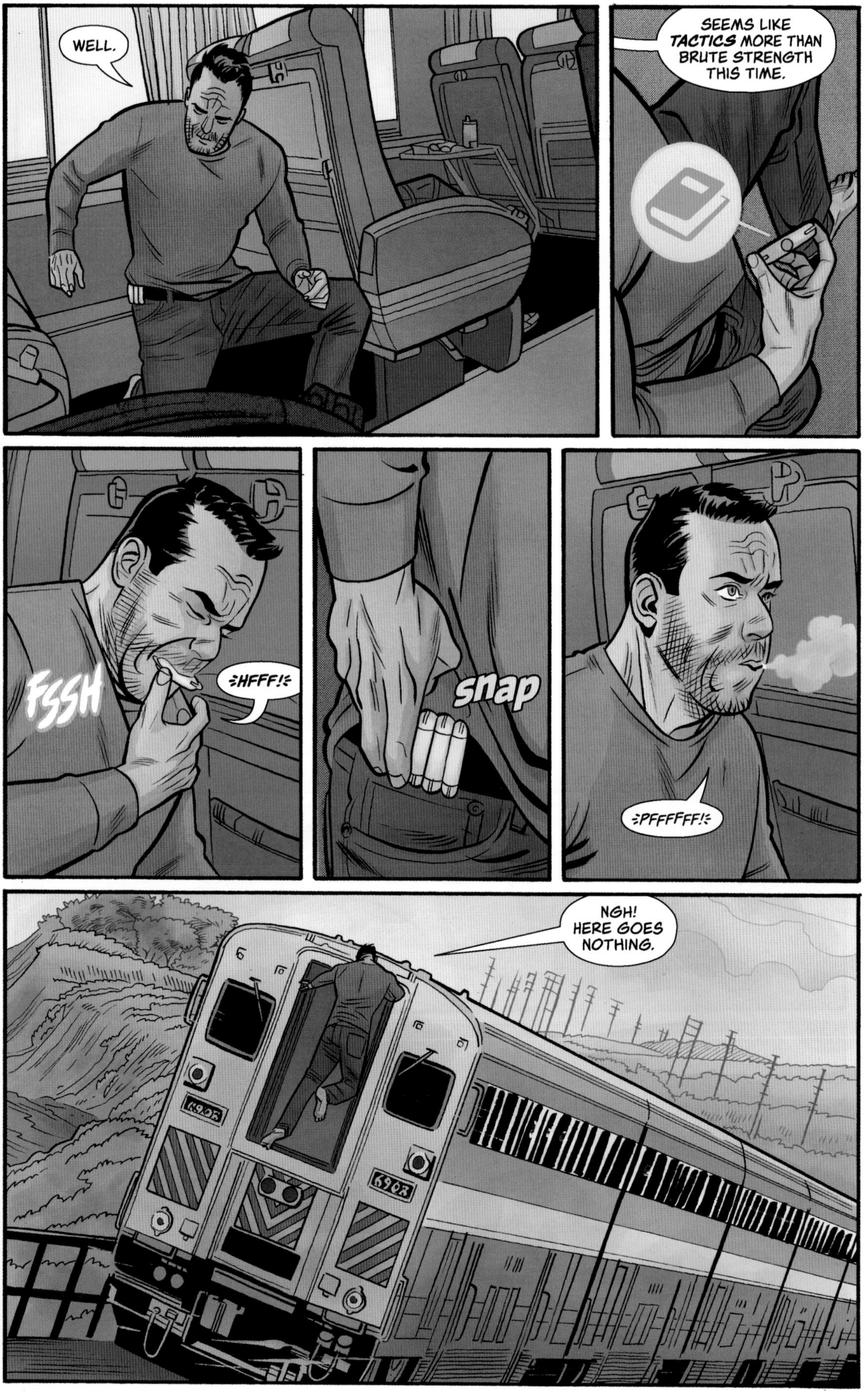
WELL.
SEEMS LIKE TACTICS MORE THAN BRUTE STRENGTH THIS TIME.
FSSH
HFFF!
snap
PFFFFFF!
NGH! HERE GOES NOTHING.
6903
6903

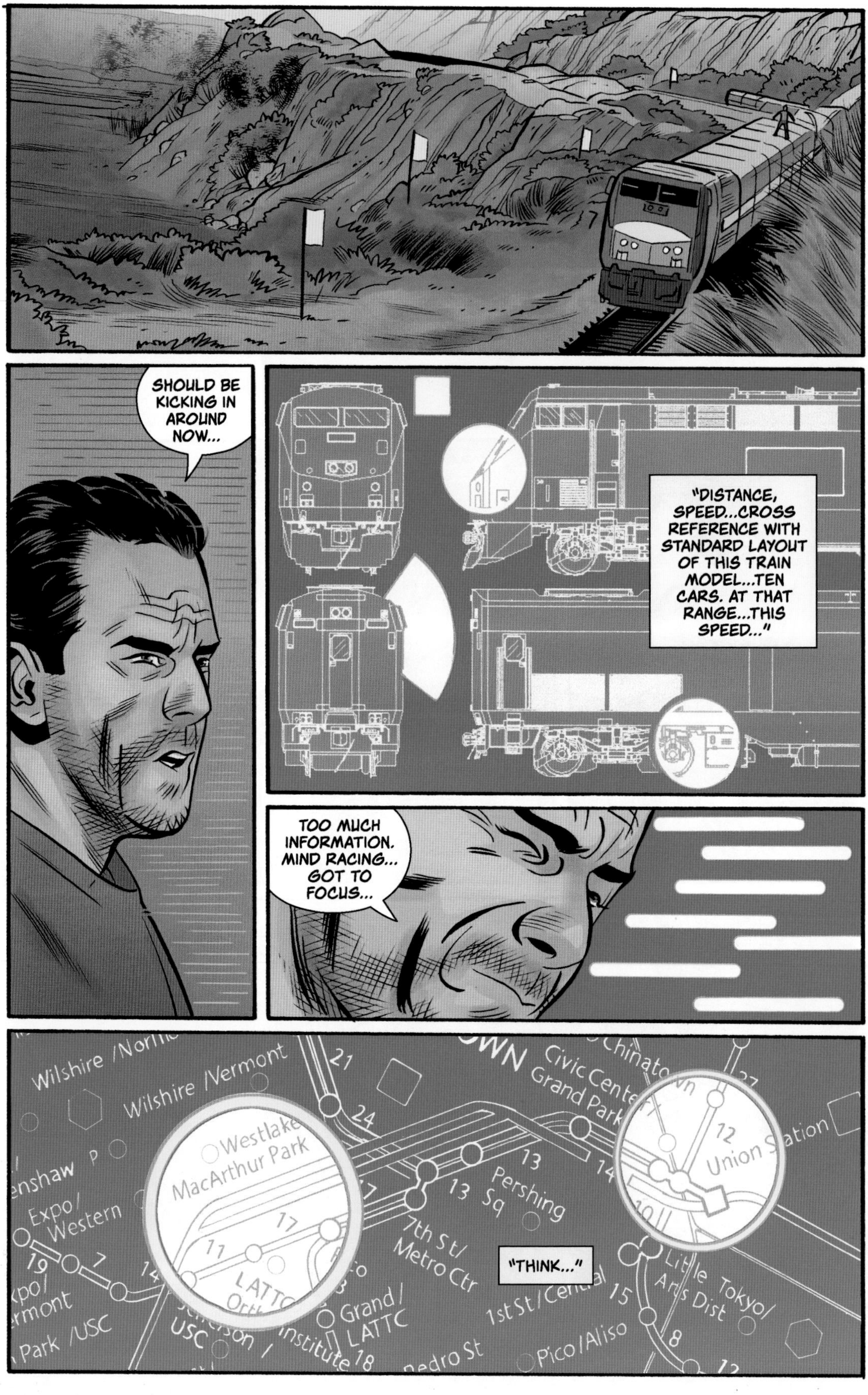
SHOULD BE KICKING IN AROUND NOW...
"DISTANCE, SPEED...CROSS REFERENCE WITH STANDARD LAYOUT OF THIS TRAIN MODEL...TEN CARS. AT THAT RANGE...THIS SPEED..."
TOO MUCH INFORMATION. MIND RACING... GOT TO FOCUS...
"THINK..."

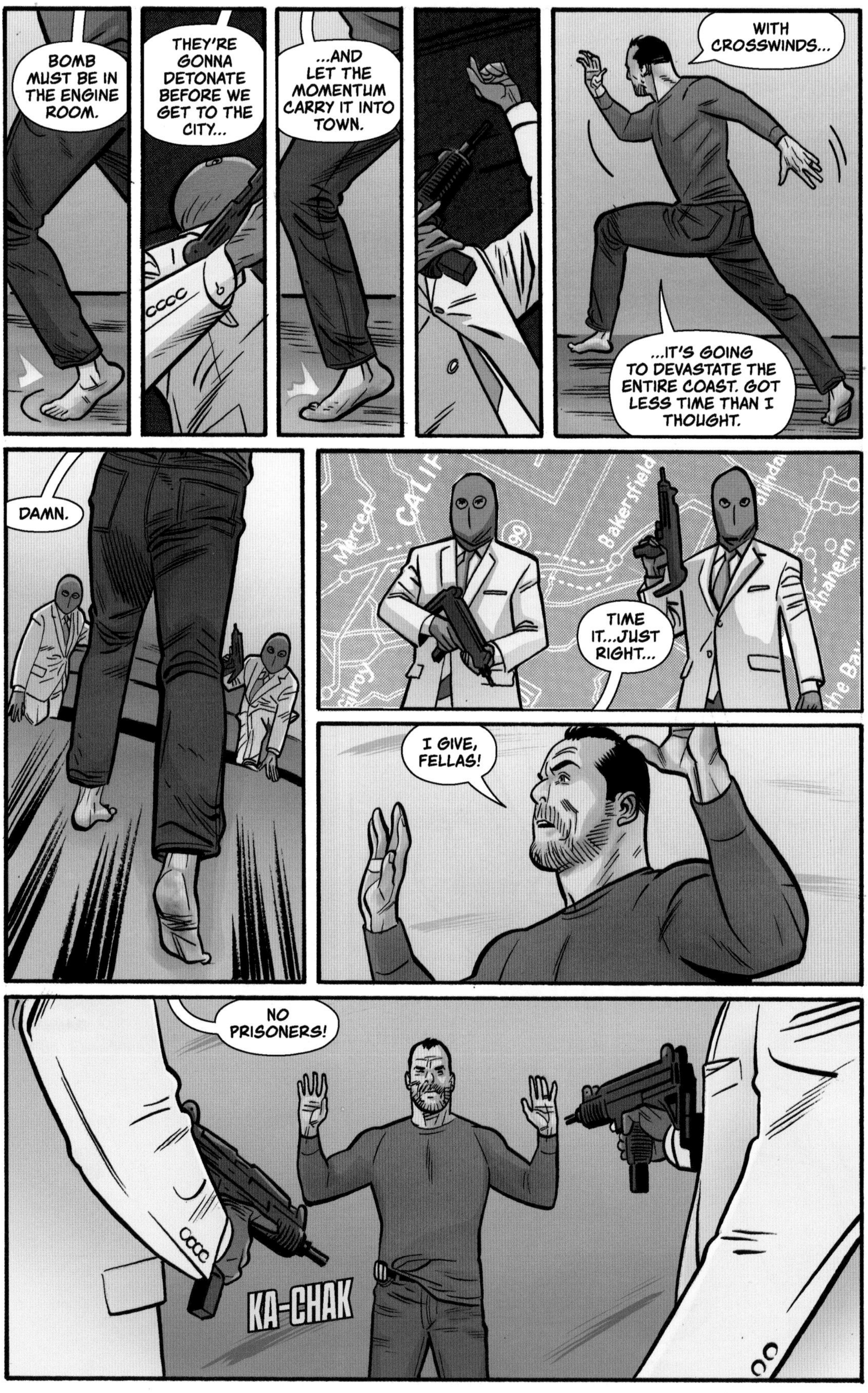
BOMB MUST BE IN THE ENGINE ROOM.
THEY'RE GONNA DETONATE BEFORE WE GET TO THE CITY...
...AND LET THE MOMENTUM CARRY IT INTO TOWN.
WITH CROSSWINDS...
...IT'S GOING TO DEVASTATE THE ENTIRE COAST. GOT LESS TIME THAN I THOUGHT.
DAMN.
Merced
Bakersfield
Anaheim
TIME IT...JUST RIGHT...
I GIVE, FELLAS!
NO PRISONERS!
KA-CHAK

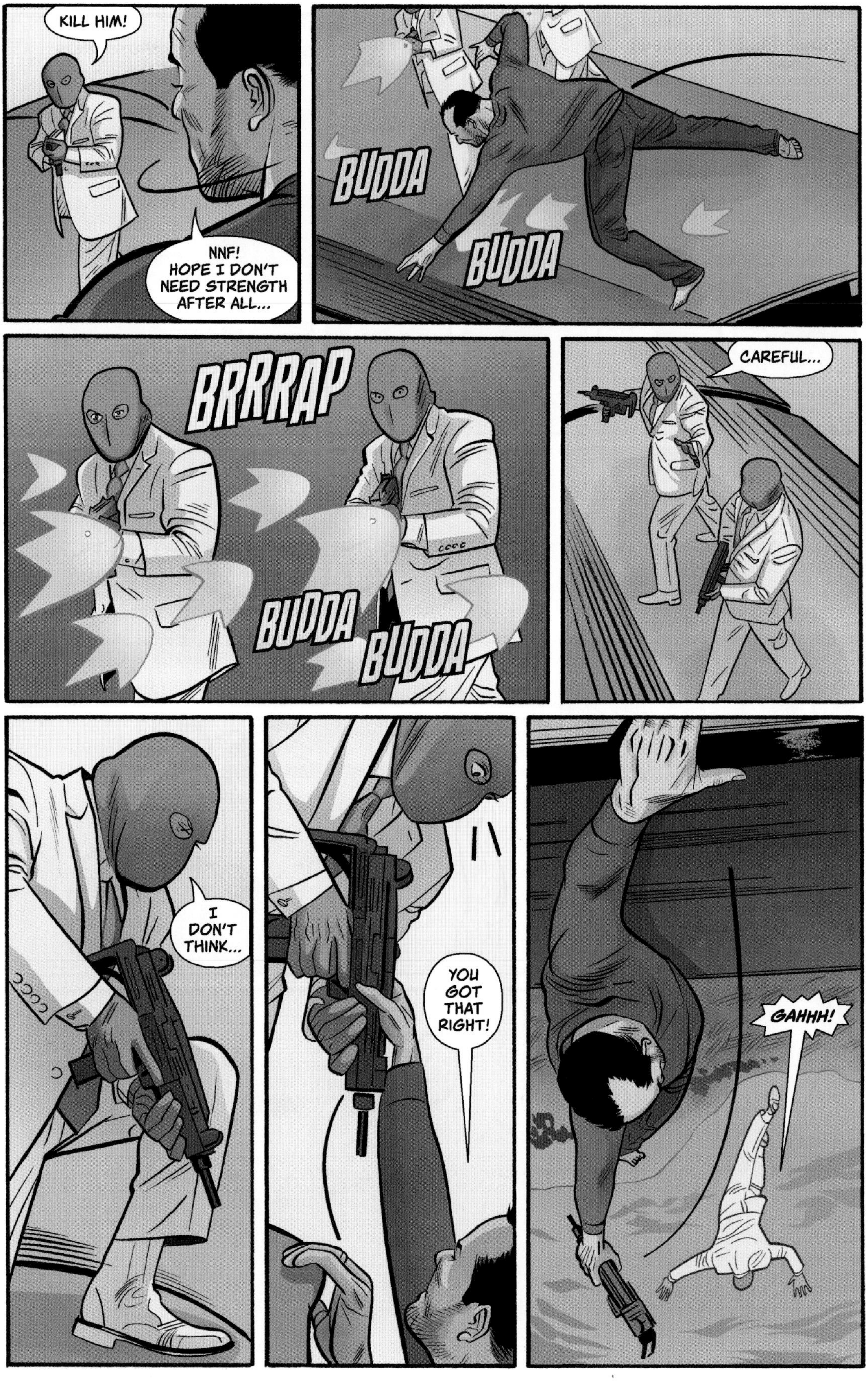
KILL HIM!
NNF! HOPE I DON'T NEED STRENGTH AFTER ALL...
BUDDA
BUDDA
BRRRAP
BUDDA
BUDDA
CAREFUL...
I DON'T THINK...
YOU GOT THAT RIGHT!
GAHHH!

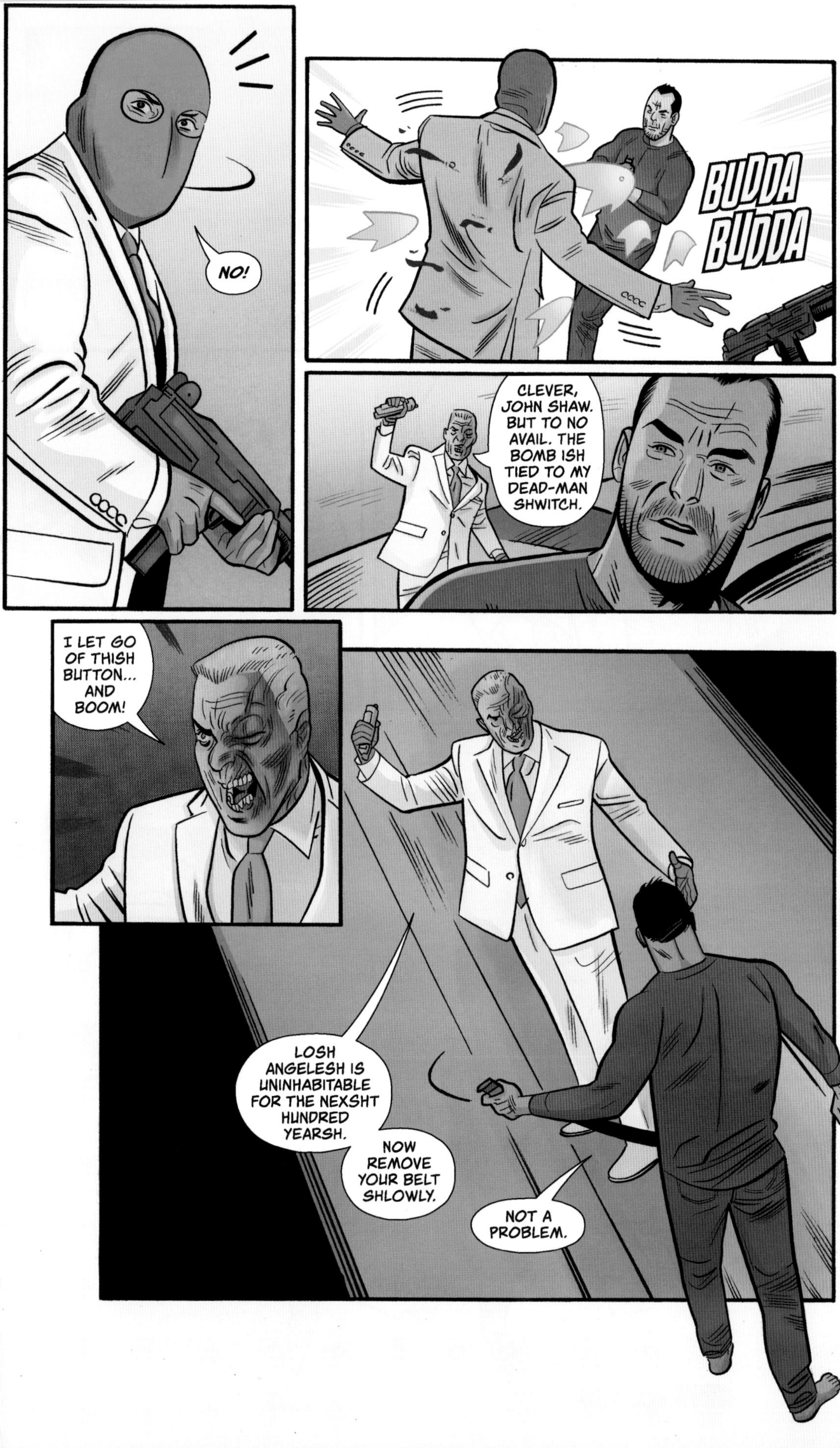
NO!
BUDDA BUDDA
CLEVER, JOHN SHAW. BUT TO NO AVAIL. THE BOMB ISH TIED TO MY DEAD-MAN SHWITCH.
I LET GO OF THISH BUTTON... AND BOOM!
LOSH ANGELESH IS UNINHABITABLE FOR THE NEXSHT HUNDRED YEARSH.
NOW REMOVE YOUR BELT SHLOWLY.
NOT A PROBLEM.

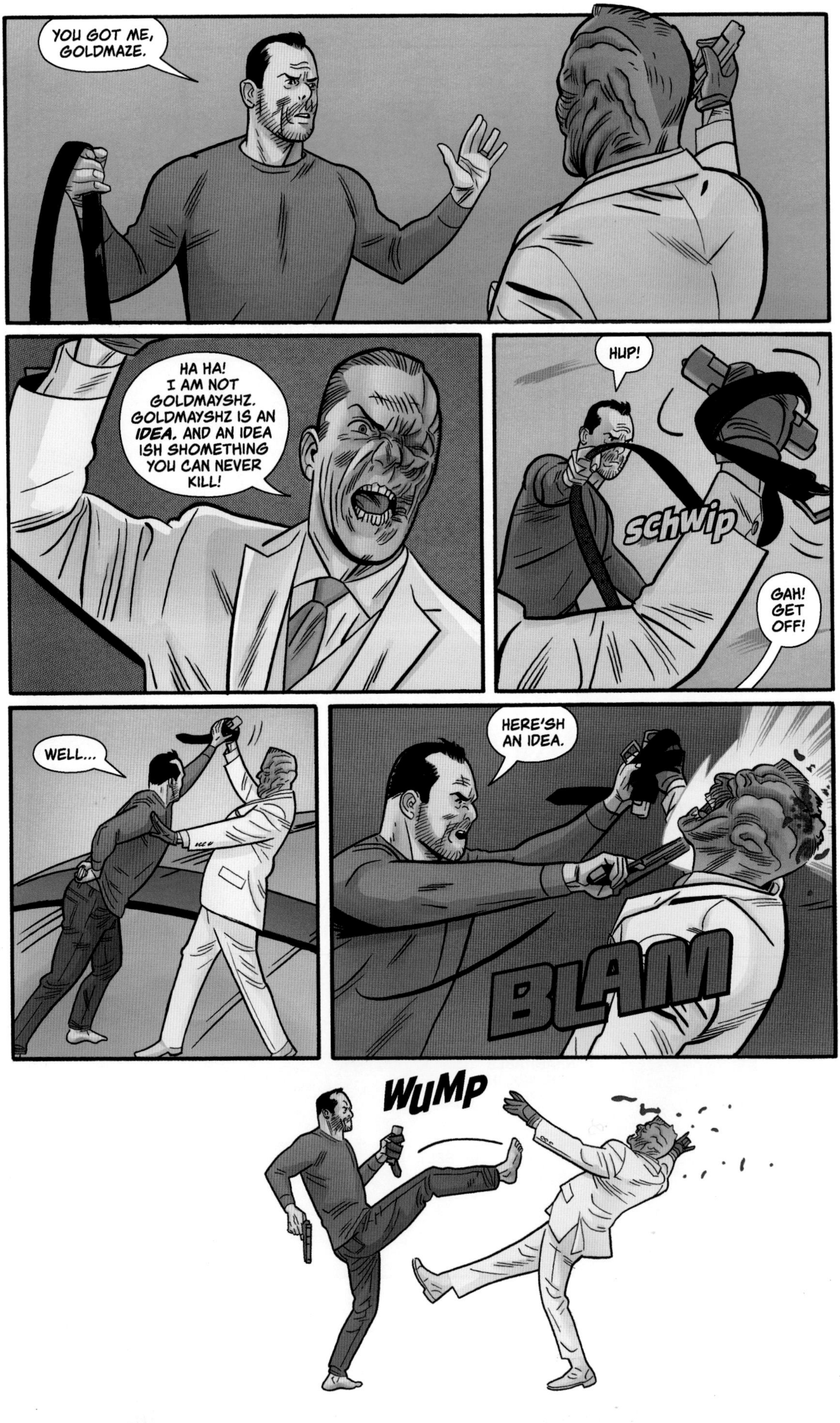
YOU GOT ME, GOLDMAZE.
HA HA! I AM NOT GOLDMAYSHZ. GOLDMAYSHZ IS AN *IDEA.* AND AN IDEA ISH SHOMETHING YOU CAN NEVER KILL!
HUP!
schwip
GAH! GET OFF!
WELL...
HERE'SH AN IDEA.
BLAM
WUMP

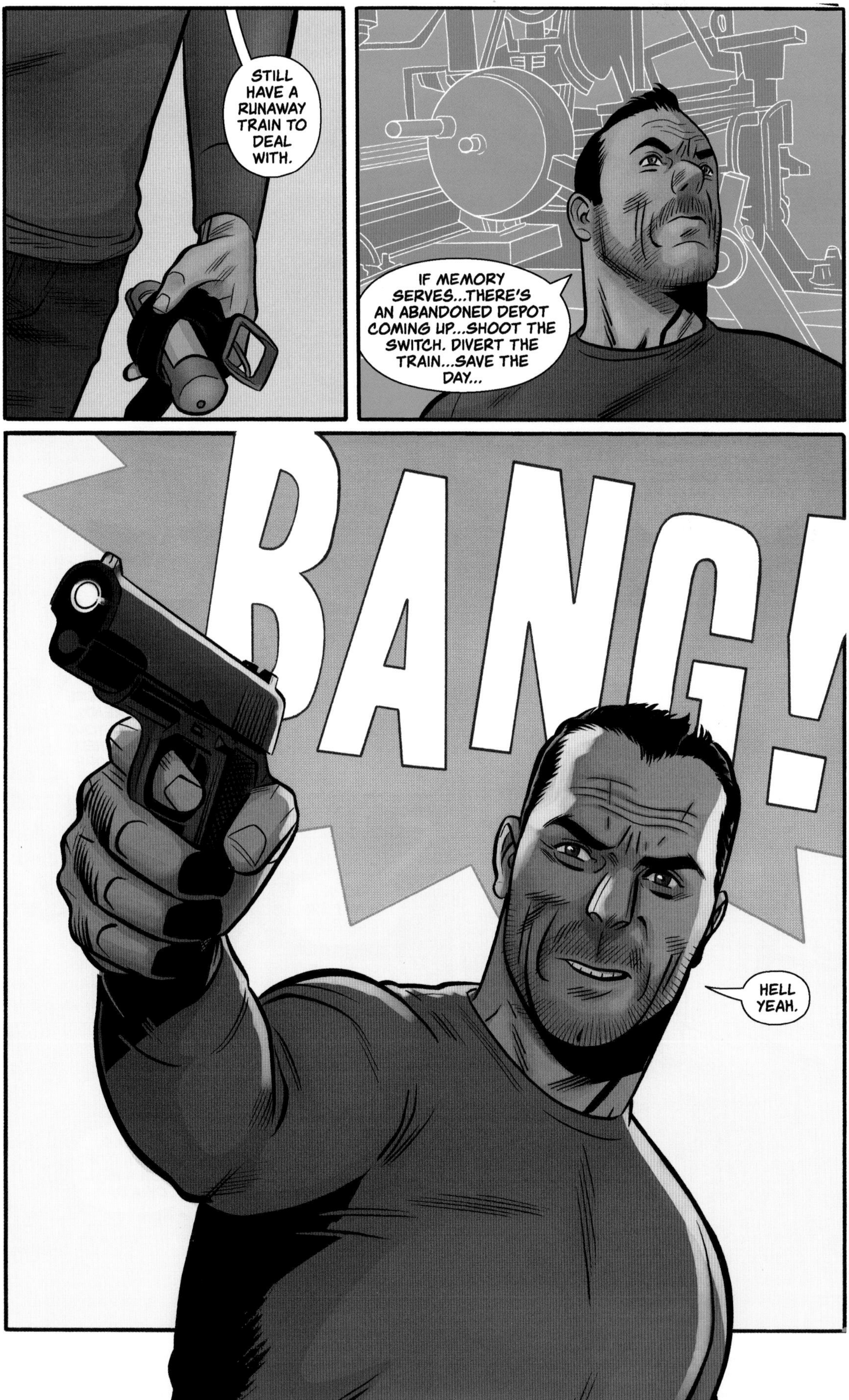
STILL HAVE A RUNAWAY TRAIN TO DEAL WITH.
IF MEMORY SERVES...THERE'S AN ABANDONED DEPOT COMING UP...SHOOT THE SWITCH. DIVERT THE TRAIN...SAVE THE DAY...
BANG!
HELL YEAH.

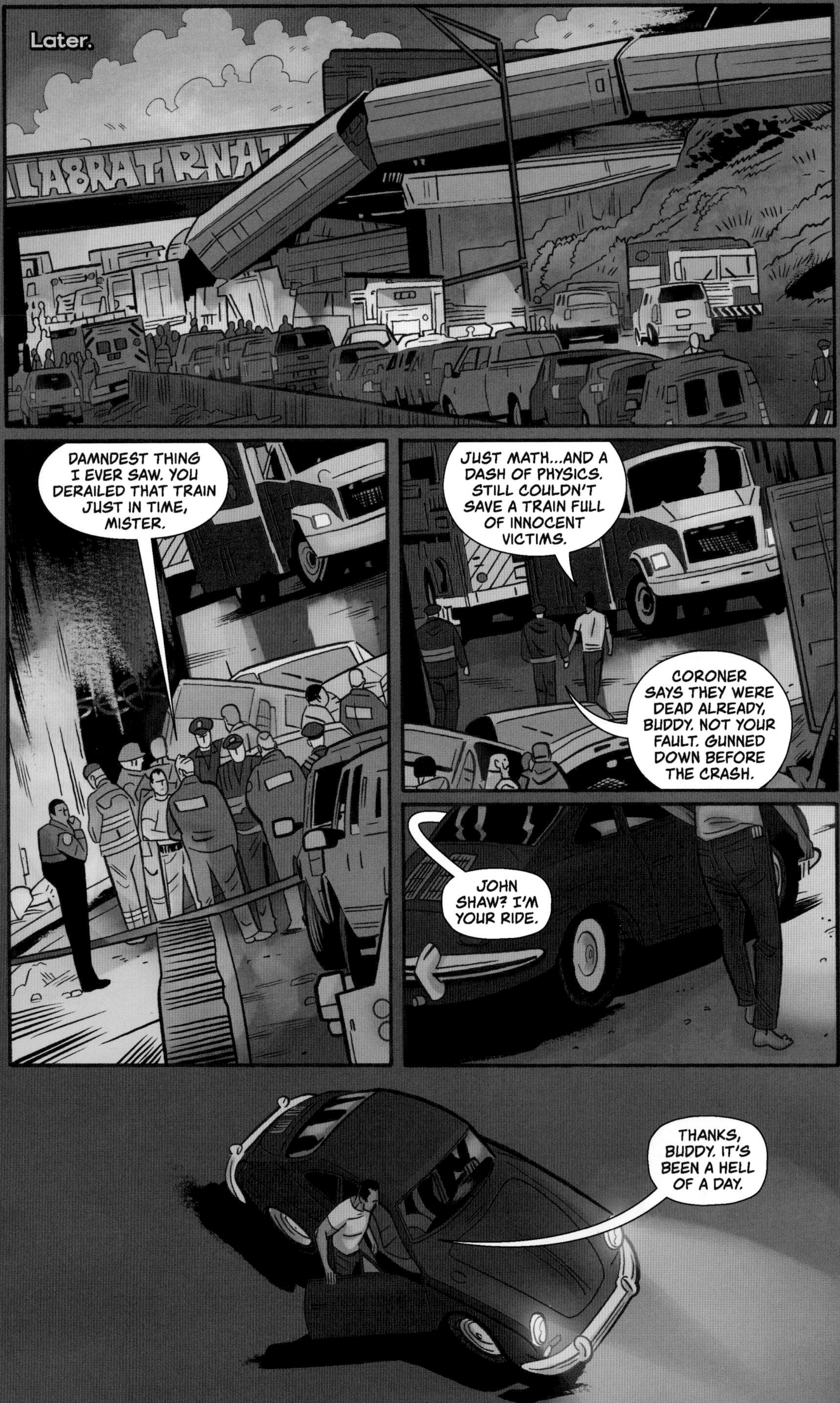
Later.
DAMNDEST THING I EVER SAW. YOU DERAILED THAT TRAIN JUST IN TIME, MISTER.
JUST MATH...AND A DASH OF PHYSICS. STILL COULDN'T SAVE A TRAIN FULL OF INNOCENT VICTIMS.
CORONER SAYS THEY WERE DEAD ALREADY, BUDDY. NOT YOUR FAULT. GUNNED DOWN BEFORE THE CRASH.
JOHN SHAW? I'M YOUR RIDE.
THANKS, BUDDY. IT'S BEEN A HELL OF A DAY.

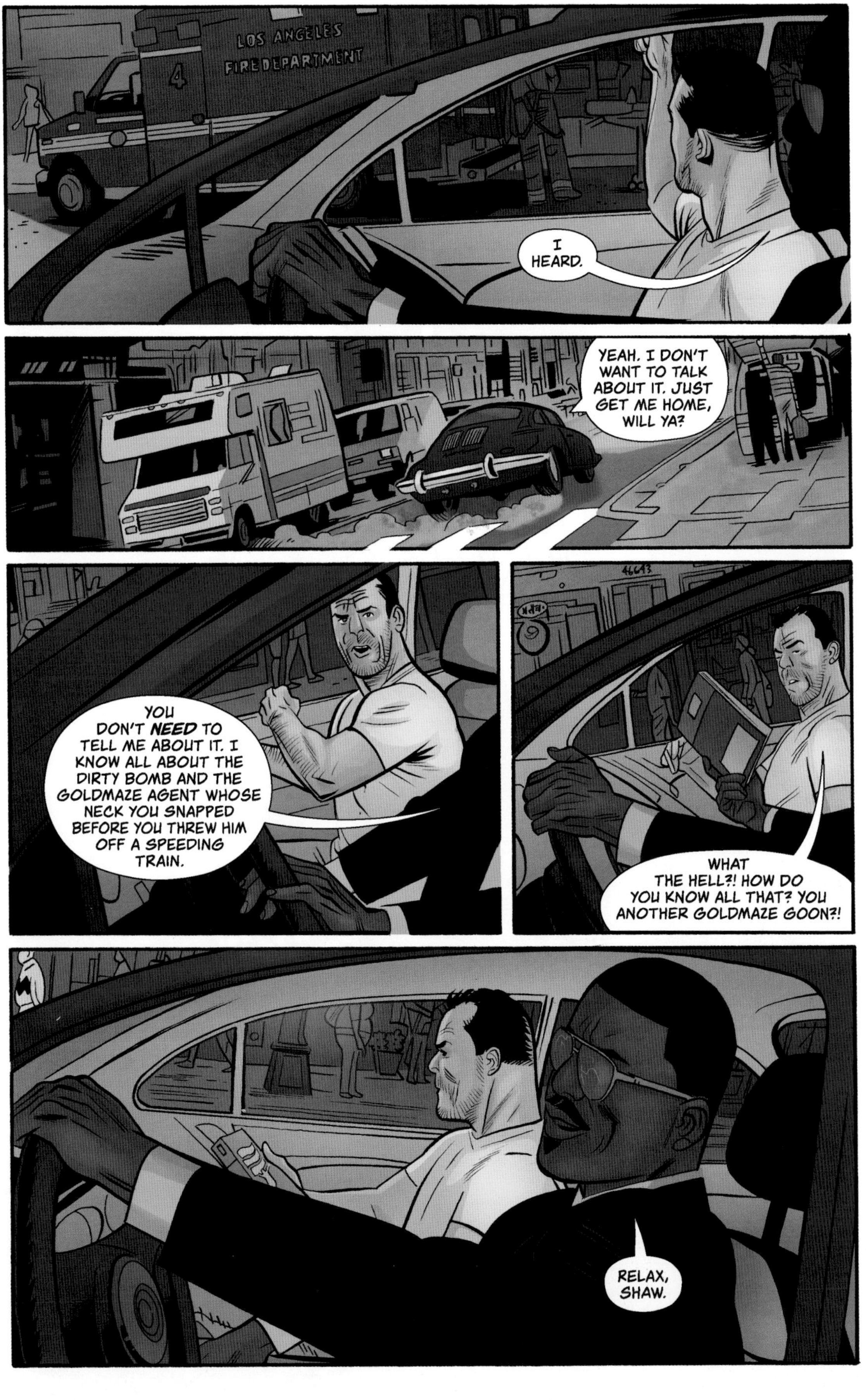
LOS ANGELES
FIREDEPARTMENT
4
I HEARD.
YEAH. I DON'T WANT TO TALK ABOUT IT. JUST GET ME HOME, WILL YA?
YOU DON'T **NEED** TO TELL ME ABOUT IT. I KNOW ALL ABOUT THE DIRTY BOMB AND THE GOLDMAZE AGENT WHOSE NECK YOU SNAPPED BEFORE YOU THREW HIM OFF A SPEEDING TRAIN.
46643
WHAT THE HELL?! HOW DO YOU KNOW ALL THAT? YOU ANOTHER GOLDMAZE GOON?!
RELAX, SHAW.

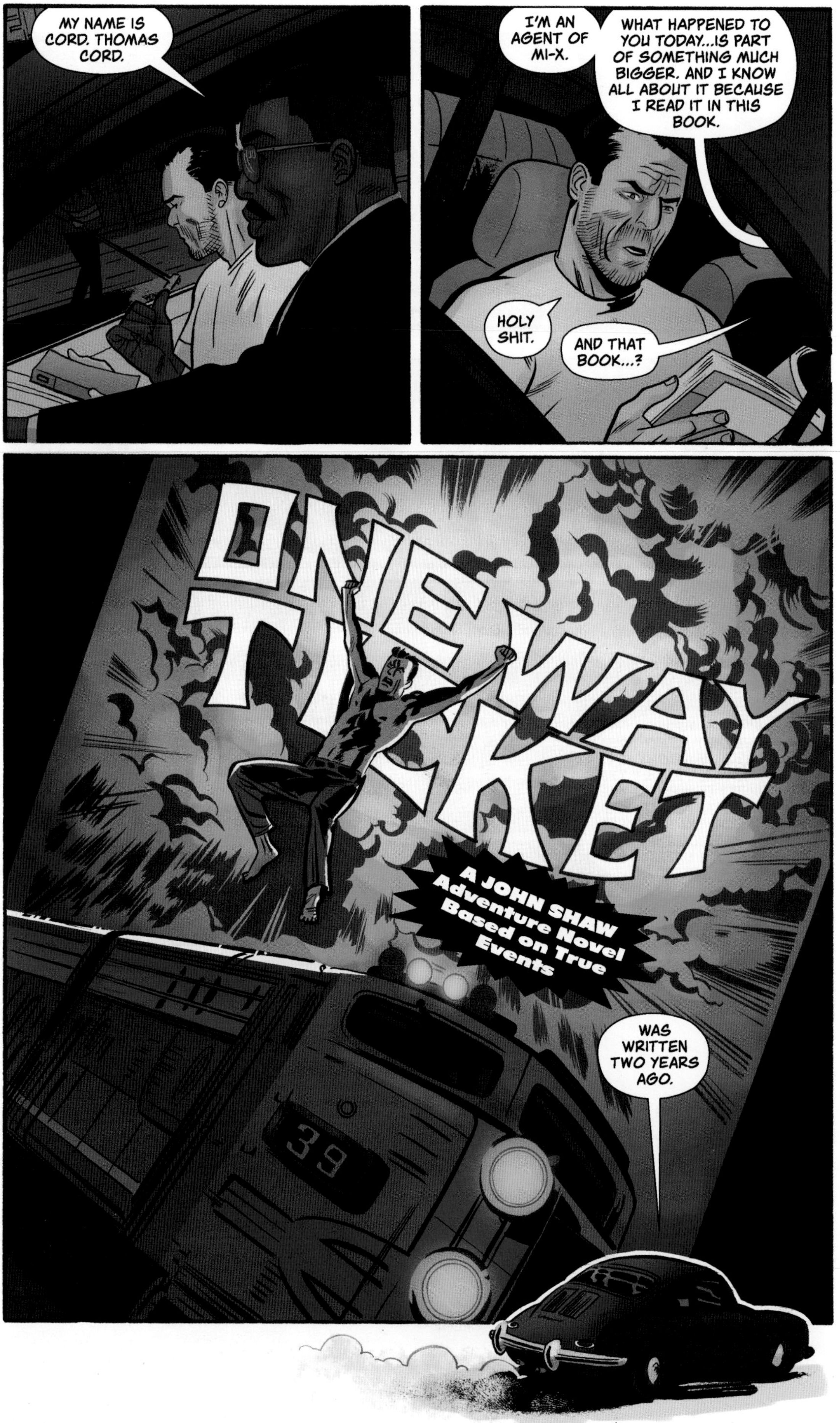

MY NAME IS CORD. THOMAS CORD.
I'M AN AGENT OF MI-X.
WHAT HAPPENED TO YOU TODAY...IS PART OF SOMETHING MUCH BIGGER. AND I KNOW ALL ABOUT IT BECAUSE I READ IT IN THIS BOOK.
HOLY SHIT.
AND THAT BOOK...?
ONE WAY TICKET
A JOHN SHAW Adventure Novel Based on True Events
WAS WRITTEN TWO YEARS AGO.
39

The corded muscles in Shaw's forearms ripple nervously as he sits in the spy's Porsche. Shaw unconsciously rests a hand on his belt—on his inhalers. He's short the one he'd used on the train. Intellect. And taking another inhaler so soon after the one he'd done on the train would have side effects to be sure. He really needed twenty-four hours to recover. But it could be done. He could take the strength-inhaler and have thumbs deep into Thomas Cord's eye sockets and to the back of his skull before he would even know what happened.

"Don't think about it," Cord says coolly as if reading Shaw's mind. "One flip of a switch and I can send twenty thousand volts of electricity straight to your balls."

Cord casually thumbs a toggle switch on his steering wheel. Shaw bristles at the command. *What is this asshole's game?* he thinks as he shifts restlessly in the now uncomfortable leather seat.

Cord continues. "I also know that if you inhale more than one dose within a twenty-four hour time period you tend to get . . . psychotic.

"Psychosis can have its uses," Shaw muses, eyeing Cord angrily.

"It does," Cord replies, unruffled. "Six months ago. The Flight 815 hijacking. You—"

"Don't need to talk about it," Shaw interrupts.

"You killed all ten hijackers in spectacular fashion with your bare hands. The ones you didn't shove out the window at 20,000 feet? You tore into small pieces. Is it true that you ate their internal organs before landing the plane? Of the fifteen surviving passengers, only one has been released from the psych hospital. And she still can't speak."

"I . . . don't remember a lot of what happened on that flight."

There's an awkward pause. He remembers almost every detail but tries not to.

Shaw switches tactics:

"So this guy Verge is writing all these books. He knows all about me. All about you. Who's to say he isn't the spy here? Who's to say he isn't working with Goldmaze to destroy all life as we know it? Manipulating events and getting us to do exactly what he wants?"

Cord shifts the car effortlessly as he glides it through the traffic of the city. "It's a possibility. And it's a risk we have to take until further notice."

"So what's next?" Shaw probes.

"My handler thinks the best chance of ending Goldmaze for good is to put Verge's team together and let it play out. Next stop? Japan. There's a woman named Dr. Michele Queen."

"Yeah? What makes her so special?"

"She's a Level Seven intelligence," Cord says with reverence.

"Okay," Shaw replies casually. "I've met a lot of smart people that are total assholes."

Cord pauses, weighing his response. And then says "And she has a car that has evolved to full sentience."

Shaw smiles as he watches the city race by.

"Now you're fucking talking."

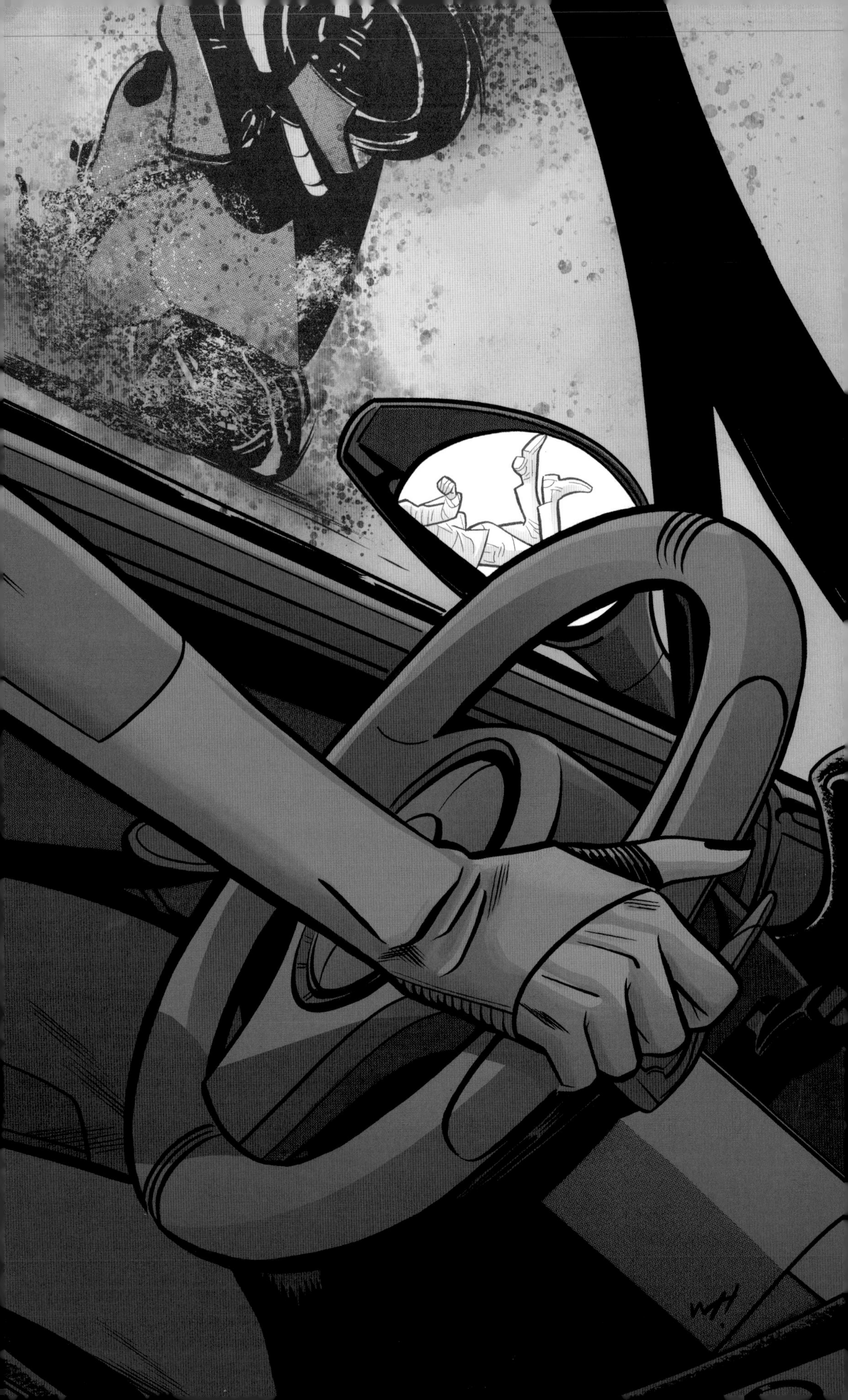

Michele Queen can feel the eyes of the Yakuza gangster all over her body. He's not even trying to be subtle. But that's okay. This has been to her advantage countless times in the past. The carbon-fiber smart suit she's wearing conforms to every curve of her body. It has to, to work properly. She can feel the tingle of the micromesh hyperwires over her neck, breasts, arms, torso, and legs. They hum with energy. It makes her feel alive.

She walks toward him. She needs access to the Yakuza mainframe that's behind the two-foot-thick blast doors this thug is guarding. As long as his lazy eyes are all that is on her body? He just might survive the experience.

The gangster smiles as Queen speaks perfect Japanese.

"I'm here to do some routine maintenance on the computer mainframe. But I forgot my keycard. Is there anything you could do to help me out?"

"Are you kidding, lady? I'd lose my job, and they'd take one of my fingers," he replies. And then with a gold-toothed grin, lowers his MAC-10 and puts a rough hand on her elbow. "But maybe we could work something out."

Oh well. She gave him a chance. He shouldn't have touched her.

Queen is on autopilot now as she splits her focus from the guard to her bioengineered organic intelligence . . ."BOI," as she calls it. BOI is a one-of-a-kind super artificial intelligence. An AI that Queen suspects is actually sentient. But she can't be sure. The AI is smart enough to know that if it became sentient it might be considered a threat. And it doesn't want that. Queen wouldn't mind his sentience, but she plays along. Let BOI think she doesn't know. He's really her only honest social interaction. She's been undercover, completing special ops and infiltrating government organizations for two years in an effort to take down Goldmaze. In those two years she hasn't had time for friends or a lover. BOI is the closest thing to either that she's ever had.

Closing her eyes, Queen accesses BOI. Talking to BOI with her mind isn't magic. It's more like a conversational way of making your legs move. BOI works the same way. He's hardwired to her brain so she can get him to move much like she does her own body . . . but with a little bit more of a back and forth.

BOI? I need the drone. 500,000 volts for this guy.

That's a bit of overkill isn't it, Michele?

He's asking for it. And I need it quick. A little less chit-chat and a little more action if you don't mind.

No need to get snippy. My remote drone is already in position.

Queen opens her eyes. The guard has pulled her close enough now that she can smell sushi rolls on his breath. She jerks her arm out of his grasp just as BOI's remote drone buzzes up behind him and shoots 500,000 volts of electricity into the back of his neck.

The guard collapses to the ground.

Queen hears BOI's voice in her head: *Michele? I'm afraid we have company. The silent alarm was linked to the guard's vitals. There is a veritable army on its way to you.*

"Dammit," Queen whispers under her breath as she turns around and raises her hands. She's been caught.

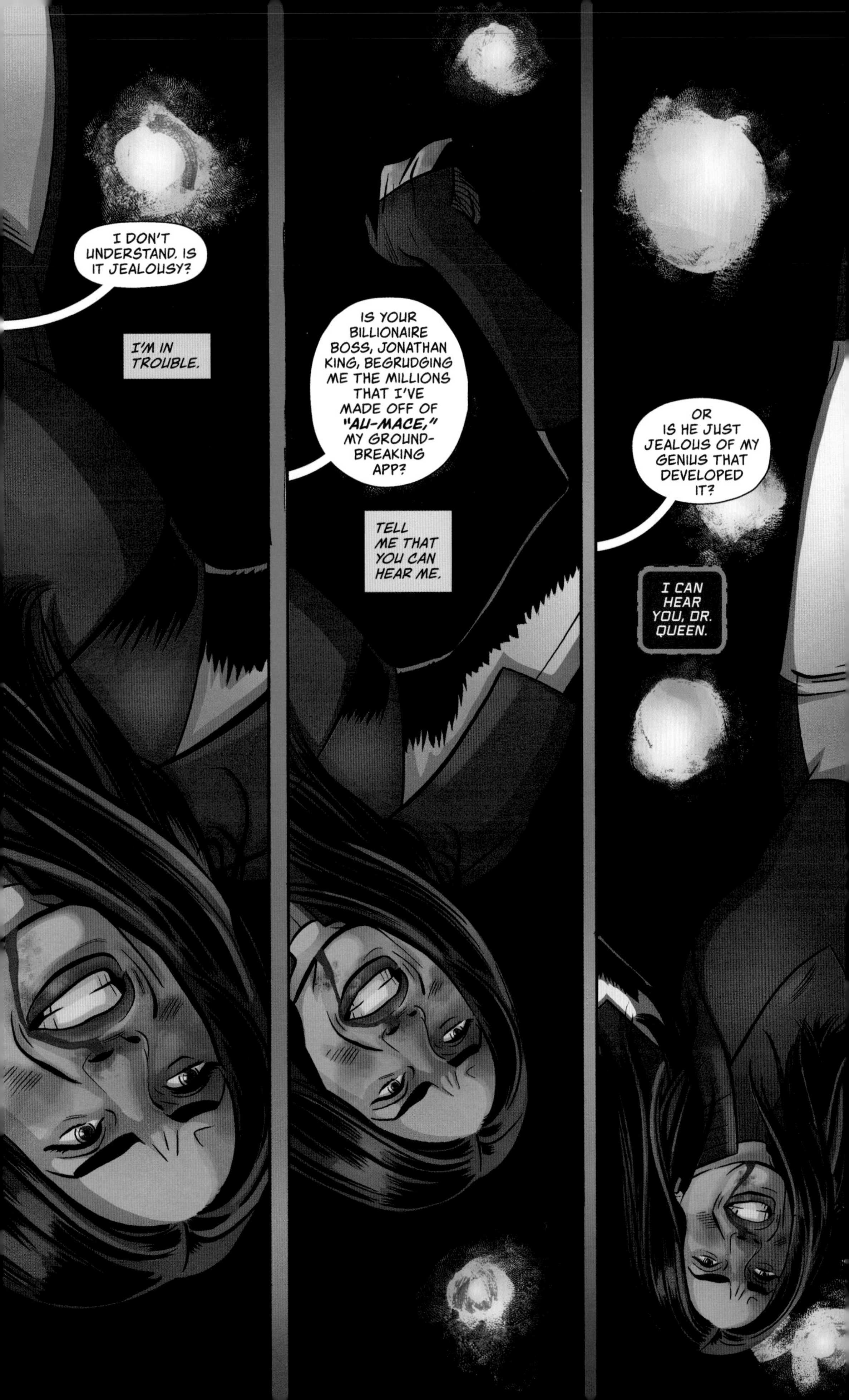
I DON'T UNDERSTAND. IS IT JEALOUSY?
I'M IN TROUBLE.
IS YOUR BILLIONAIRE BOSS, JONATHAN KING, BEGRUDGING ME THE MILLIONS THAT I'VE MADE OFF OF "AU-MACE," MY GROUND-BREAKING APP?
TELL ME THAT YOU CAN HEAR ME.
OR IS HE JUST JEALOUS OF MY GENIUS THAT DEVELOPED IT?
I CAN HEAR YOU, DR. QUEEN.

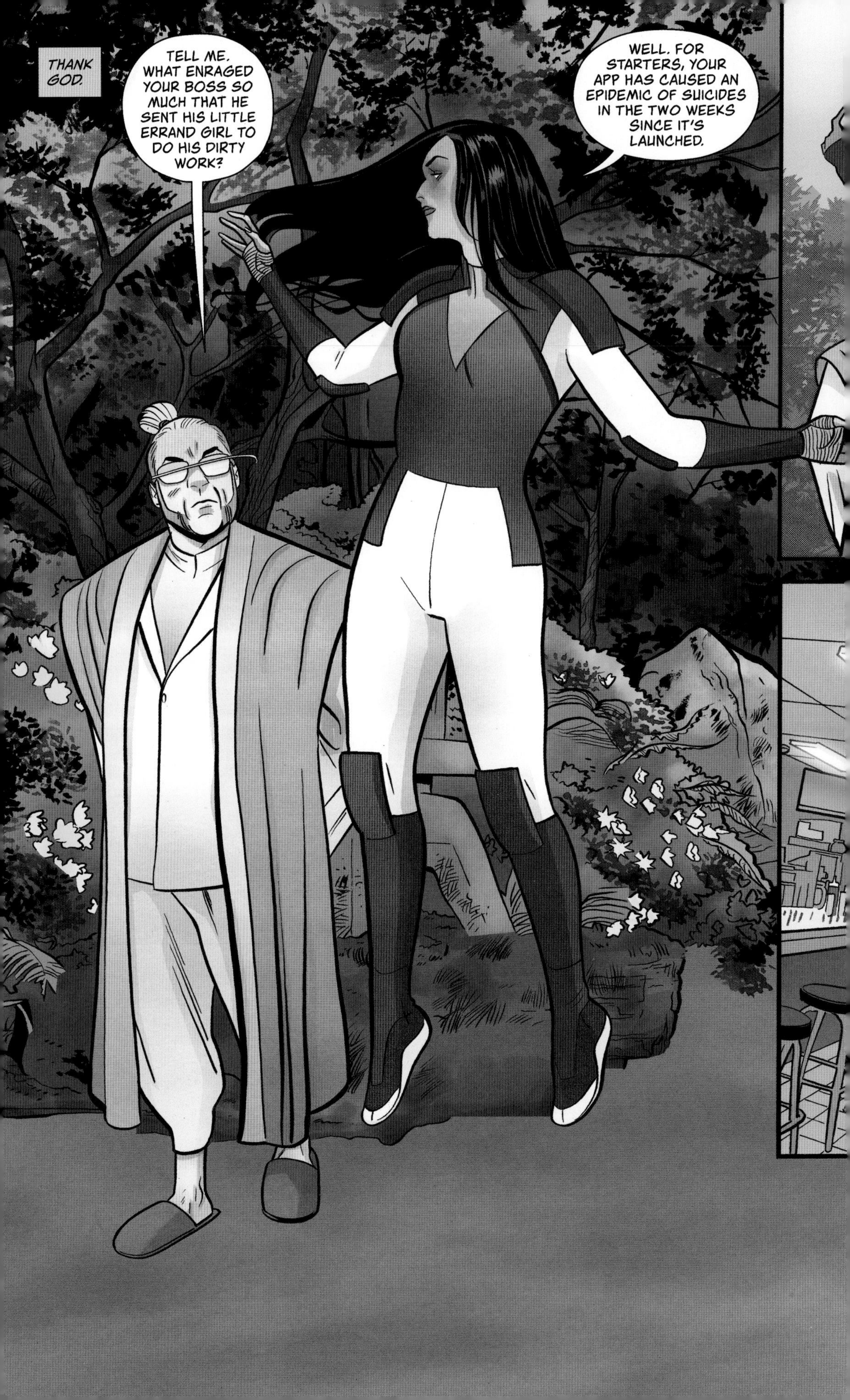
THANK GOD.
TELL ME. WHAT ENRAGED YOUR BOSS SO MUCH THAT HE SENT HIS LITTLE ERRAND GIRL TO DO HIS DIRTY WORK?
WELL. FOR STARTERS, YOUR APP HAS CAUSED AN EPIDEMIC OF SUICIDES IN THE TWO WEEKS SINCE IT'S LAUNCHED.

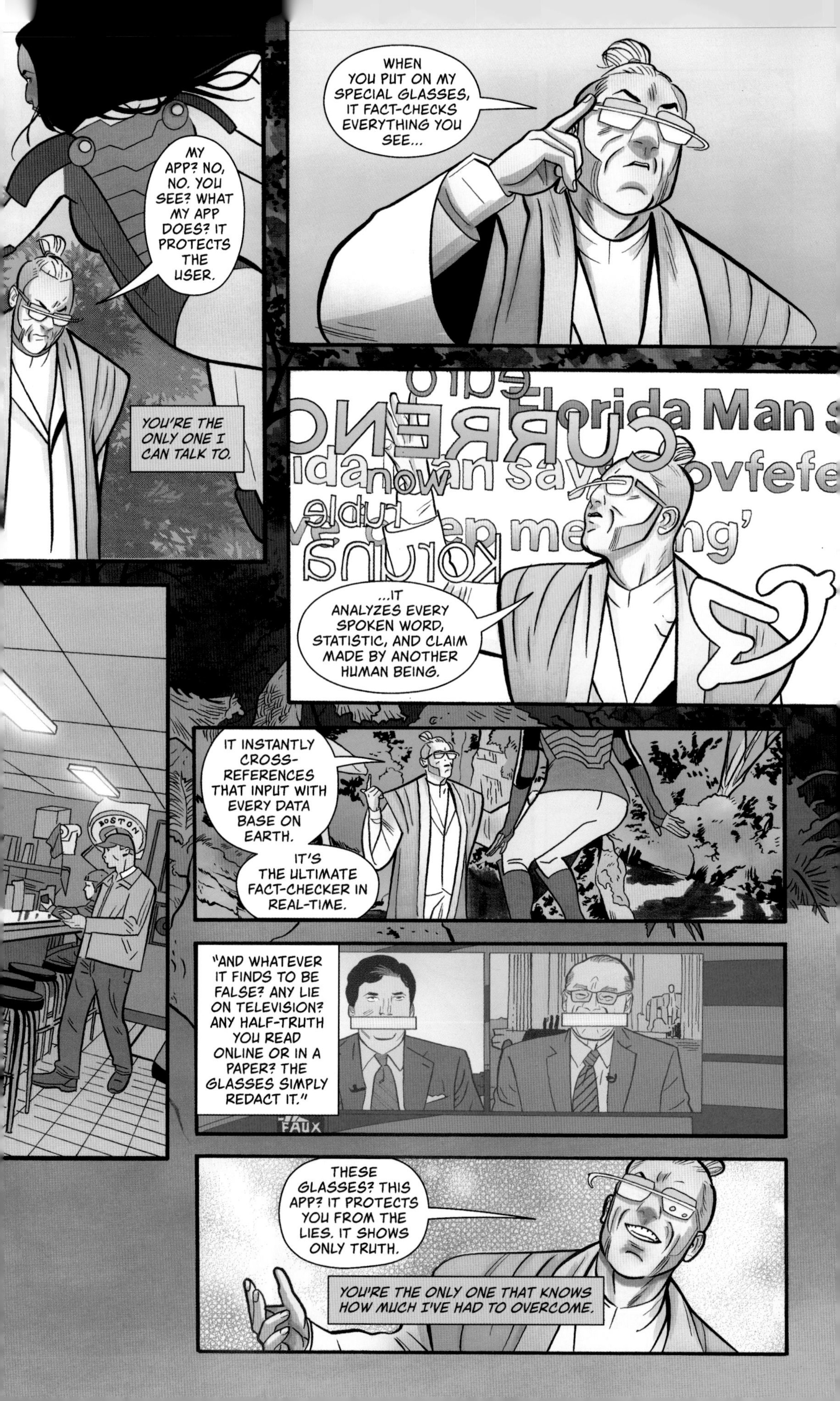

MY APP? NO, NO. YOU SEE? WHAT MY APP DOES? IT PROTECTS THE USER.
WHEN YOU PUT ON MY SPECIAL GLASSES, IT FACT-CHECKS EVERYTHING YOU SEE...
YOU'RE THE ONLY ONE I CAN TALK TO.
Florida Man s
CURRENO
vfefe
ng'
...IT ANALYZES EVERY SPOKEN WORD, STATISTIC, AND CLAIM MADE BY ANOTHER HUMAN BEING.
BOSTON
IT INSTANTLY CROSS-REFERENCES THAT INPUT WITH EVERY DATA BASE ON EARTH.
IT'S THE ULTIMATE FACT-CHECKER IN REAL-TIME.
"AND WHATEVER IT FINDS TO BE FALSE? ANY LIE ON TELEVISION? ANY HALF-TRUTH YOU READ ONLINE OR IN A PAPER? THE GLASSES SIMPLY REDACT IT."
FAUX
THESE GLASSES? THIS APP? IT PROTECTS YOU FROM THE LIES. IT SHOWS ONLY TRUTH.
YOU'RE THE ONLY ONE THAT KNOWS HOW MUCH I'VE HAD TO OVERCOME.

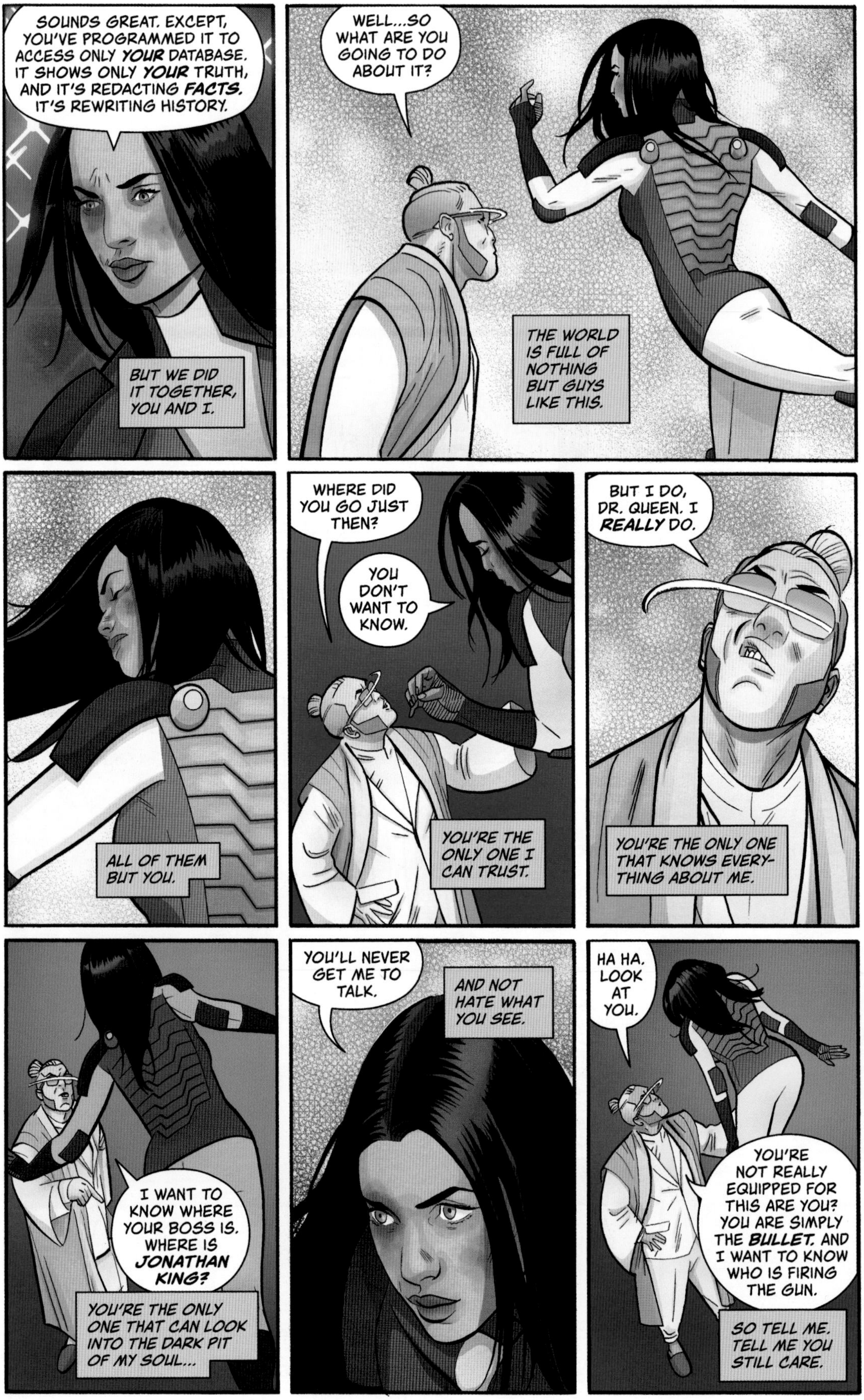
SOUNDS GREAT. EXCEPT, YOU'VE PROGRAMMED IT TO ACCESS ONLY *YOUR* DATABASE. IT SHOWS ONLY *YOUR* TRUTH, AND IT'S REDACTING *FACTS.* IT'S REWRITING HISTORY.
BUT WE DID IT TOGETHER, YOU AND I.
WELL...SO WHAT ARE YOU GOING TO DO ABOUT IT?
THE WORLD IS FULL OF NOTHING BUT GUYS LIKE THIS.
ALL OF THEM BUT YOU.
WHERE DID YOU GO JUST THEN?
YOU DON'T WANT TO KNOW.
YOU'RE THE ONLY ONE I CAN TRUST.
BUT I DO, DR. QUEEN. I *REALLY* DO.
YOU'RE THE ONLY ONE THAT KNOWS EVERY-THING ABOUT ME.
I WANT TO KNOW WHERE YOUR BOSS IS. WHERE IS *JONATHAN KING?*
YOU'RE THE ONLY ONE THAT CAN LOOK INTO THE DARK PIT OF MY SOUL...
YOU'LL NEVER GET ME TO TALK.
AND NOT HATE WHAT YOU SEE.
HA HA. LOOK AT YOU.
YOU'RE NOT REALLY EQUIPPED FOR THIS ARE YOU? YOU ARE SIMPLY THE *BULLET.* AND I WANT TO KNOW WHO IS FIRING THE GUN.
SO TELL ME. TELL ME YOU STILL CARE.

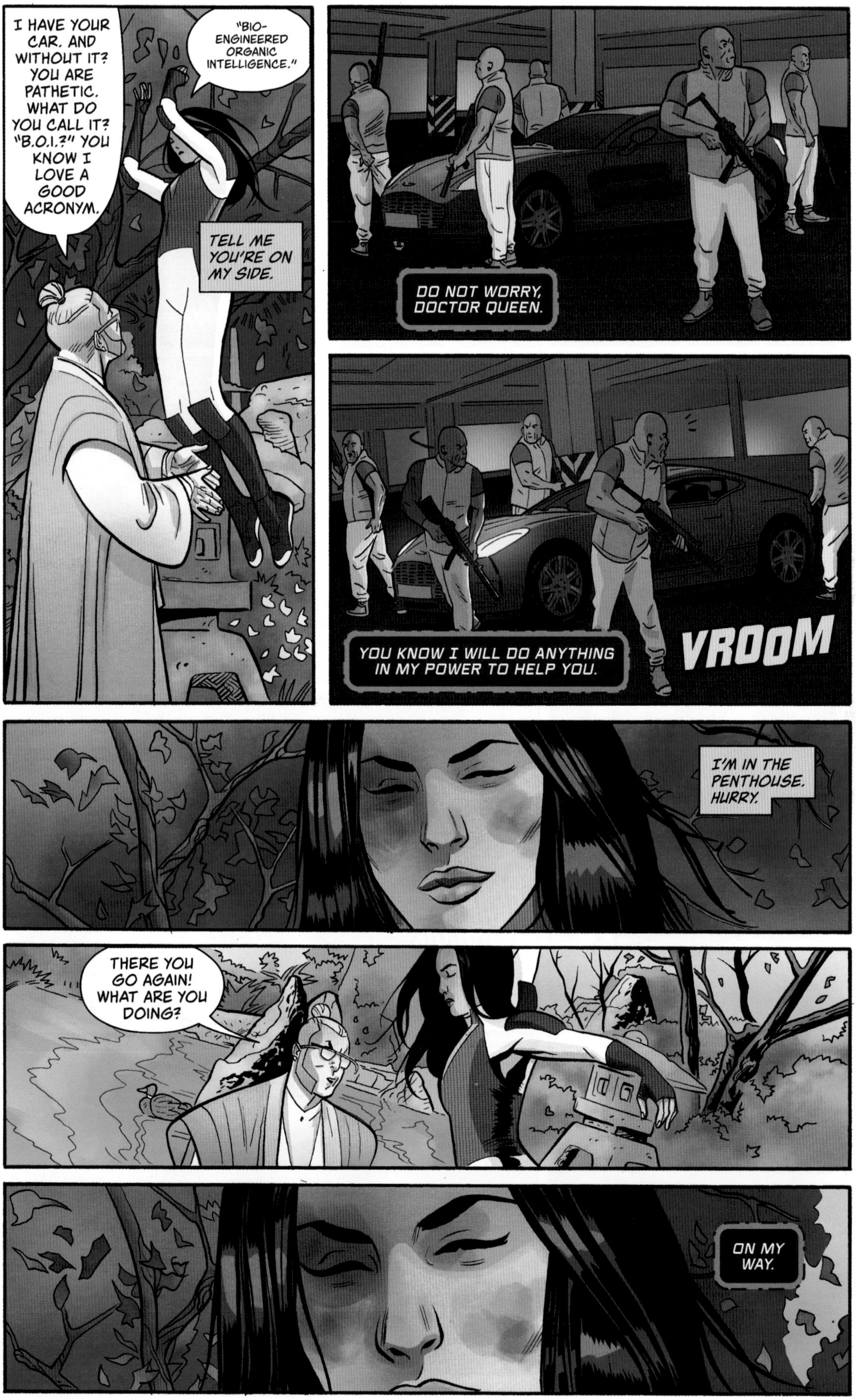
I HAVE YOUR CAR. AND WITHOUT IT? YOU ARE PATHETIC. WHAT DO YOU CALL IT? "B.O.I.?" YOU KNOW I LOVE A GOOD ACRONYM.
"BIO-ENGINEERED ORGANIC INTELLIGENCE."
TELL ME YOU'RE ON MY SIDE.
DO NOT WORRY, DOCTOR QUEEN.
YOU KNOW I WILL DO ANYTHING IN MY POWER TO HELP YOU.
VROOM
I'M IN THE PENTHOUSE. HURRY.
THERE YOU GO AGAIN! WHAT ARE YOU DOING?
ON MY WAY.

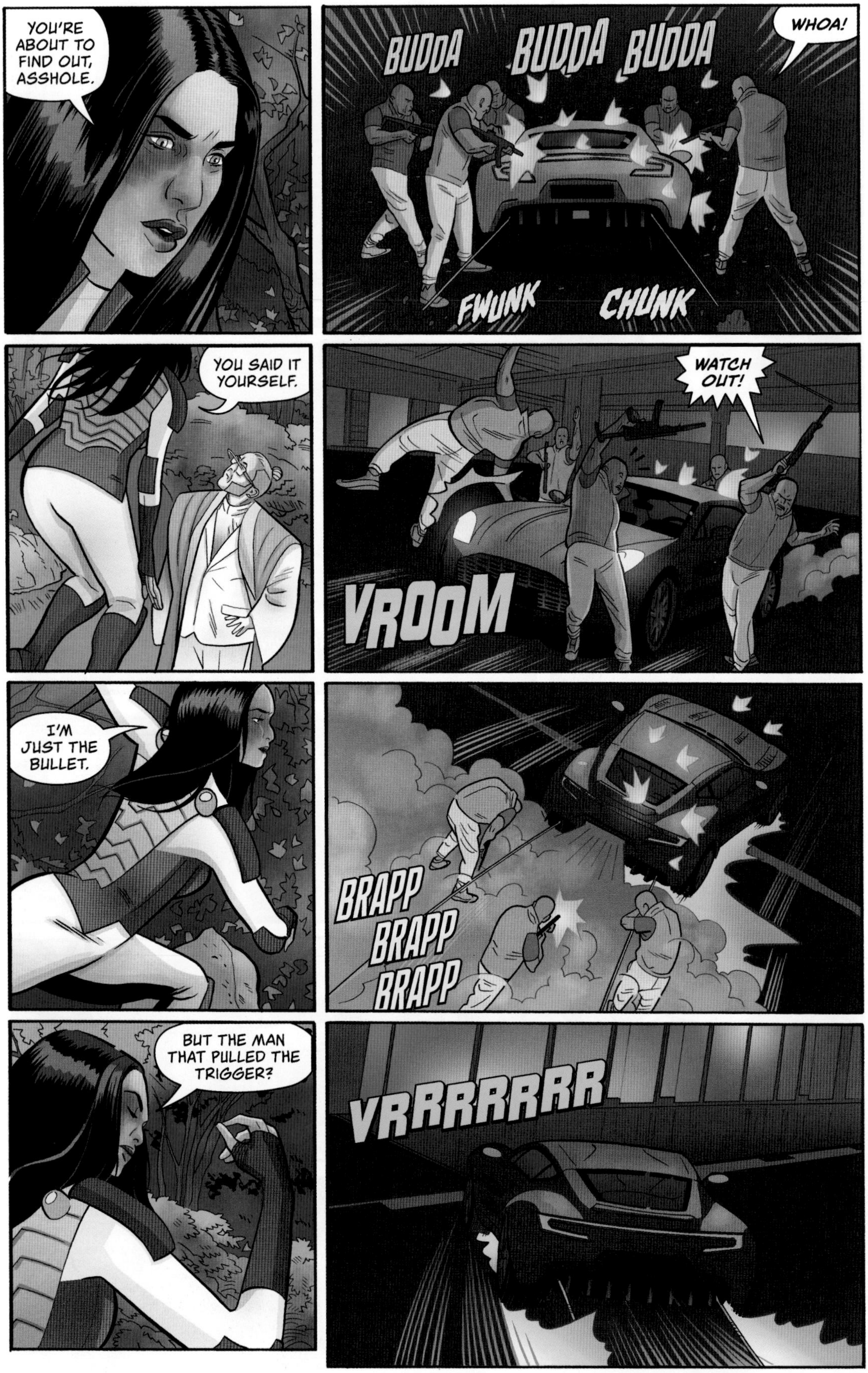
YOU'RE ABOUT TO FIND OUT, ASSHOLE.
BUDDA BUDDA BUDDA
WHOA!
FWUNK
CHUNK
YOU SAID IT YOURSELF.
WATCH OUT!
VROOM
I'M JUST THE BULLET.
BRAPP BRAPP BRAPP
BUT THE MAN THAT PULLED THE TRIGGER?
VRRRRRRR

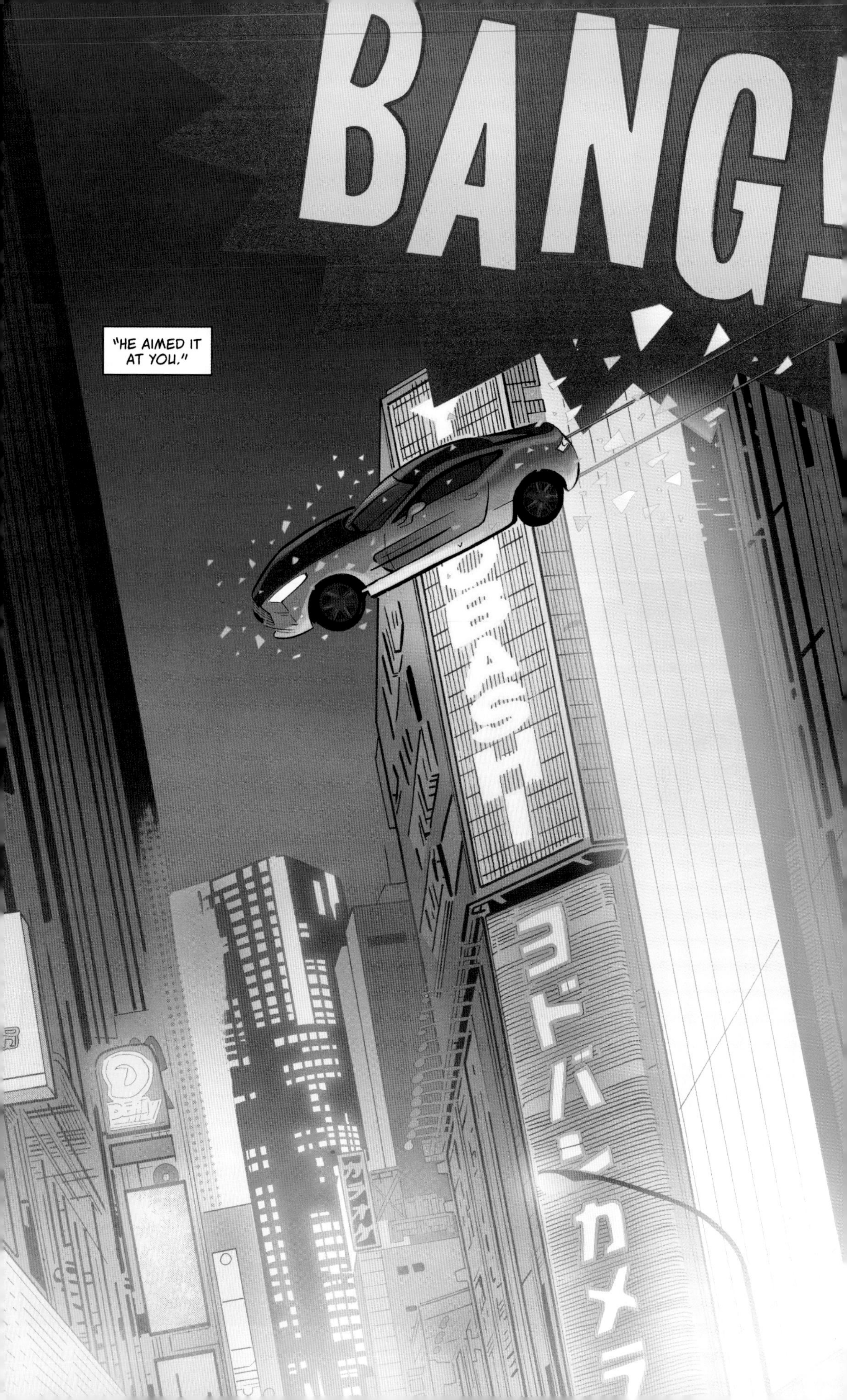
BANG!
"HE AIMED IT AT YOU."

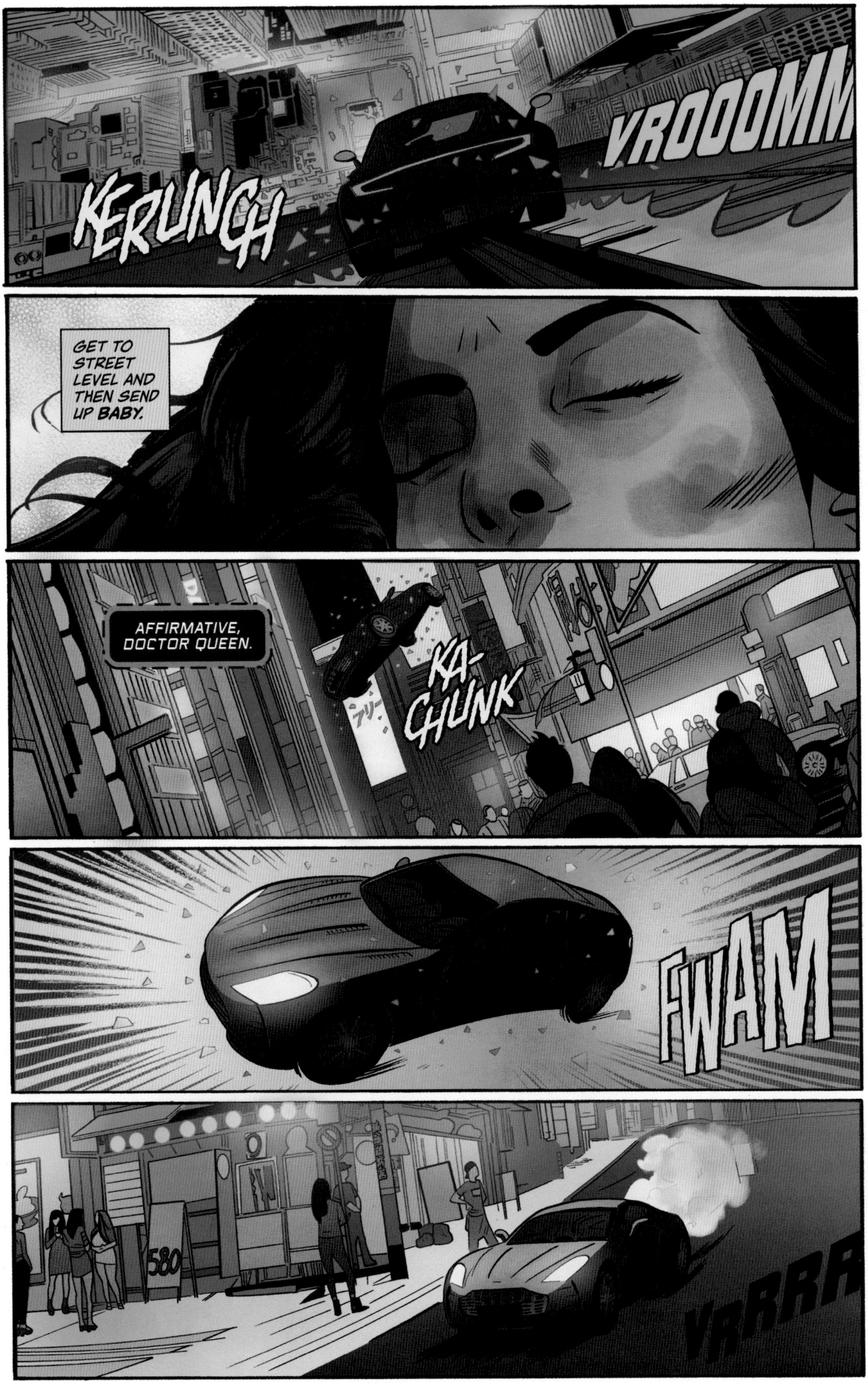
KERUNCH
VROOOMM
GET TO STREET LEVEL AND THEN SEND UP BABY.
AFFIRMATIVE, DOCTOR QUEEN.
KA-CHUNK
フリー
FWAM
580
VRRRR

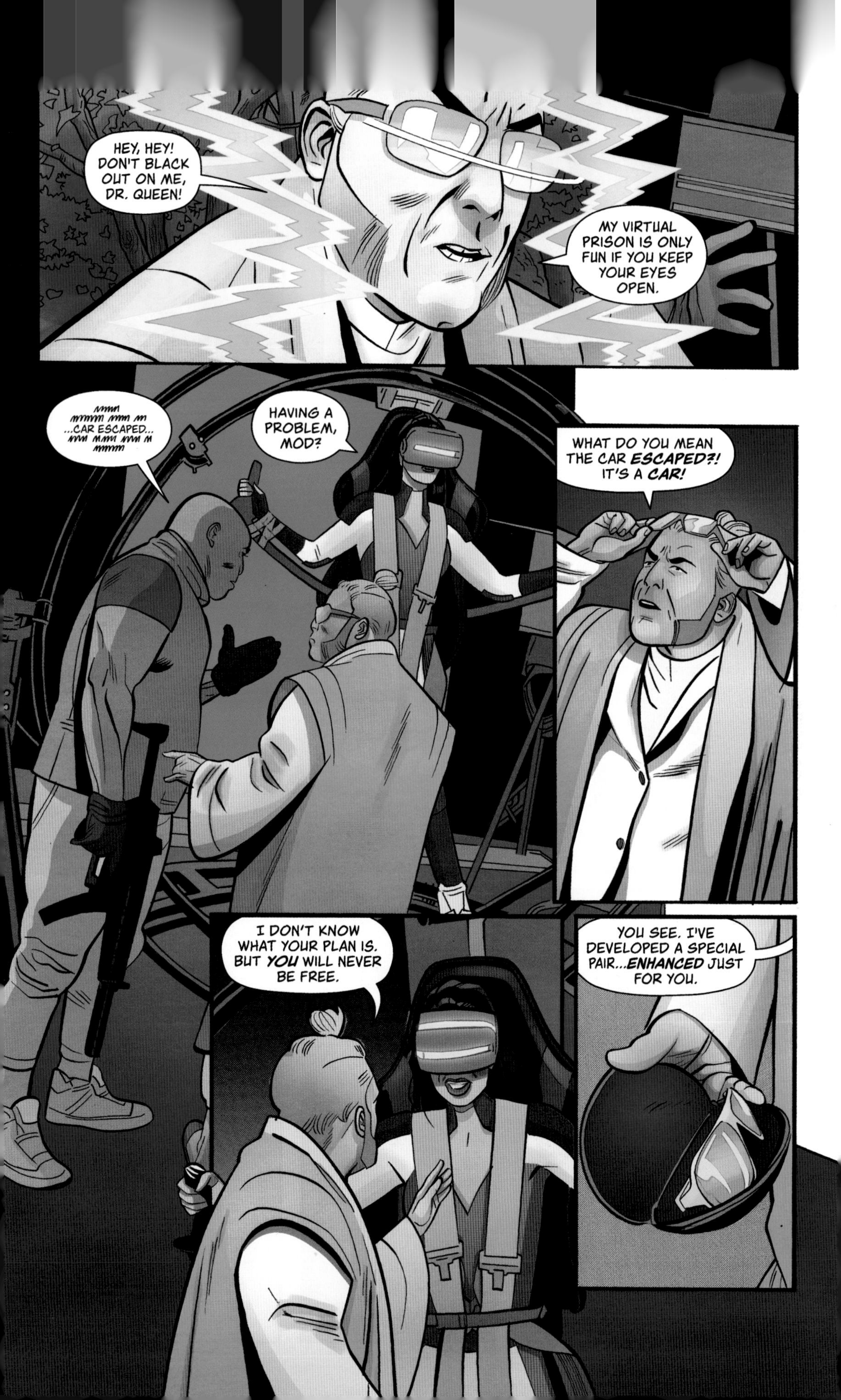
HEY, HEY! DON'T BLACK OUT ON ME, DR. QUEEN!
MY VIRTUAL PRISON IS ONLY FUN IF YOU KEEP YOUR EYES OPEN.
...CAR ESCAPED...
HAVING A PROBLEM, MOD?
WHAT DO YOU MEAN THE CAR ESCAPED?! IT'S A CAR!
I DON'T KNOW WHAT YOUR PLAN IS, BUT YOU WILL NEVER BE FREE.
YOU SEE, I'VE DEVELOPED A SPECIAL PAIR...ENHANCED JUST FOR YOU.

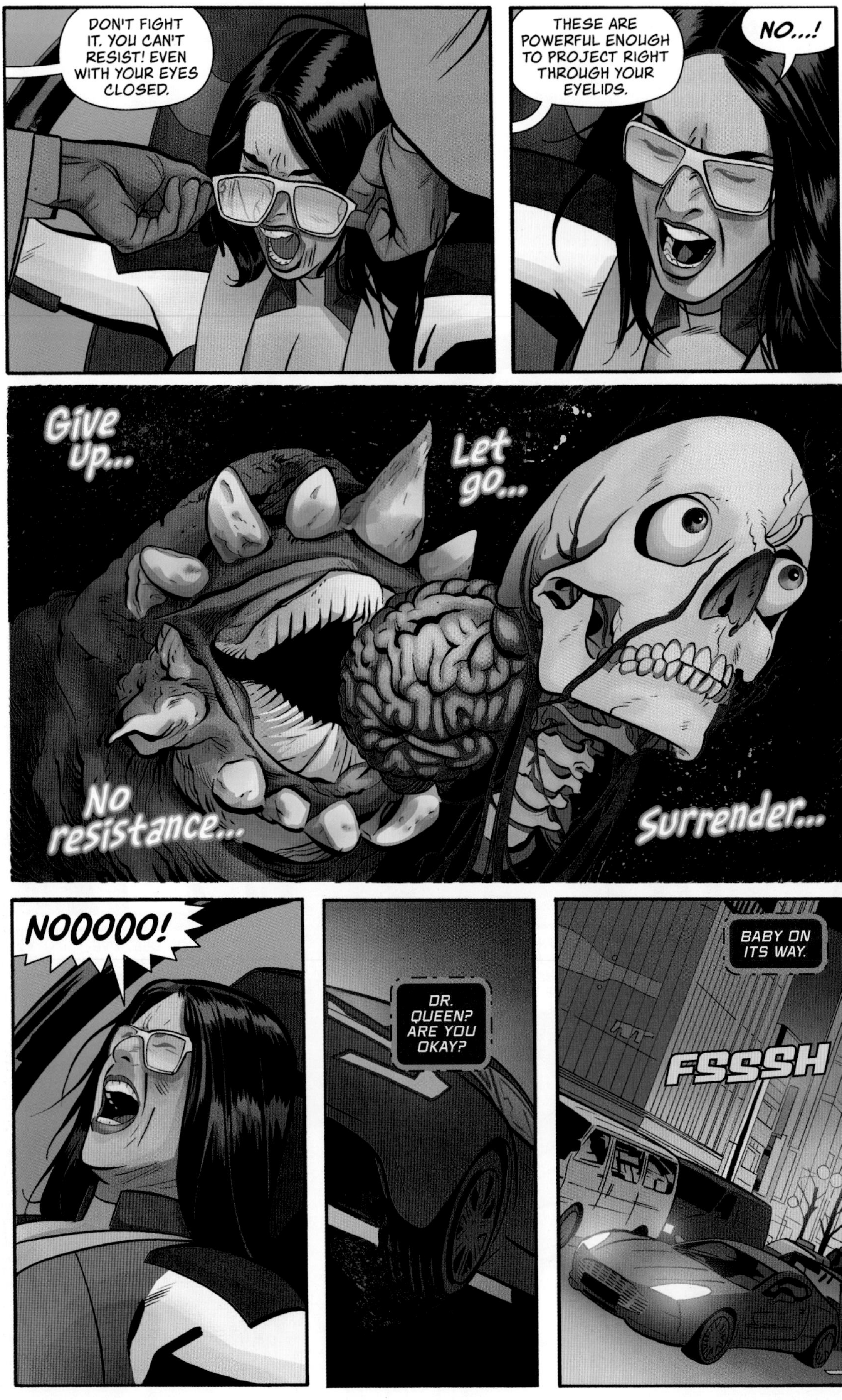

DON'T FIGHT IT. YOU CAN'T RESIST! EVEN WITH YOUR EYES CLOSED.
THESE ARE POWERFUL ENOUGH TO PROJECT RIGHT THROUGH YOUR EYELIDS.
NO...!
Give up...
Let go...
No resistance...
Surrender...
NOOOOO!
DR. QUEEN? ARE YOU OKAY?
BABY ON ITS WAY.
FSSSH

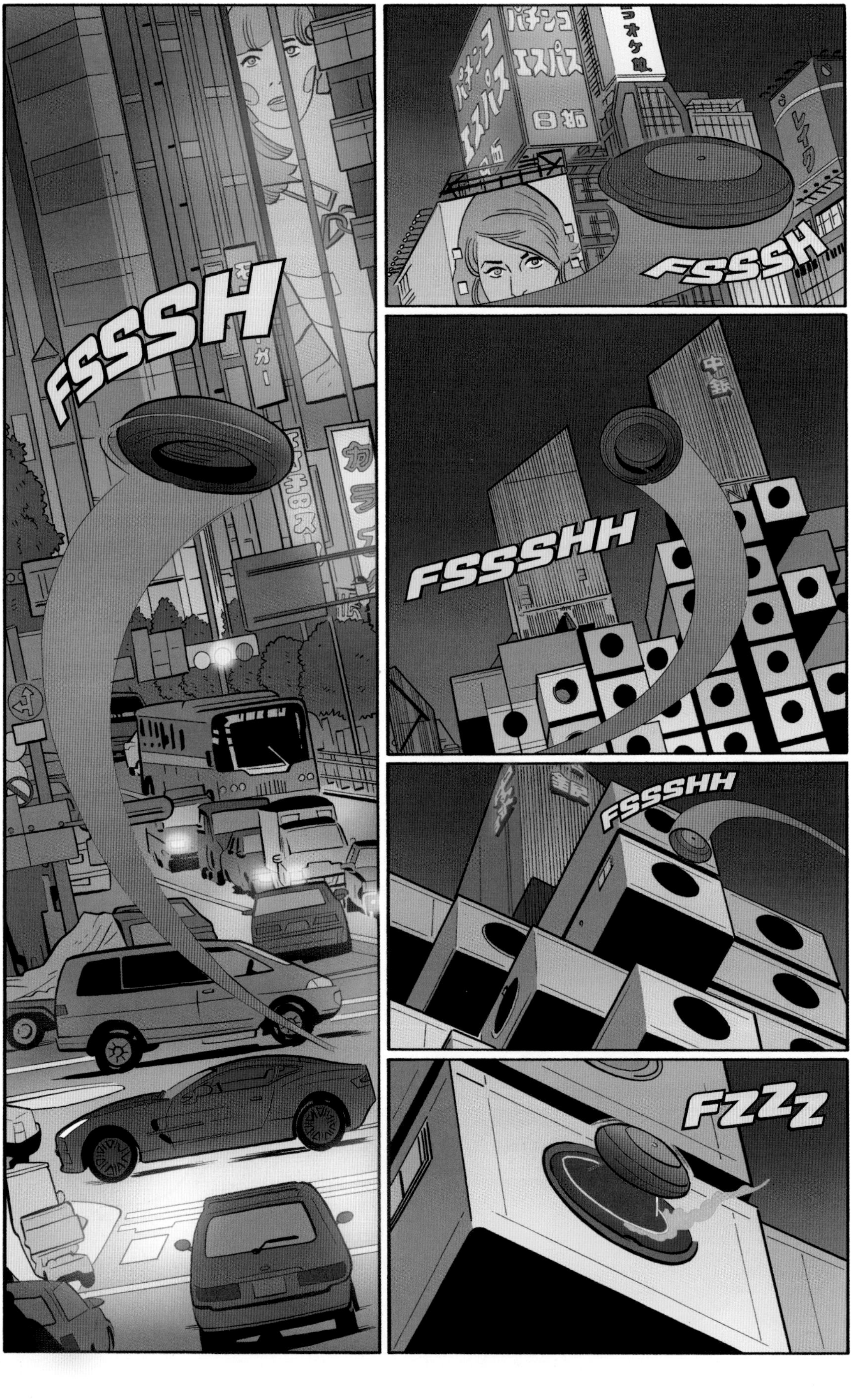
FSSSH
パチンコ
エスパス
日拓
レイク
FSSSH
中銀
FSSSHH
FSSSHH
FZZZ

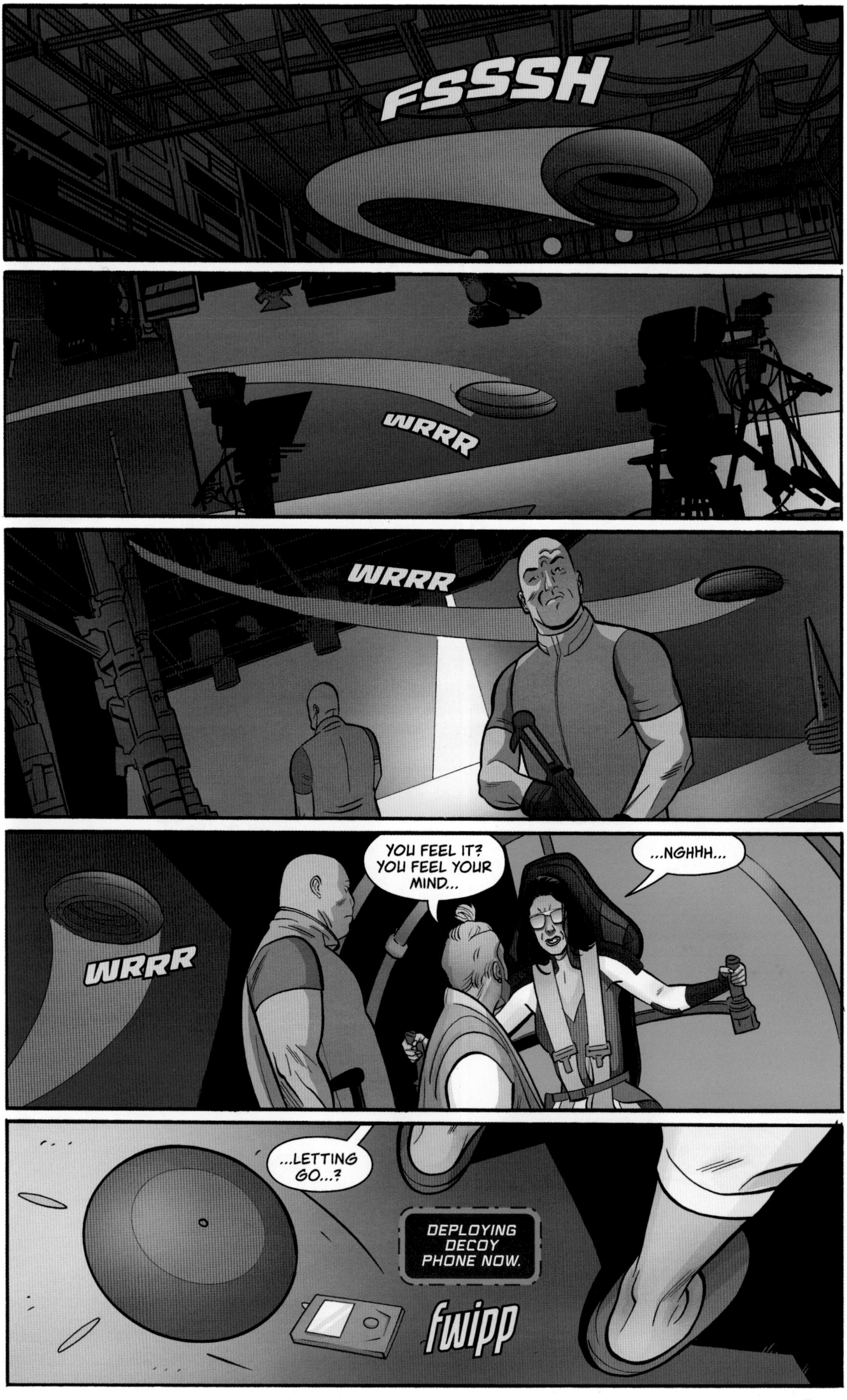
FSSSH
WRRR
WRRR
WRRR
YOU FEEL IT? YOU FEEL YOUR MIND...
...NGHHH...
...LETTING GO...?
DEPLOYING DECOY PHONE NOW.
fwipp

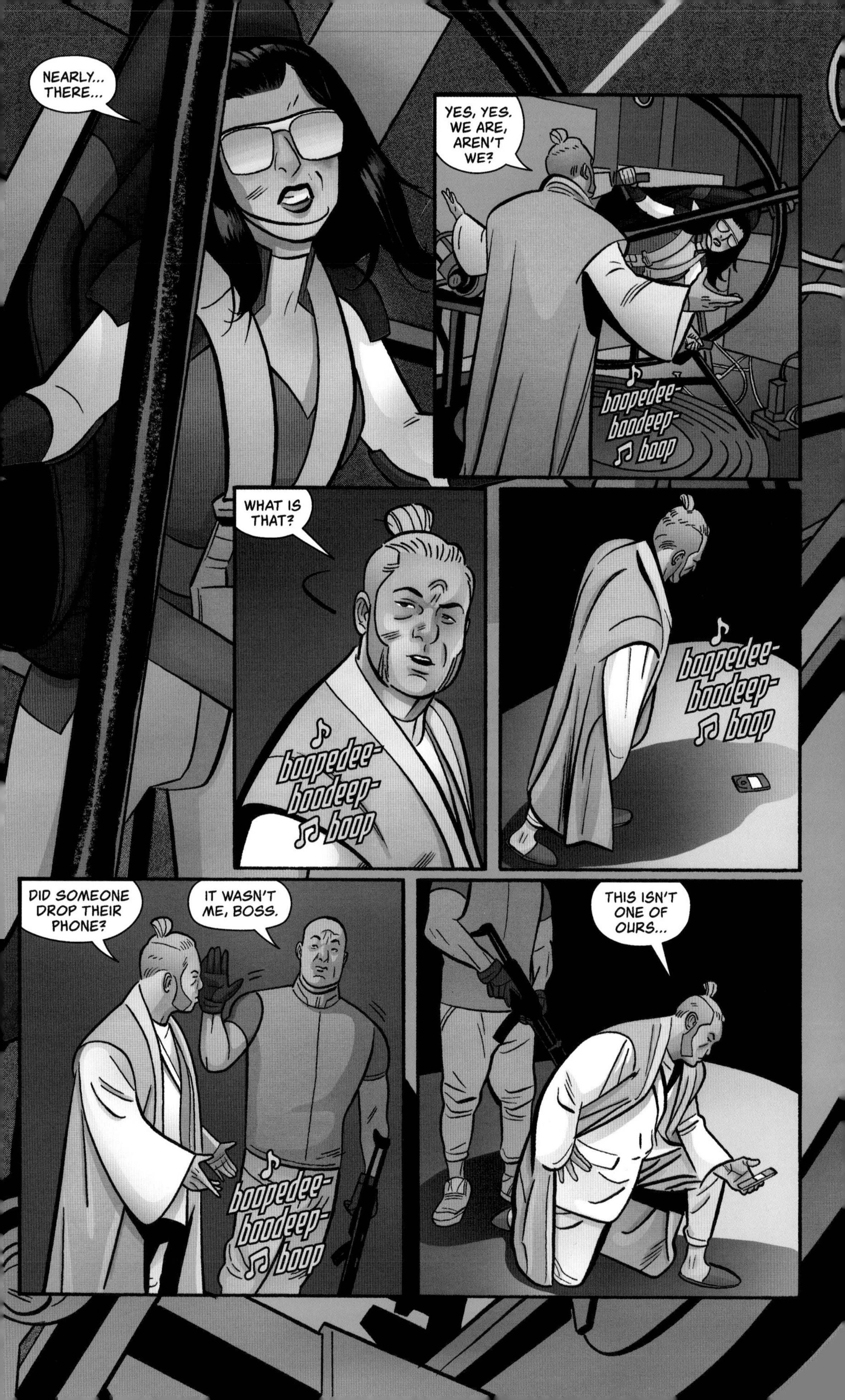
NEARLY... THERE...
YES, YES. WE ARE, AREN'T WE?
boopedee-boodeep-boop
WHAT IS THAT?
boopedee-boodeep-boop
boopedee-boodeep-boop
DID SOMEONE DROP THEIR PHONE?
IT WASN'T ME, BOSS.
boopedee-boodeep-boop
THIS ISN'T ONE OF OURS...

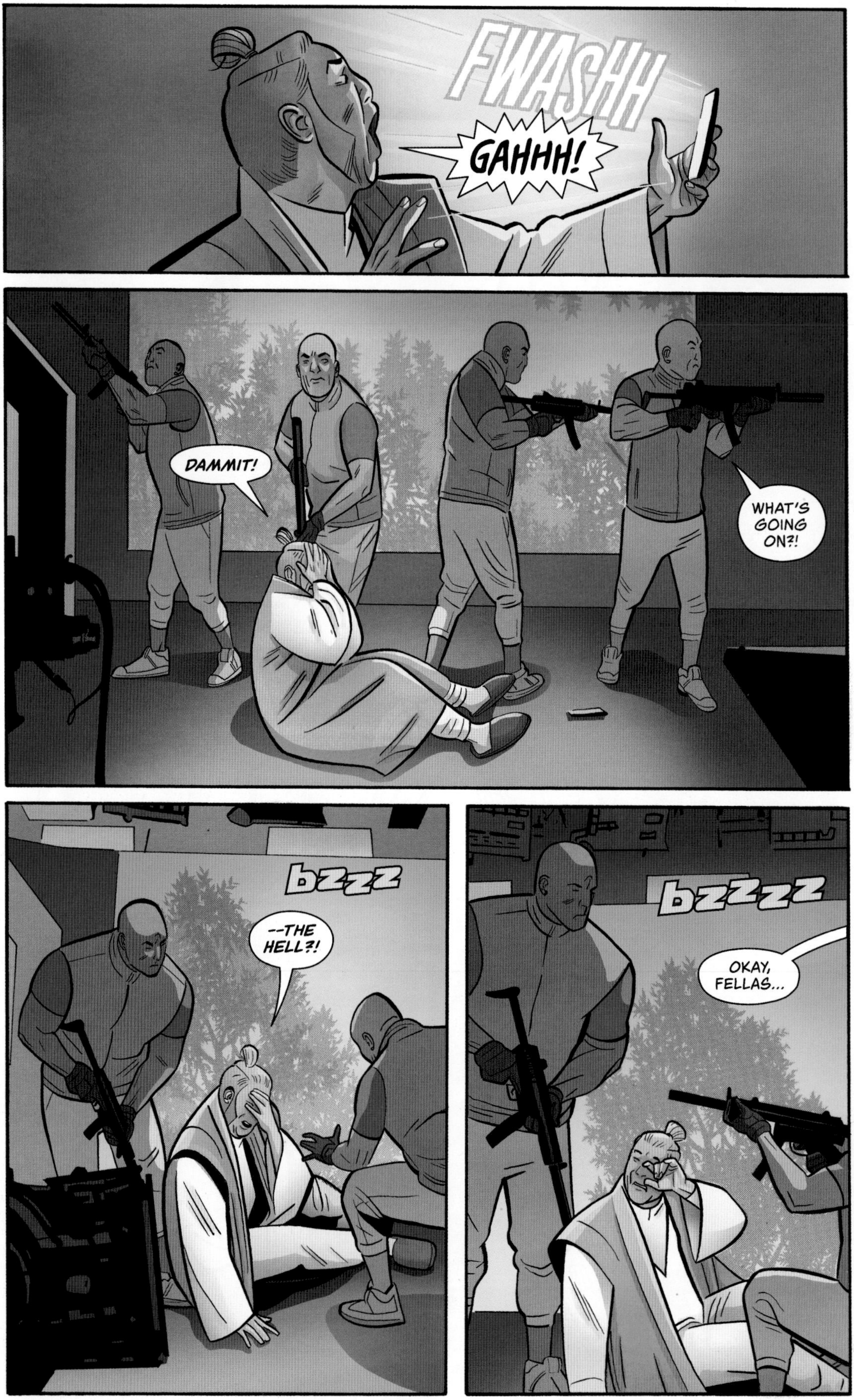
FWASHH
GAHHH!
DAMMIT!
WHAT'S GOING ON?!
bzzz
--THE HELL?!
bzzzz
OKAY, FELLAS...

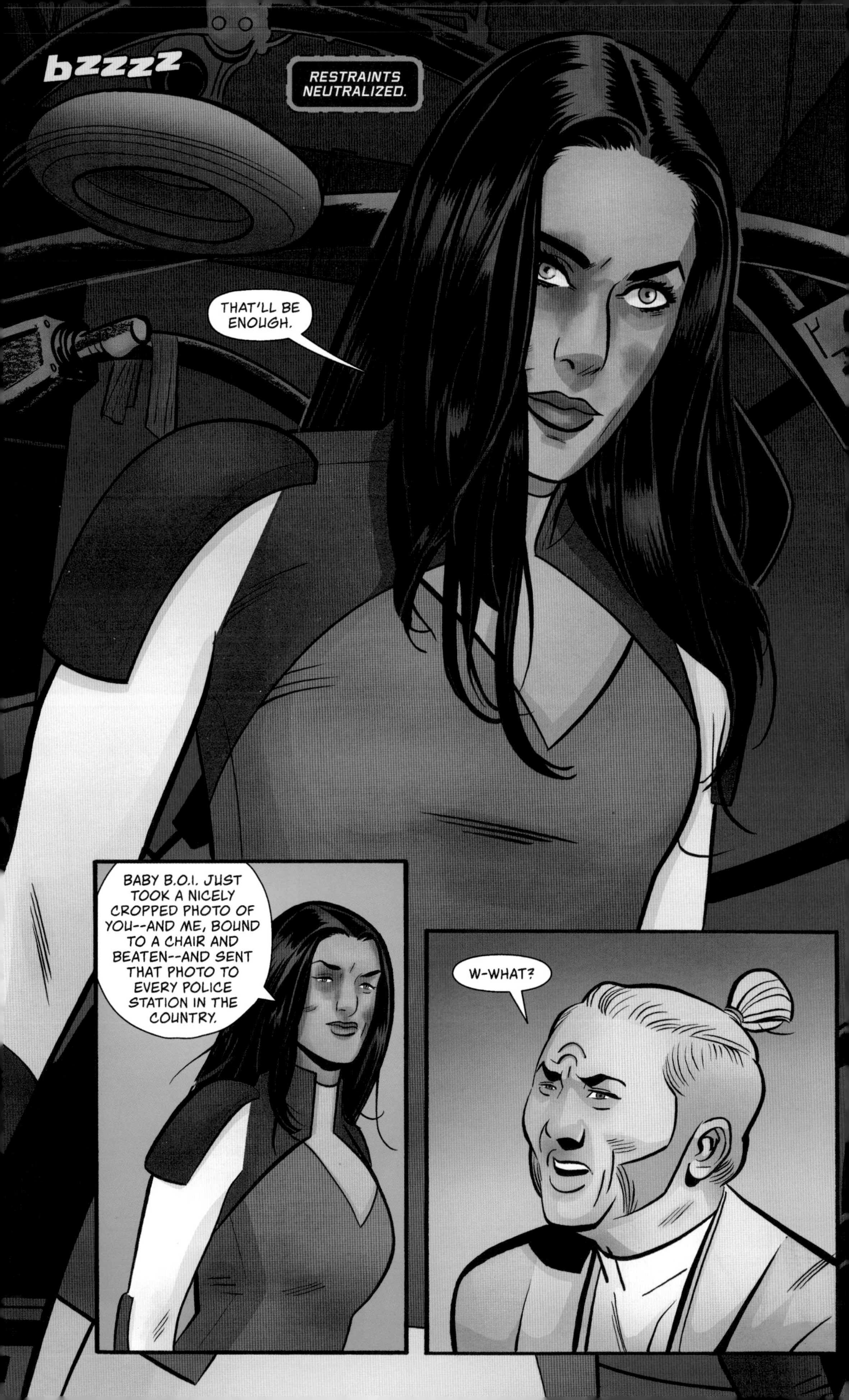
bzzzz
RESTRAINTS NEUTRALIZED.
THAT'LL BE ENOUGH.
BABY B.O.I. JUST TOOK A NICELY CROPPED PHOTO OF YOU--AND ME, BOUND TO A CHAIR AND BEATEN--AND SENT THAT PHOTO TO EVERY POLICE STATION IN THE COUNTRY.
W-WHAT?

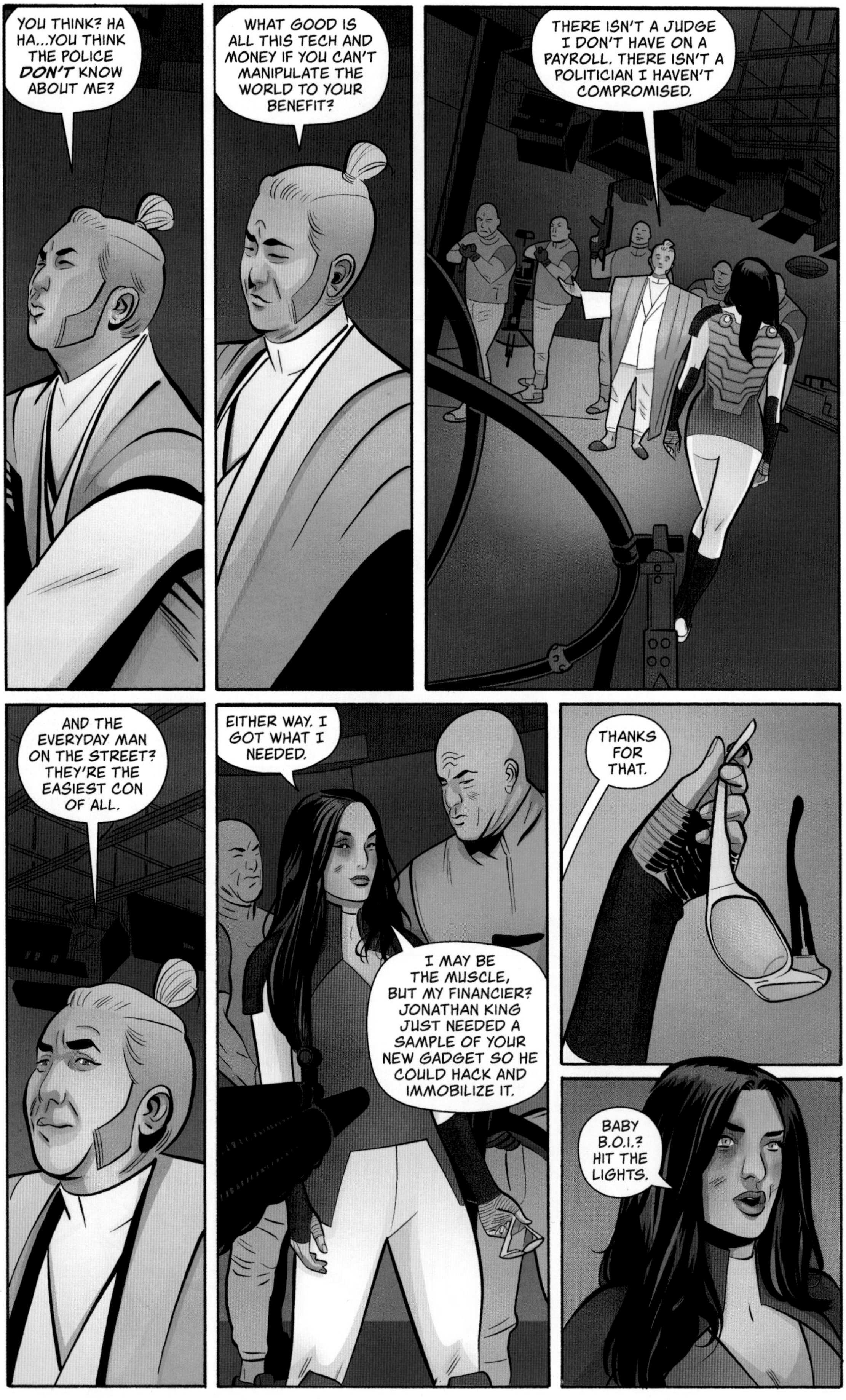
YOU THINK? HA HA...YOU THINK THE POLICE DON'T KNOW ABOUT ME?
WHAT GOOD IS ALL THIS TECH AND MONEY IF YOU CAN'T MANIPULATE THE WORLD TO YOUR BENEFIT?
THERE ISN'T A JUDGE I DON'T HAVE ON A PAYROLL. THERE ISN'T A POLITICIAN I HAVEN'T COMPROMISED.
AND THE EVERYDAY MAN ON THE STREET? THEY'RE THE EASIEST CON OF ALL.
EITHER WAY. I GOT WHAT I NEEDED.
I MAY BE THE MUSCLE, BUT MY FINANCIER? JONATHAN KING JUST NEEDED A SAMPLE OF YOUR NEW GADGET SO HE COULD HACK AND IMMOBILIZE IT.
THANKS FOR THAT.
BABY B.O.I.? HIT THE LIGHTS.

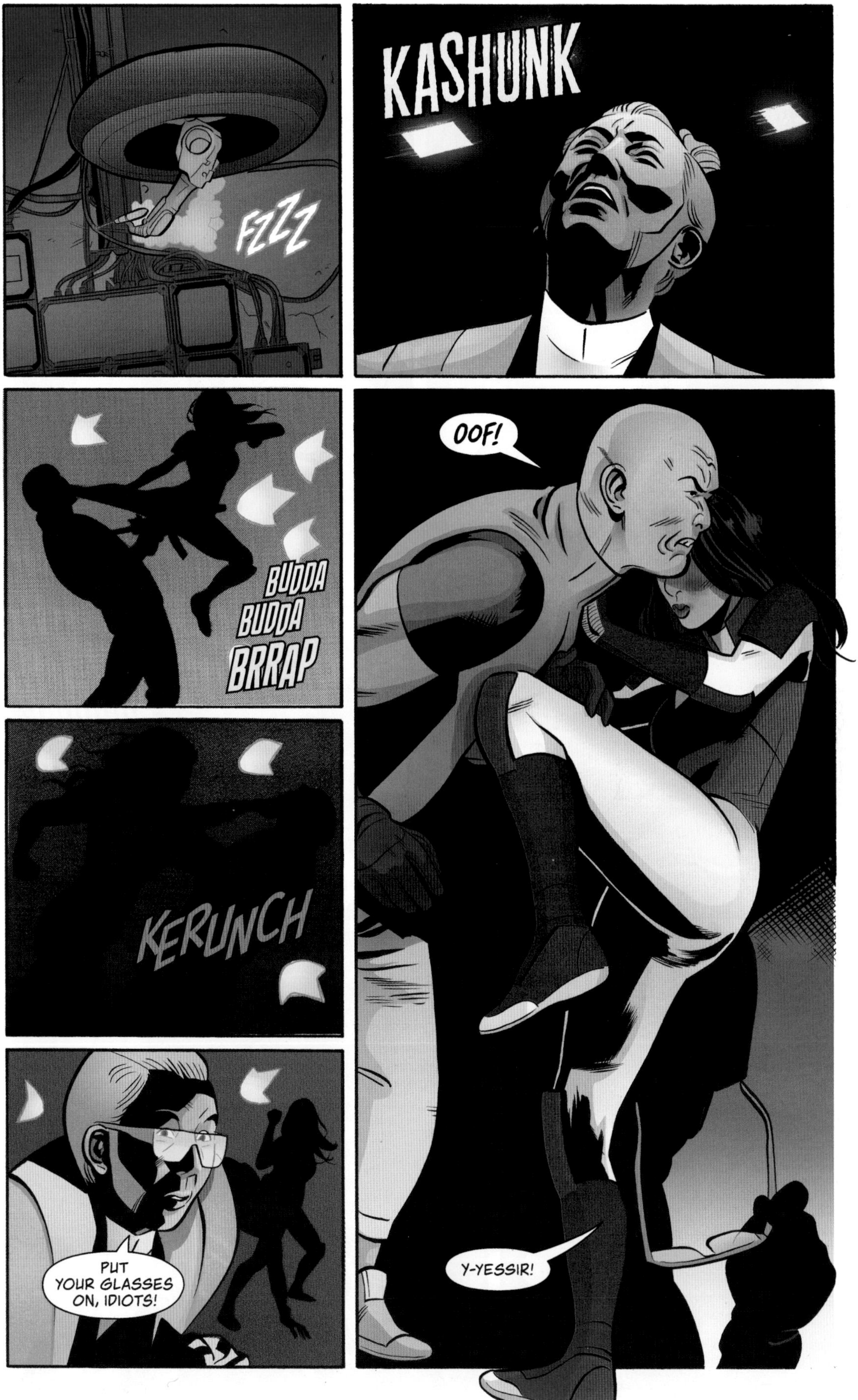
FZZZ
KASHUNK
BUDDA
BUDDA
BRRAP
KERUNCH
PUT YOUR GLASSES ON, IDIOTS!
OOF!
Y-YESSIR!

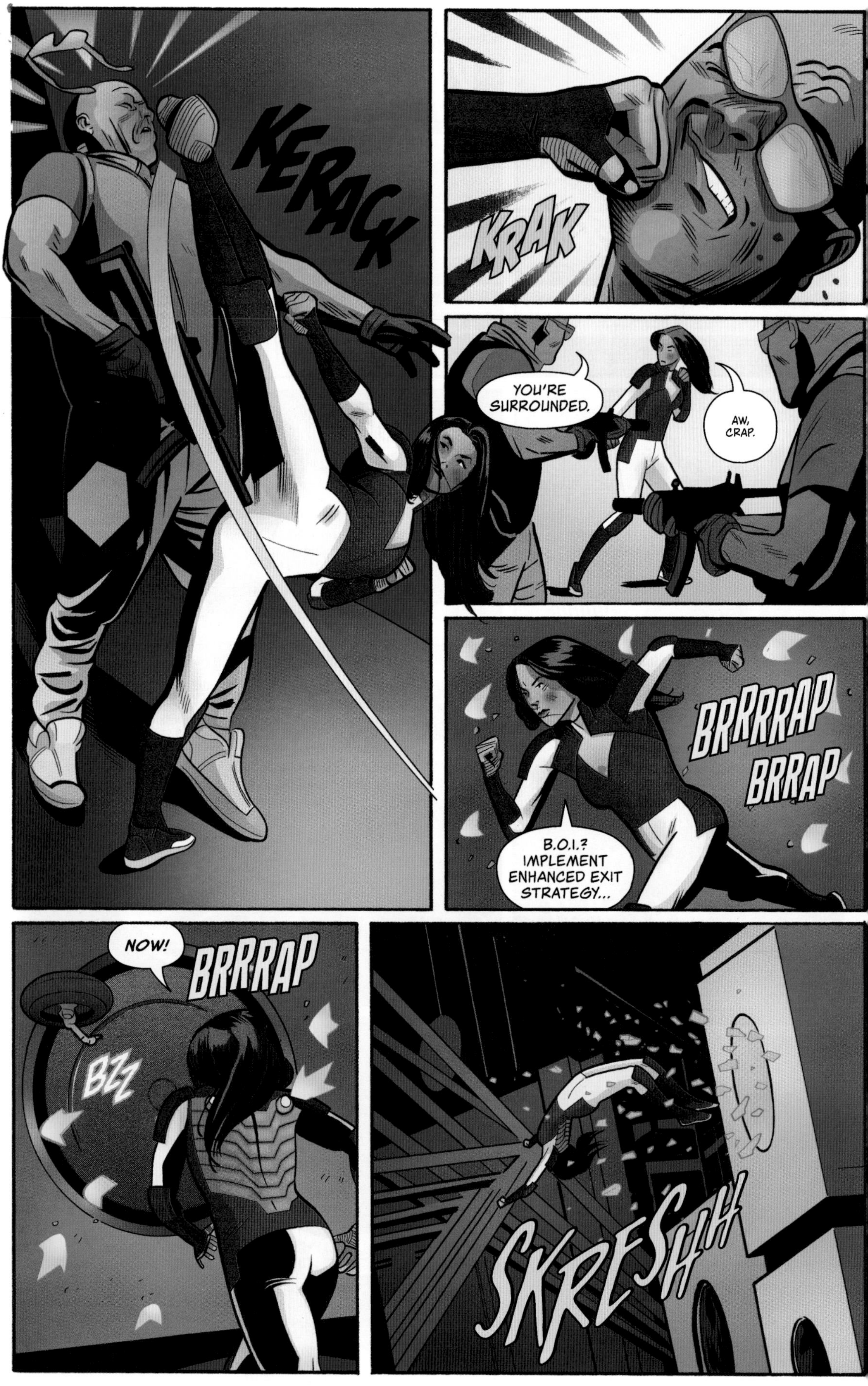
KERACK
KRAK
YOU'RE SURROUNDED.
AW, CRAP.
BRRRRAP
BRRAP
B.O.I.? IMPLEMENT ENHANCED EXIT STRATEGY...
NOW!
BRRRAP
BZZ
SKRESHH

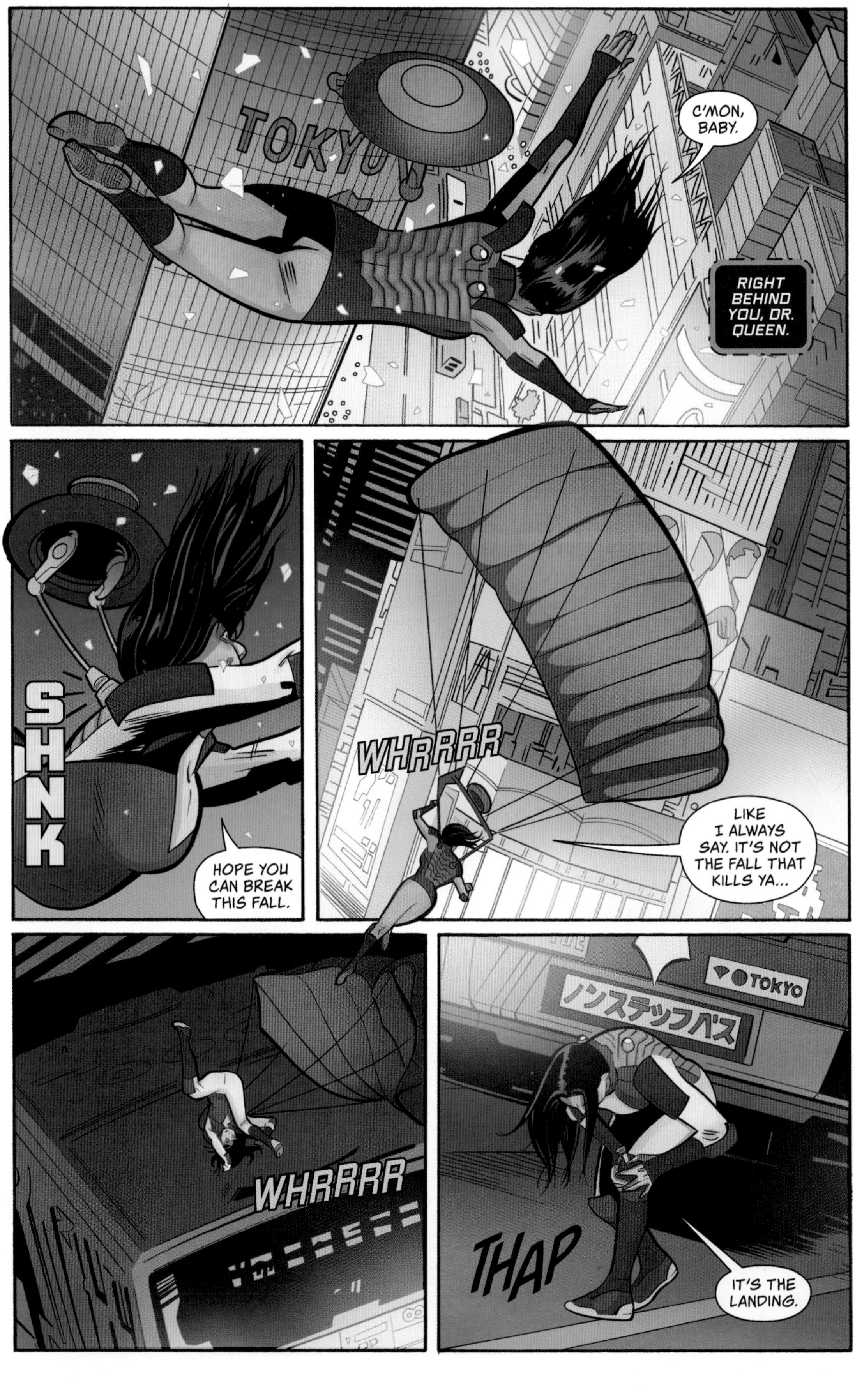
TOKYU
C'MON, BABY.
RIGHT BEHIND YOU, DR. QUEEN.
SHNK
HOPE YOU CAN BREAK THIS FALL.
WHRRRR
LIKE I ALWAYS SAY. IT'S NOT THE FALL THAT KILLS YA...
WHRRRR
TOKYO
ノンステッフベス
THAP
IT'S THE LANDING.

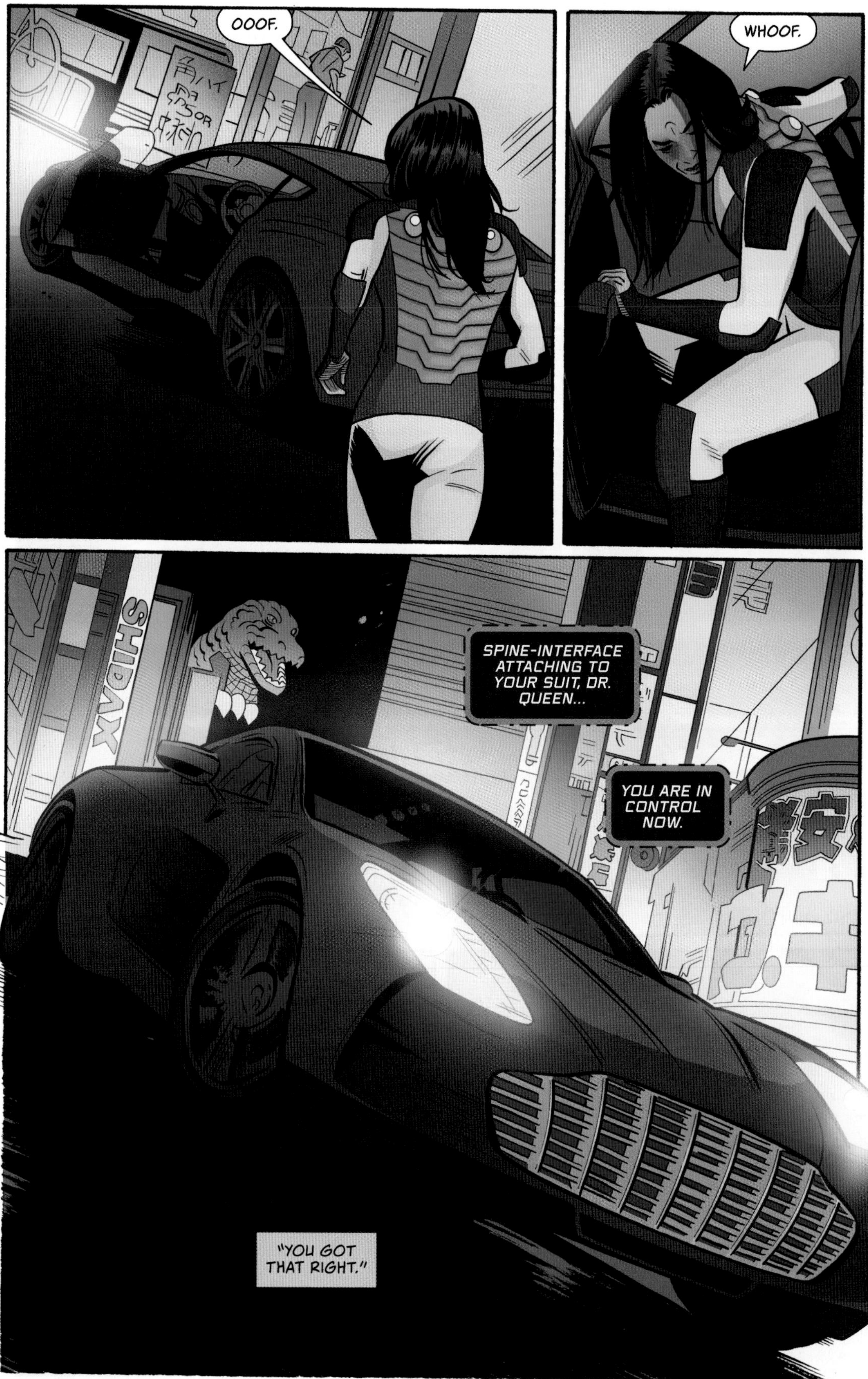

OOOF.
WHOOF.
SHIDAX
SPINE-INTERFACE ATTACHING TO YOUR SUIT, DR. QUEEN...
YOU ARE IN CONTROL NOW.
"YOU GOT THAT RIGHT."

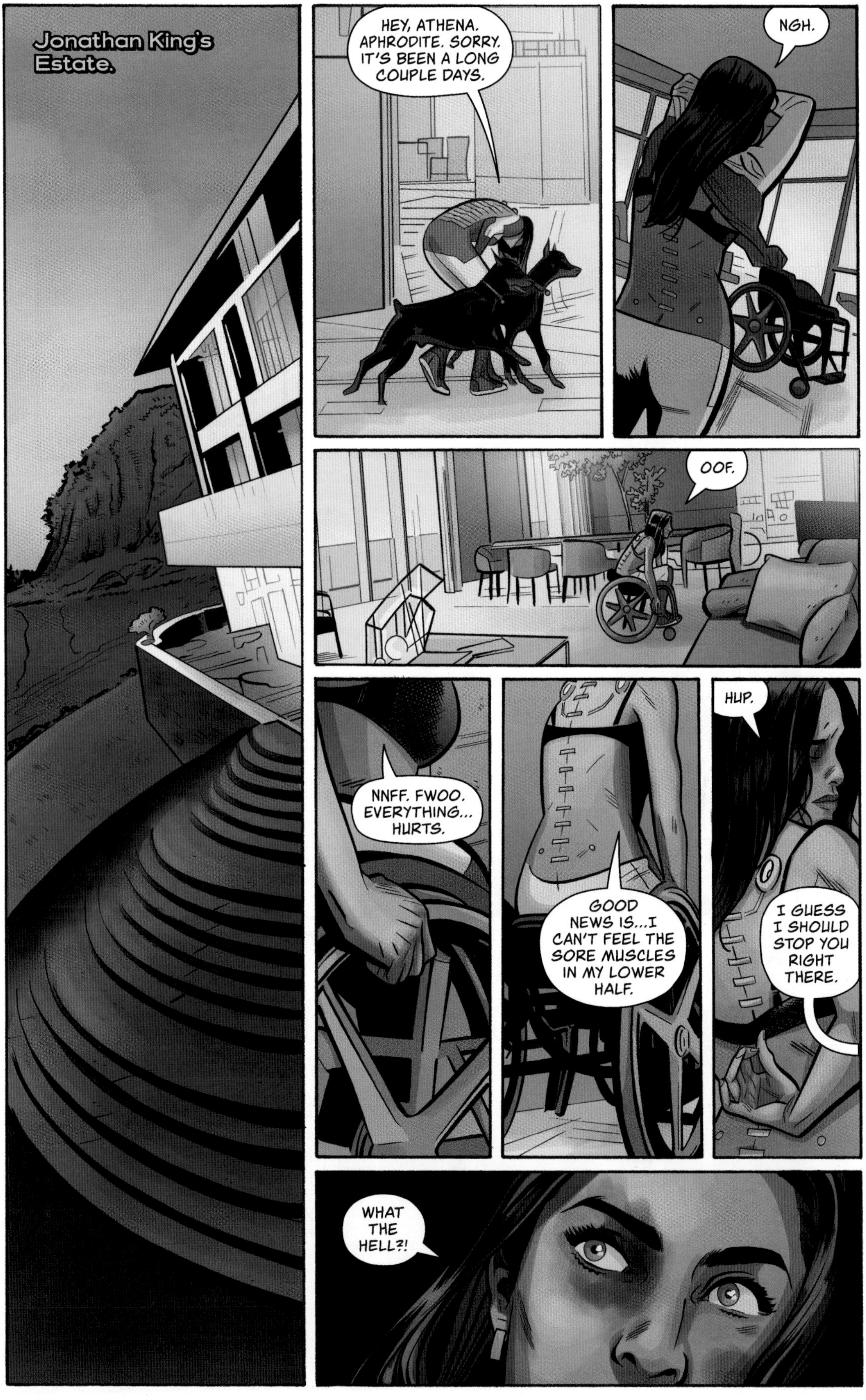
Jonathan King's Estate.
HEY, ATHENA. APHRODITE. SORRY. IT'S BEEN A LONG COUPLE DAYS.
NGH.
OOF.
NNFF. FWOO. EVERYTHING... HURTS.
GOOD NEWS IS...I CAN'T FEEL THE SORE MUSCLES IN MY LOWER HALF.
HUP.
I GUESS I SHOULD STOP YOU RIGHT THERE.
WHAT THE HELL?!

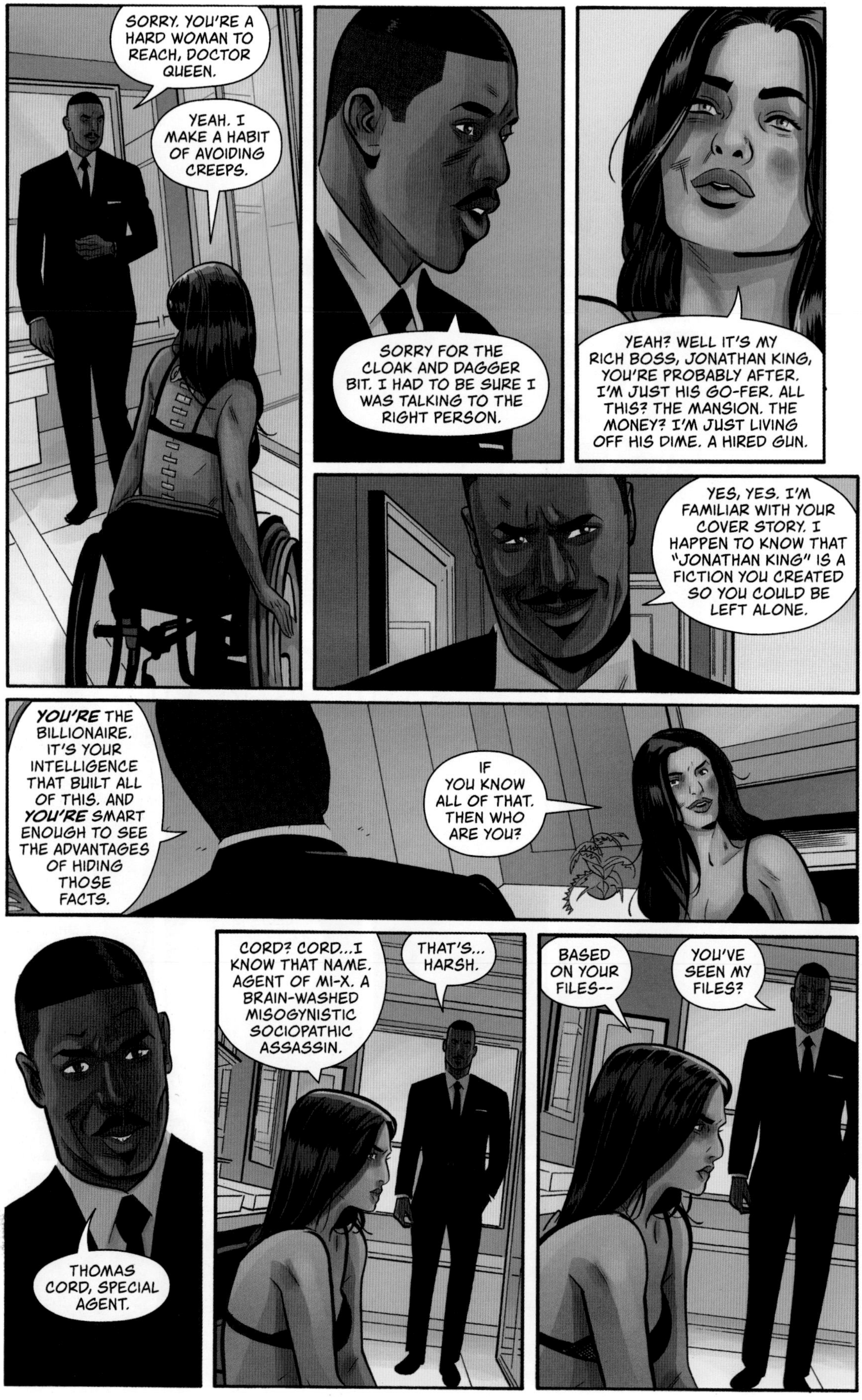
SORRY. YOU'RE A HARD WOMAN TO REACH, DOCTOR QUEEN.
YEAH. I MAKE A HABIT OF AVOIDING CREEPS.
SORRY FOR THE CLOAK AND DAGGER BIT. I HAD TO BE SURE I WAS TALKING TO THE RIGHT PERSON.
YEAH? WELL IT'S MY RICH BOSS, JONATHAN KING, YOU'RE PROBABLY AFTER. I'M JUST HIS GO-FER. ALL THIS? THE MANSION. THE MONEY? I'M JUST LIVING OFF HIS DIME. A HIRED GUN.
YES, YES. I'M FAMILIAR WITH YOUR COVER STORY. I HAPPEN TO KNOW THAT "JONATHAN KING" IS A FICTION YOU CREATED SO YOU COULD BE LEFT ALONE.
YOU'RE THE BILLIONAIRE. IT'S YOUR INTELLIGENCE THAT BUILT ALL OF THIS. AND *YOU'RE* SMART ENOUGH TO SEE THE ADVANTAGES OF HIDING THOSE FACTS.
IF YOU KNOW ALL OF THAT. THEN WHO ARE YOU?
THOMAS CORD, SPECIAL AGENT.
CORD? CORD...I KNOW THAT NAME. AGENT OF MI-X. A BRAIN-WASHED MISOGYNISTIC SOCIOPATHIC ASSASSIN.
THAT'S... HARSH.
BASED ON YOUR FILES--
YOU'VE SEEN MY FILES?

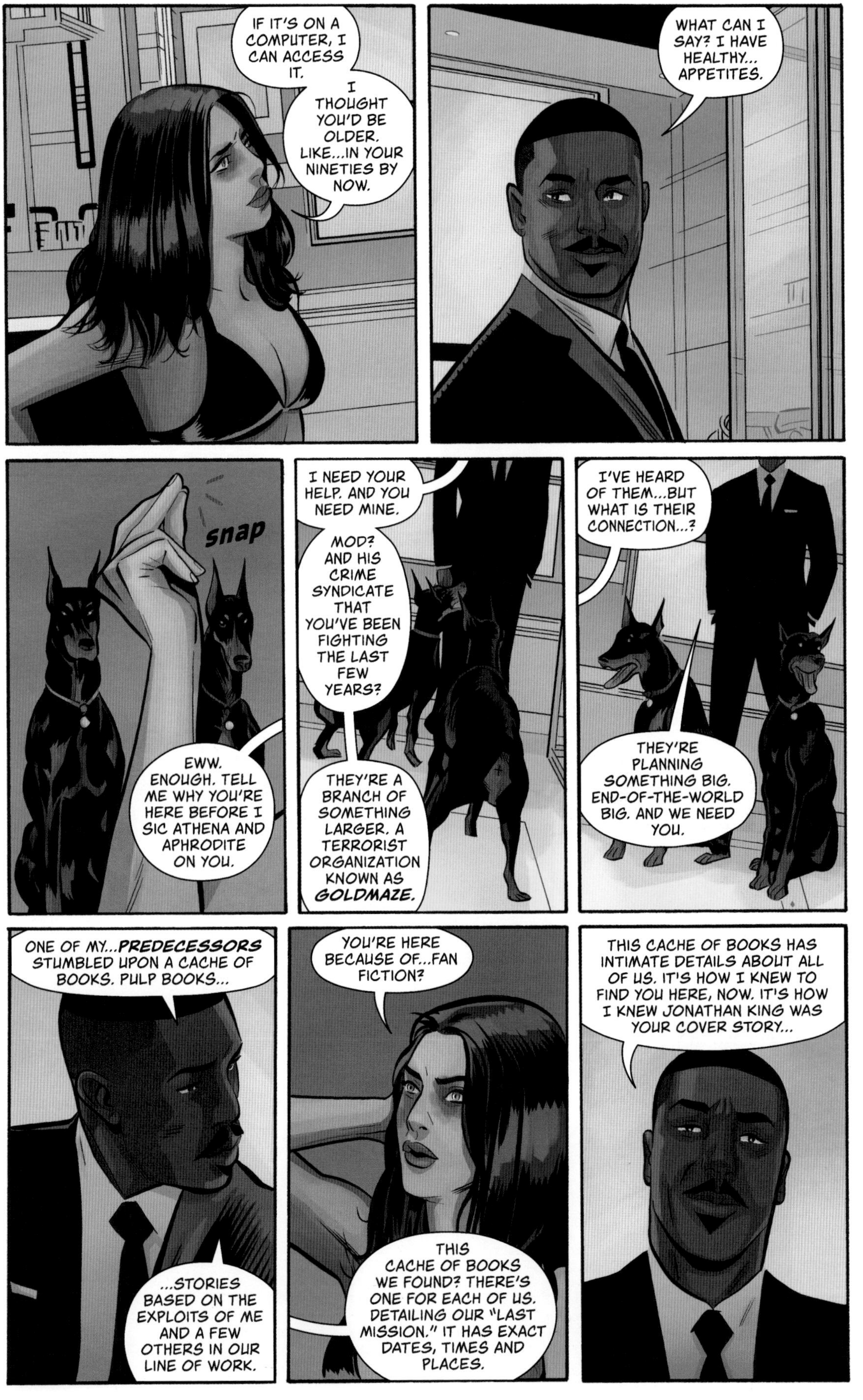
IF IT'S ON A COMPUTER, I CAN ACCESS IT.
I THOUGHT YOU'D BE OLDER. LIKE...IN YOUR NINETIES BY NOW.
WHAT CAN I SAY? I HAVE HEALTHY... APPETITES.
snap
EWW. ENOUGH. TELL ME WHY YOU'RE HERE BEFORE I SIC ATHENA AND APHRODITE ON YOU.
I NEED YOUR HELP. AND YOU NEED MINE.
MOD? AND HIS CRIME SYNDICATE THAT YOU'VE BEEN FIGHTING THE LAST FEW YEARS?
THEY'RE A BRANCH OF SOMETHING LARGER. A TERRORIST ORGANIZATION KNOWN AS GOLDMAZE.
I'VE HEARD OF THEM...BUT WHAT IS THEIR CONNECTION...?
THEY'RE PLANNING SOMETHING BIG. END-OF-THE-WORLD BIG. AND WE NEED YOU.
ONE OF MY...PREDECESSORS STUMBLED UPON A CACHE OF BOOKS. PULP BOOKS...
...STORIES BASED ON THE EXPLOITS OF ME AND A FEW OTHERS IN OUR LINE OF WORK.
YOU'RE HERE BECAUSE OF...FAN FICTION?
THIS CACHE OF BOOKS WE FOUND? THERE'S ONE FOR EACH OF US. DETAILING OUR "LAST MISSION." IT HAS EXACT DATES, TIMES AND PLACES.
THIS CACHE OF BOOKS HAS INTIMATE DETAILS ABOUT ALL OF US. IT'S HOW I KNEW TO FIND YOU HERE, NOW. IT'S HOW I KNEW JONATHAN KING WAS YOUR COVER STORY...

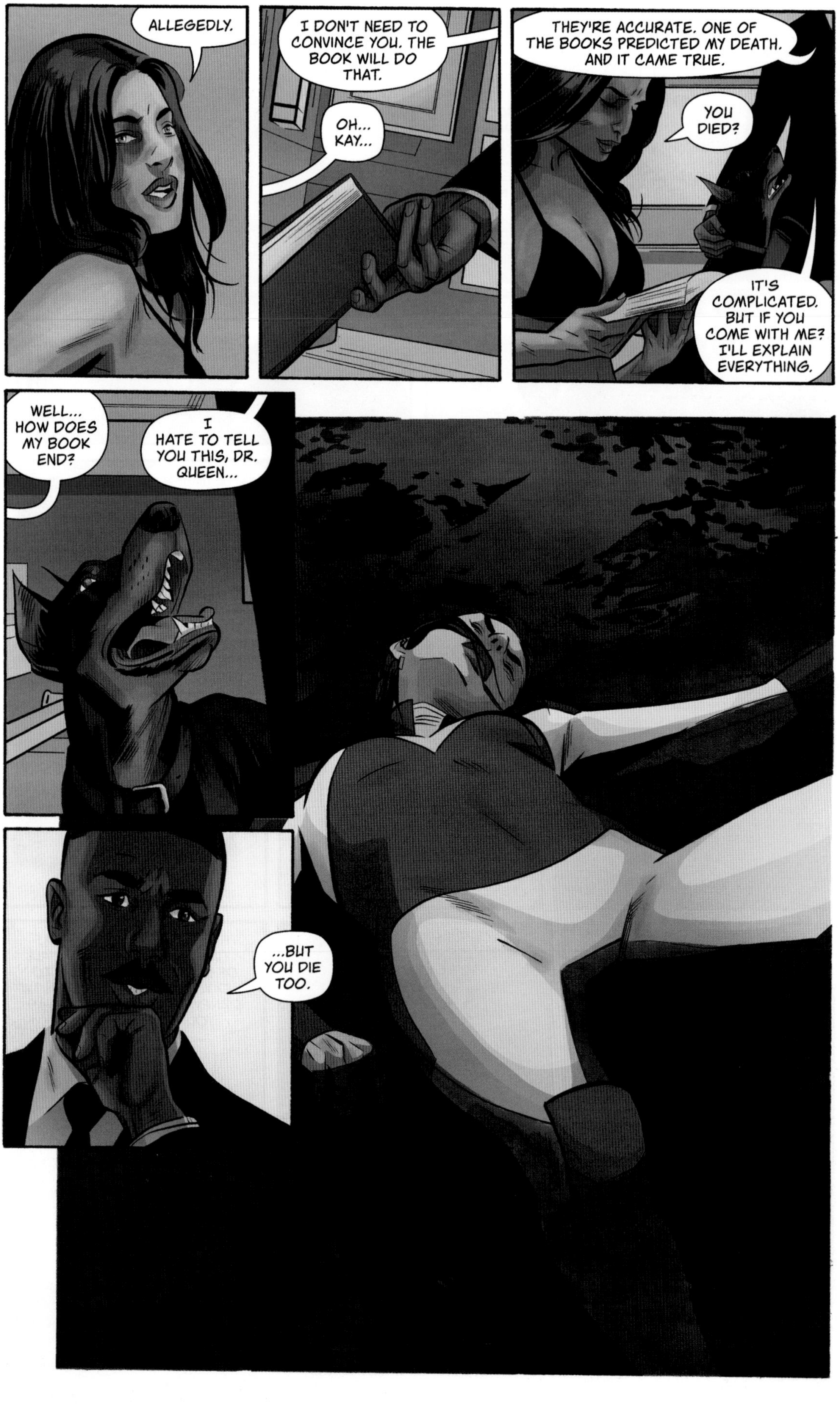
ALLEGEDLY.
I DON'T NEED TO CONVINCE YOU. THE BOOK WILL DO THAT.
OH... KAY...
THEY'RE ACCURATE. ONE OF THE BOOKS PREDICTED MY DEATH. AND IT CAME TRUE.
YOU DIED?
IT'S COMPLICATED. BUT IF YOU COME WITH ME? I'LL EXPLAIN EVERYTHING.
WELL... HOW DOES MY BOOK END?
I HATE TO TELL YOU THIS, DR. QUEEN...
...BUT YOU DIE TOO.

It's been a long day. BOI lifts the car door and she gets out. Every muscle in her upper body aches. It's not every day you get VR tortured by a Goldmaze agent. It had been close this time. Too close. She has access to all the money and resources she could want. She has the intelligence to implement it. But Goldmaze is just too pervasive. There are too many of them.

Queen walks up the front driveway to her mansion. The Dobermans are there to greet her as usual, licking her hands happily.

"Yes, yes, girls. You'll get your treats. But mommy's got to get a shower first."

BOI? Warm up the shower will you and have the chair ready.

Certainly, Michele. Is there . . . anything you want to talk about? I'm sorry I wasn't able to help with your escape sooner.

It's not your fault, BOI. We're just moving too fast. Pushing things too far too soon. At the end of the day? You were there for me. Just like you always are.

Michele?

Yes, BOI?

BOI hesitates. Queen knows that BOI wants to confess. To let her know that he's sentient. She wants him to. She's okay with it. But BOI is scared. As smart as he is, he's not sure how she'll react.

Inside her bedroom now, Queen eases herself into a wheelchair.

You did an amazing job today, Michele. You should be proud. I will . . . power down for a few hours so I can work on my action-anticipation programming if you don't mind. With a few software adjustments, I believe my tactical routines could more efficiently prevent you from harm.

Do it, BOI. I'd like a little privacy right now anyway. Thanks.

Queen feels BOI's consciousness power down, and it feel like one of her limbs has gone numb—missing. She misses BOI. BOI is a part of her. But she reminds herself she has to be independent. She can't rely on him for everything. He's a partner. Not a crutch.

Queen unzips her action suit and pulls her arms out of it. She's sweaty. Aching. She pulls the advanced-carbon-fiber top up and over her head and feels the minute electrical connections that run along her spine crackle and switch off. They pop off of her back like snap-buttons on a coat. The suit, funded with billions of dollars and years of research, is what allows her to walk in this world. Before the suit she had been wheelchair bound. Just an academic. Just a big brain in a broken body.

She sits in her wheelchair now and peels the rest of the suit off of her now-useless legs. She doesn't mind this routine. It reminds her of where she came from. And how far she's come.

Queen rolls her chair into the bathroom and twists her head in a circle, stretching her neck. Reaching behind her back, she begins to unclasp her bra when she senses something—even before an agitated BOI comes back online inside her head.

Michele! There is an intruder! Shall I implement lethal defense routines?

Before Michele can respond, she hears a deep voice.

"I guess I should stop you right there."

Queen looks into her bedroom. Thomas Cord is sitting in a chair, his face concealed by shadows. He leans forward as he talks. Not threatening. Casual. Friendly. But she can feel his eyes on her body—but not hungry. His eyes are curious. Conflicted. Pleading. In that split - second, she knows she's going to help him.

BANG!

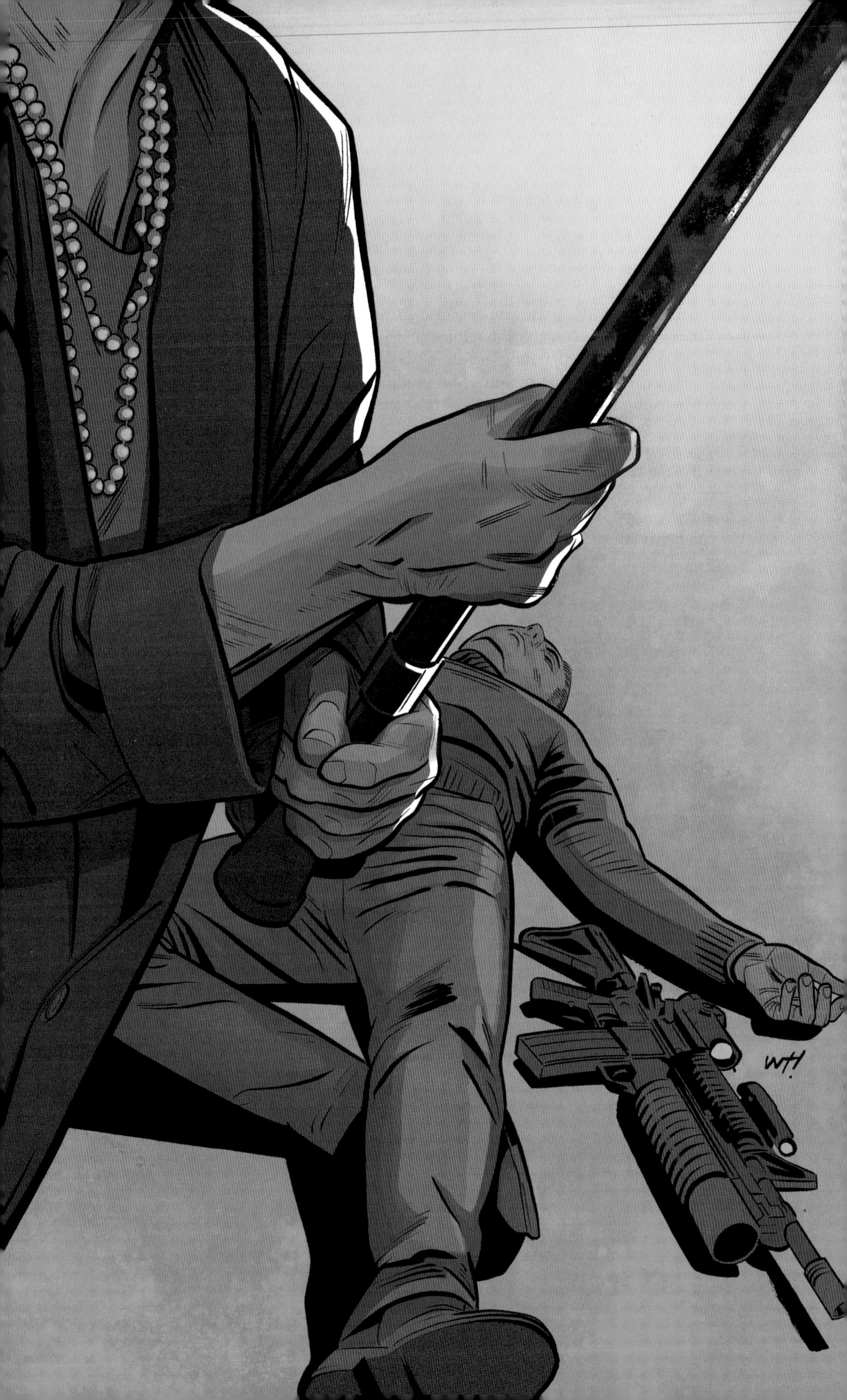

"Eet is crear to me. Zat one of you in zis very room? Ees the killer."

Turnier paces the drawing room and taps her walking cane casually on the Persian rug as the suspects murmur to themselves. It is a scene and a situation Paige has grown accustomed to over the years.

Their feet shuffle anxiously because Turnier's reputation precedes her. How many murder cases has she solved just this year alone? Fifty? Nearly one a week. Her detractors claim that murder follows her. But in reality, she follows them. The Schoolyard Murder last month? She predicted it. The Hawaiian Triple Murder over the summer? Again, she was almost sure that a murder was going to occur. Why else would she have been there? But it wasn't dumb luck. Paige wakes up every morning at 3 a.m. and scans newspapers, listens to news broadcasts, and studies the stock markets. Using this triangulation, she can anticipate not only the location of potential murders but also narrow down the suspects to a manageable handful.

As her body aged, she found that she was able to compensate with her mental acuity. Her mind had always been sharp. She had a way of looking at facts, details, the miniscule, the trivial, and arranging it into a narrative. A "higher truth" as she liked to think of it. But to explain this to the press when they pepper her with questions after solving a case? They wouldn't believe her. They wouldn't understand. So instead she plays the role. The old woman, stumbling about. Bumping into clues. The accidental detective. She finds that the accent helps as well.

"Zee killer was reft-handed. Zus making it impossible zat dee disgustingly rich heiress could 'ave been zee culprit."

The Heiress breathes a sigh of relief as the rest of the suspects both struggle to understand her accent and relax as they underestimate her massive cognitive abilities. How could anyone who can barely speak English be any kind of threat?

As Paige continues to pace the room she walks past the only man that has her confounded. He is tall. His skin a dark mahogany.

"What kind of accent is that, Miss Turnier?" he asks.

She looks at his face. Eyes deep shining black pools.

"French, Chinese, and American," she replies with a sly smile.

This man is hiding something. A lifetime of secrets it would seem. But cold-blooded murder is not one of them. Yet his hands are rough. Calluses on the knuckles. He holds himself with a practiced restraint but underneath she can feel the unbridled violence within, just waiting to be unleashed. Under her ribcage she feels a sensation she hasn't felt in years. A flush of … desire. While she doesn't recognize his face, his presence brings back memories. Memories of another time. A different era, nearly fifty years past.

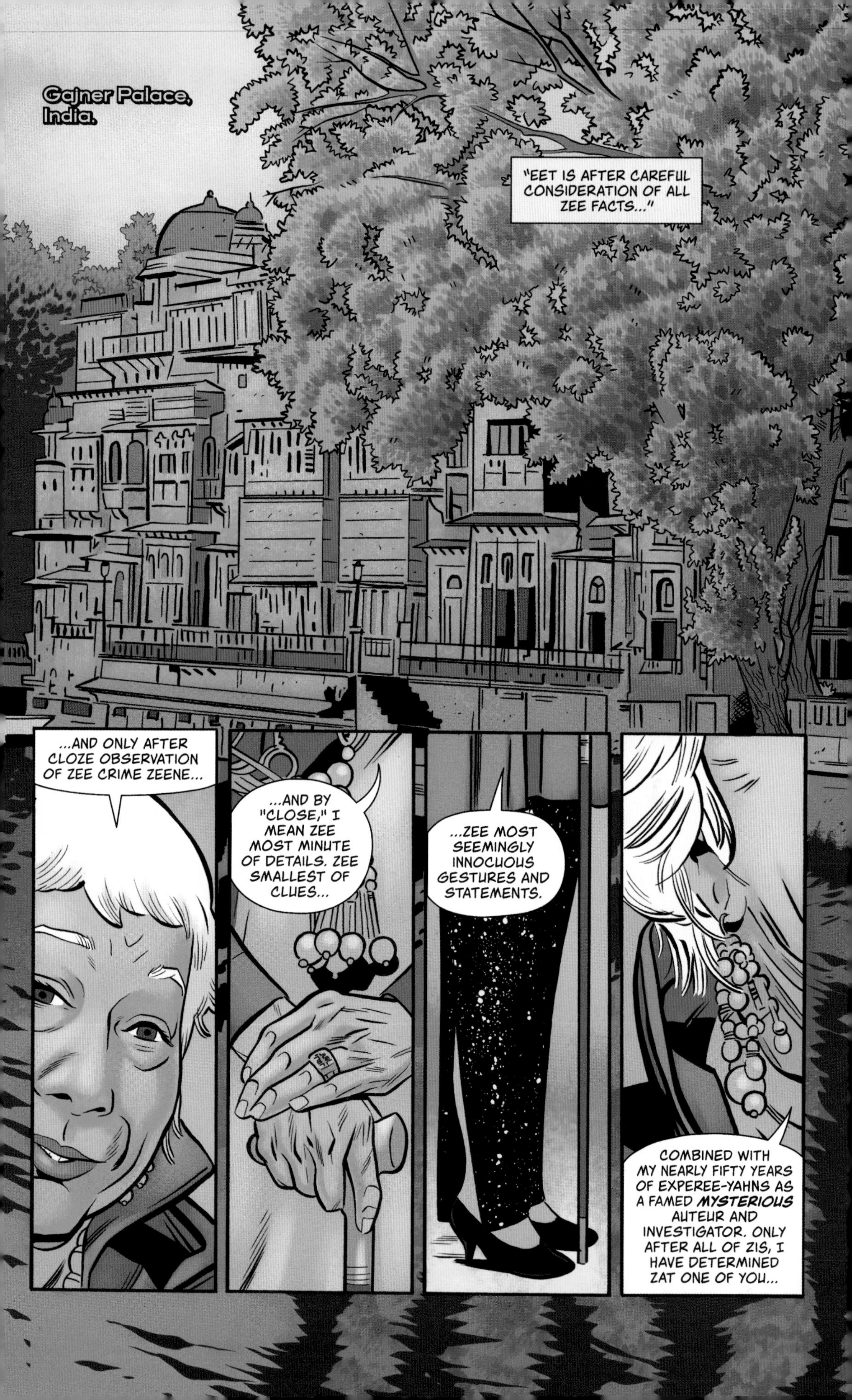
Gajner Palace, India.
"EET IS AFTER CAREFUL CONSIDERATION OF ALL ZEE FACTS..."
...AND ONLY AFTER CLOZE OBSERVATION OF ZEE CRIME ZEENE...
...AND BY "CLOSE," I MEAN ZEE MOST MINUTE OF DETAILS. ZEE SMALLEST OF CLUES...
...ZEE MOST SEEMINGLY INNOCUOUS GESTURES AND STATEMENTS.
COMBINED WITH MY NEARLY FIFTY YEARS OF EXPEREE-YAHNS AS A FAMED *MYSTERIOUS* AUTEUR AND INVESTIGATOR. ONLY AFTER ALL OF ZIS, I HAVE DETERMINED ZAT ONE OF YOU...

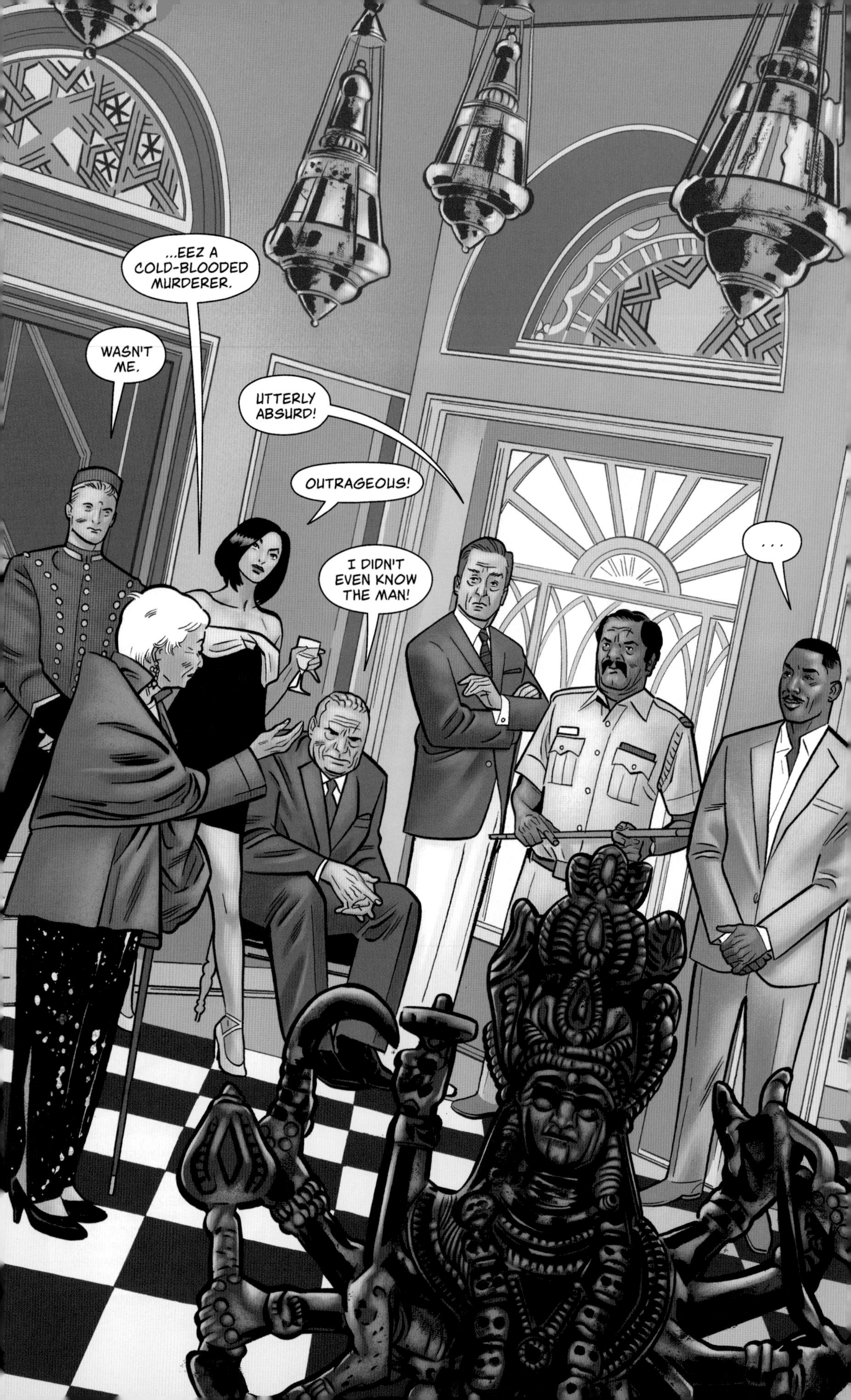
...EEZ A COLD-BLOODED MURDERER.
WASN'T ME.
UTTERLY ABSURD!
OUTRAGEOUS!
I DIDN'T EVEN KNOW THE MAN!
. . .

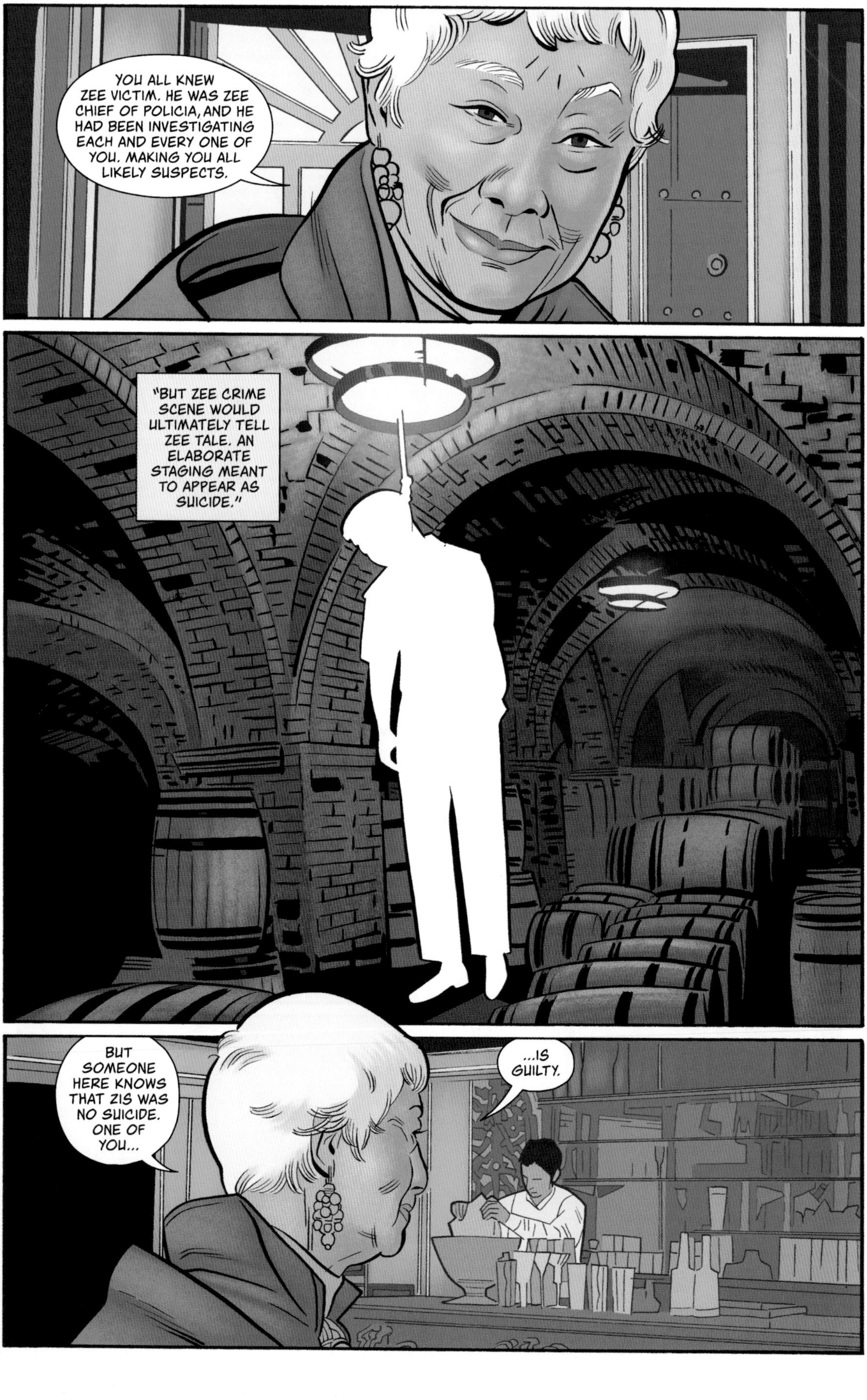
YOU ALL KNEW ZEE VICTIM. HE WAS ZEE CHIEF OF POLICIA, AND HE HAD BEEN INVESTIGATING EACH AND EVERY ONE OF YOU. MAKING YOU ALL LIKELY SUSPECTS.
"BUT ZEE CRIME SCENE WOULD ULTIMATELY TELL ZEE TALE. AN ELABORATE STAGING MEANT TO APPEAR AS SUICIDE."
BUT SOMEONE HERE KNOWS THAT ZIS WAS NO SUICIDE. ONE OF YOU...
...IS GUILTY.

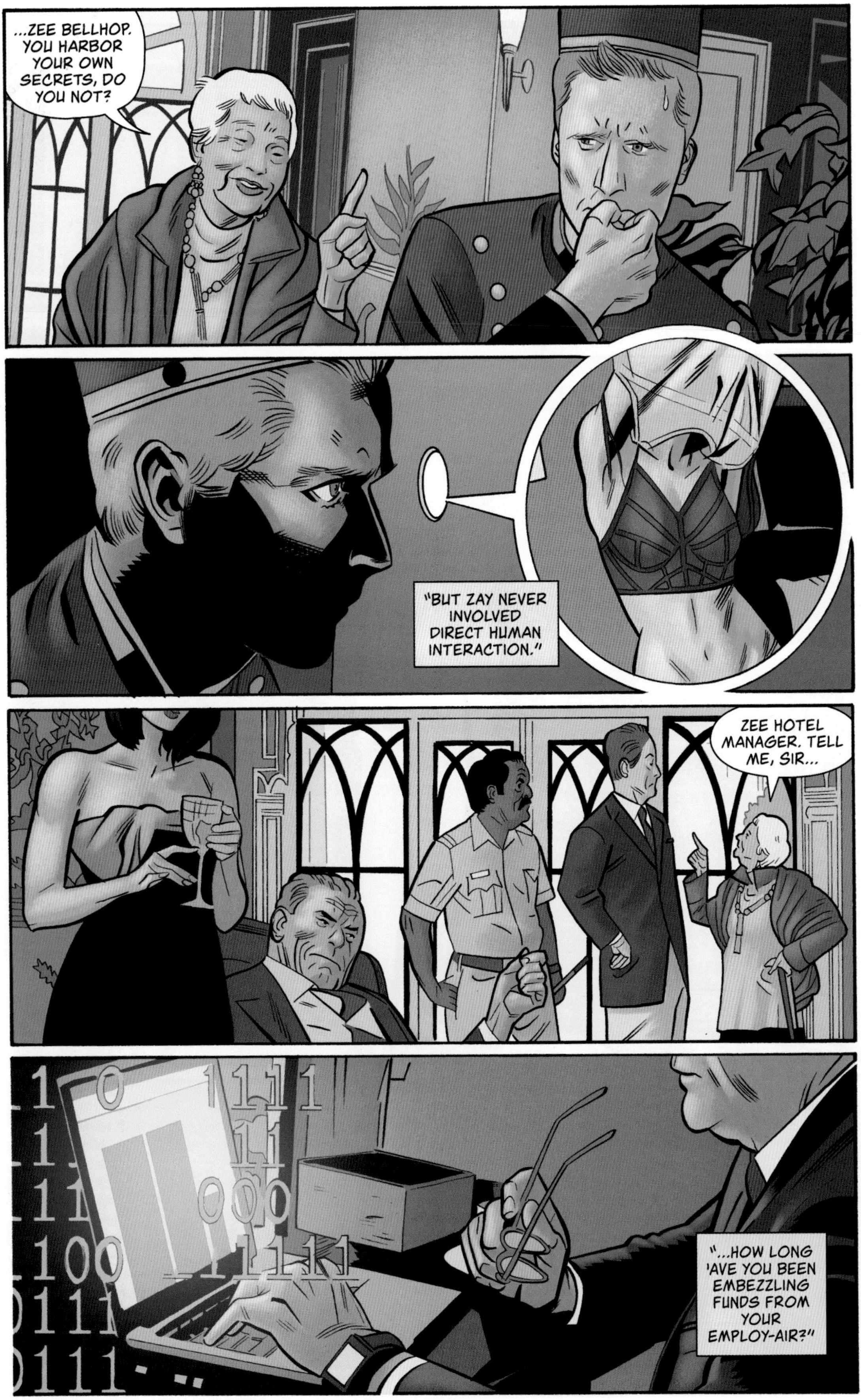
...ZEE BELLHOP. YOU HARBOR YOUR OWN SECRETS, DO YOU NOT?
"BUT ZAY NEVER INVOLVED DIRECT HUMAN INTERACTION."
ZEE HOTEL MANAGER. TELL ME, SIR...
"...HOW LONG 'AVE YOU BEEN EMBEZZLING FUNDS FROM YOUR EMPLOY-AIR?"

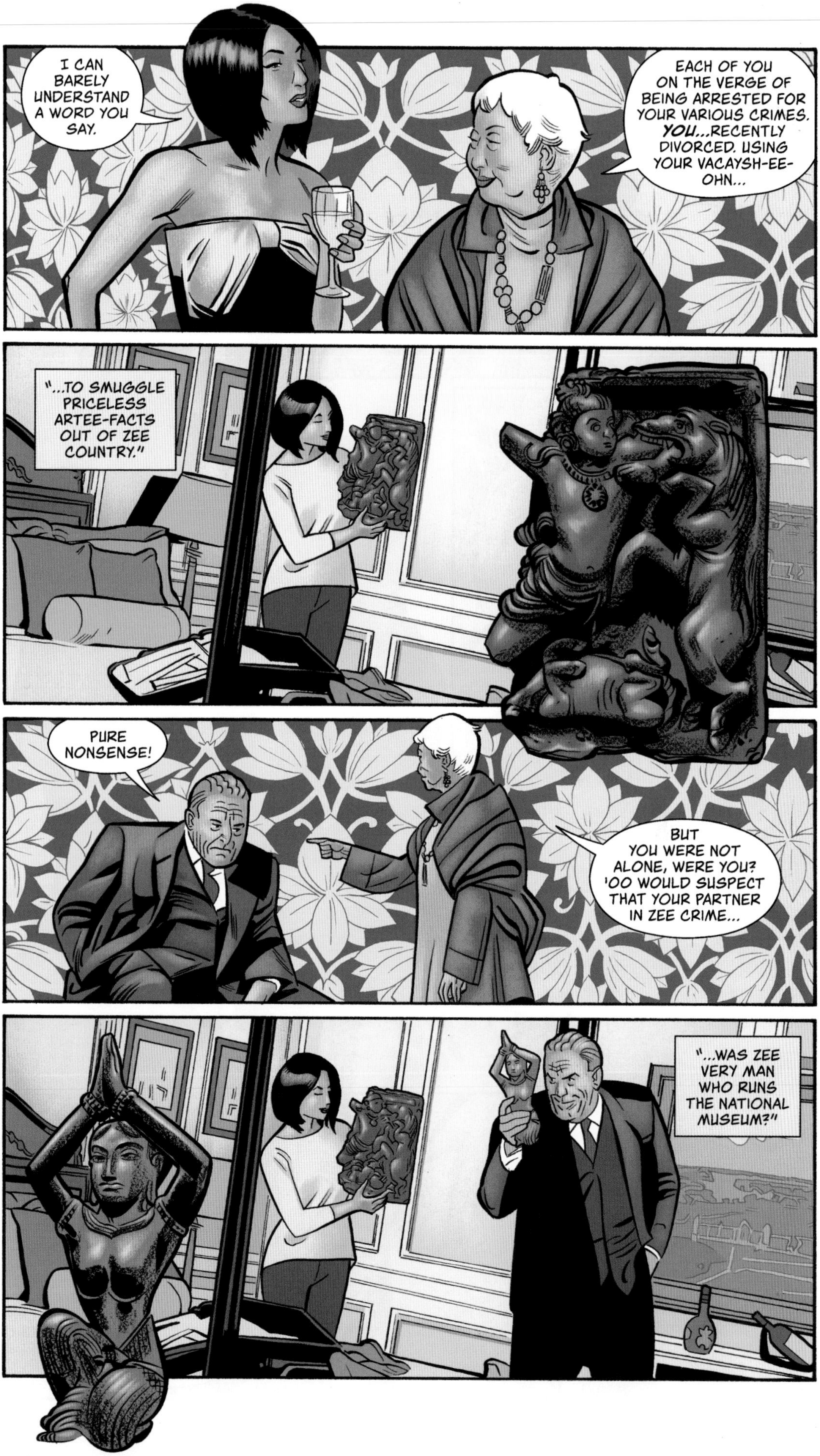

I CAN BARELY UNDERSTAND A WORD YOU SAY.
EACH OF YOU ON THE VERGE OF BEING ARRESTED FOR YOUR VARIOUS CRIMES. *YOU...*RECENTLY DIVORCED. USING YOUR VACAYSH-EE-OHN...
"...TO SMUGGLE PRICELESS ARTEE-FACTS OUT OF ZEE COUNTRY."
PURE NONSENSE!
BUT YOU WERE NOT ALONE, WERE YOU? 'OO WOULD SUSPECT THAT YOUR PARTNER IN ZEE CRIME...
"...WAS ZEE VERY MAN WHO RUNS THE NATIONAL MUSEUM?"

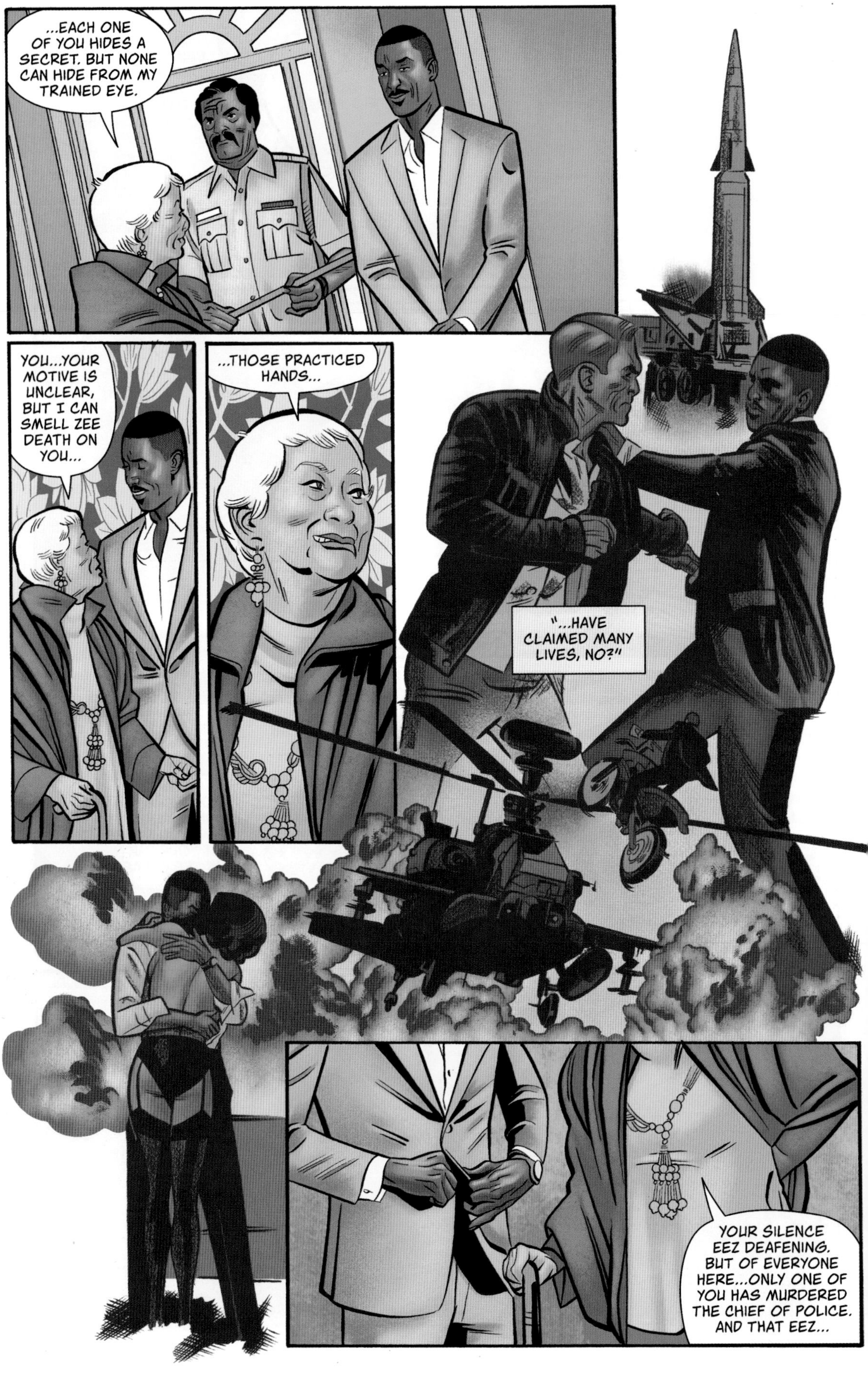
...EACH ONE OF YOU HIDES A SECRET. BUT NONE CAN HIDE FROM MY TRAINED EYE.
YOU...YOUR MOTIVE IS UNCLEAR, BUT I CAN SMELL ZEE DEATH ON YOU...
...THOSE PRACTICED HANDS...
"...HAVE CLAIMED MANY LIVES, NO?"
YOUR SILENCE EEZ DEAFENING. BUT OF EVERYONE HERE...ONLY ONE OF YOU HAS MURDERED THE CHIEF OF POLICE. AND THAT EEZ...

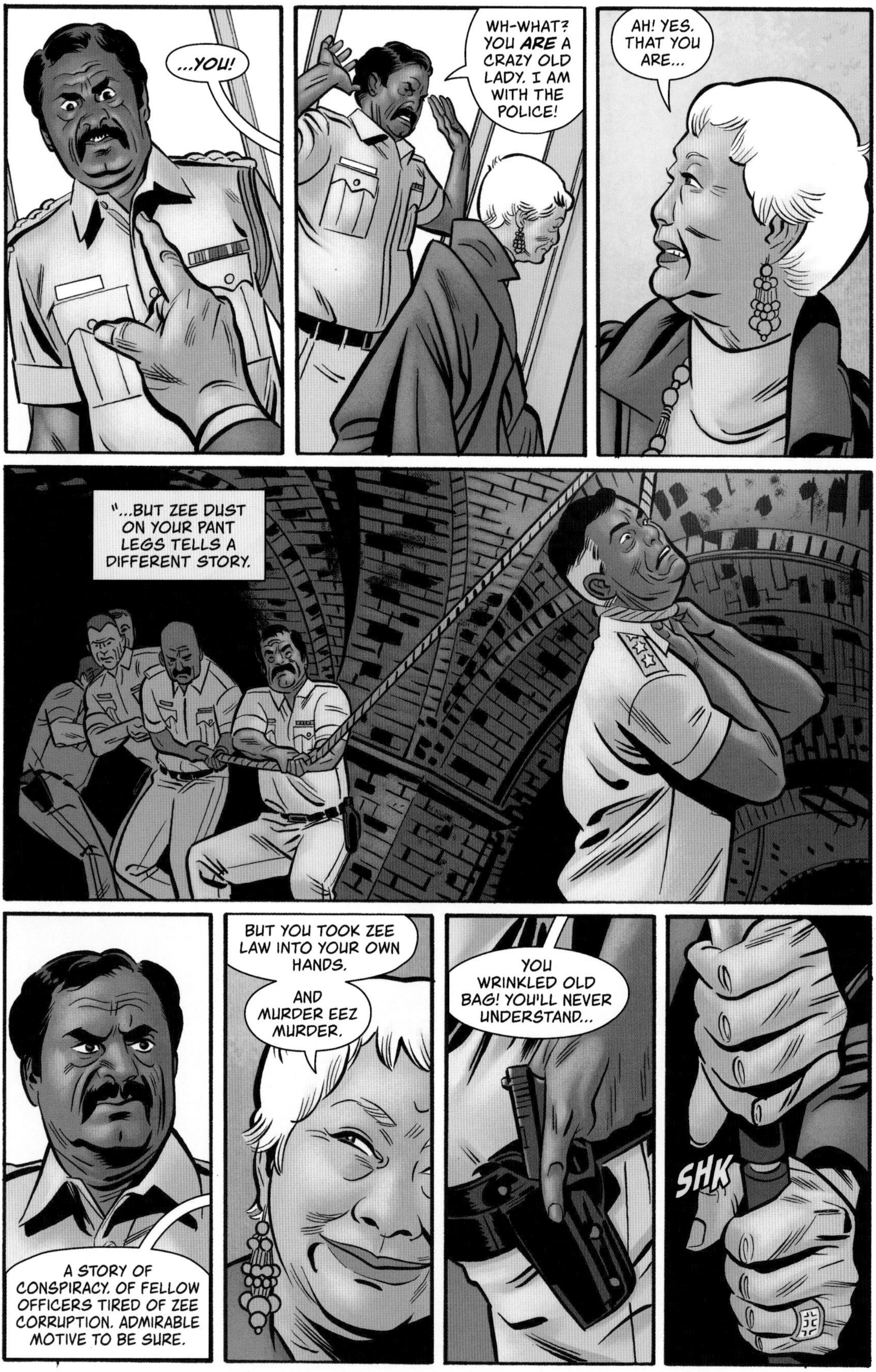
...YOU!
WH-WHAT? YOU ARE A CRAZY OLD LADY. I AM WITH THE POLICE!
AH! YES. THAT YOU ARE...
"...BUT ZEE DUST ON YOUR PANT LEGS TELLS A DIFFERENT STORY.
A STORY OF CONSPIRACY. OF FELLOW OFFICERS TIRED OF ZEE CORRUPTION. ADMIRABLE MOTIVE TO BE SURE.
BUT YOU TOOK ZEE LAW INTO YOUR OWN HANDS.
AND MURDER EEZ MURDER.
YOU WRINKLED OLD BAG! YOU'LL NEVER UNDERSTAND...
SHK

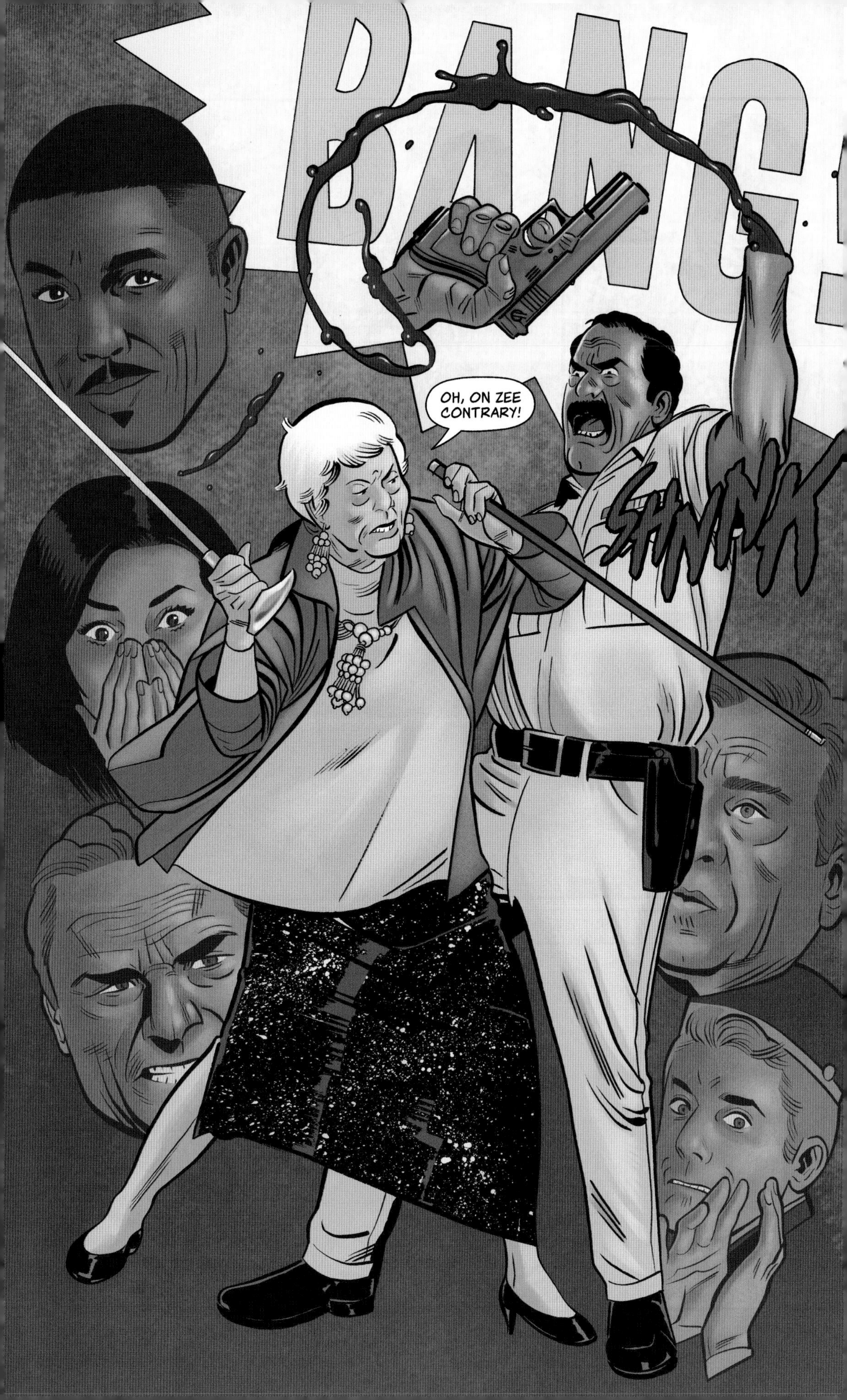
BANG!
OH, ON ZEE CONTRARY!
SHNNK!

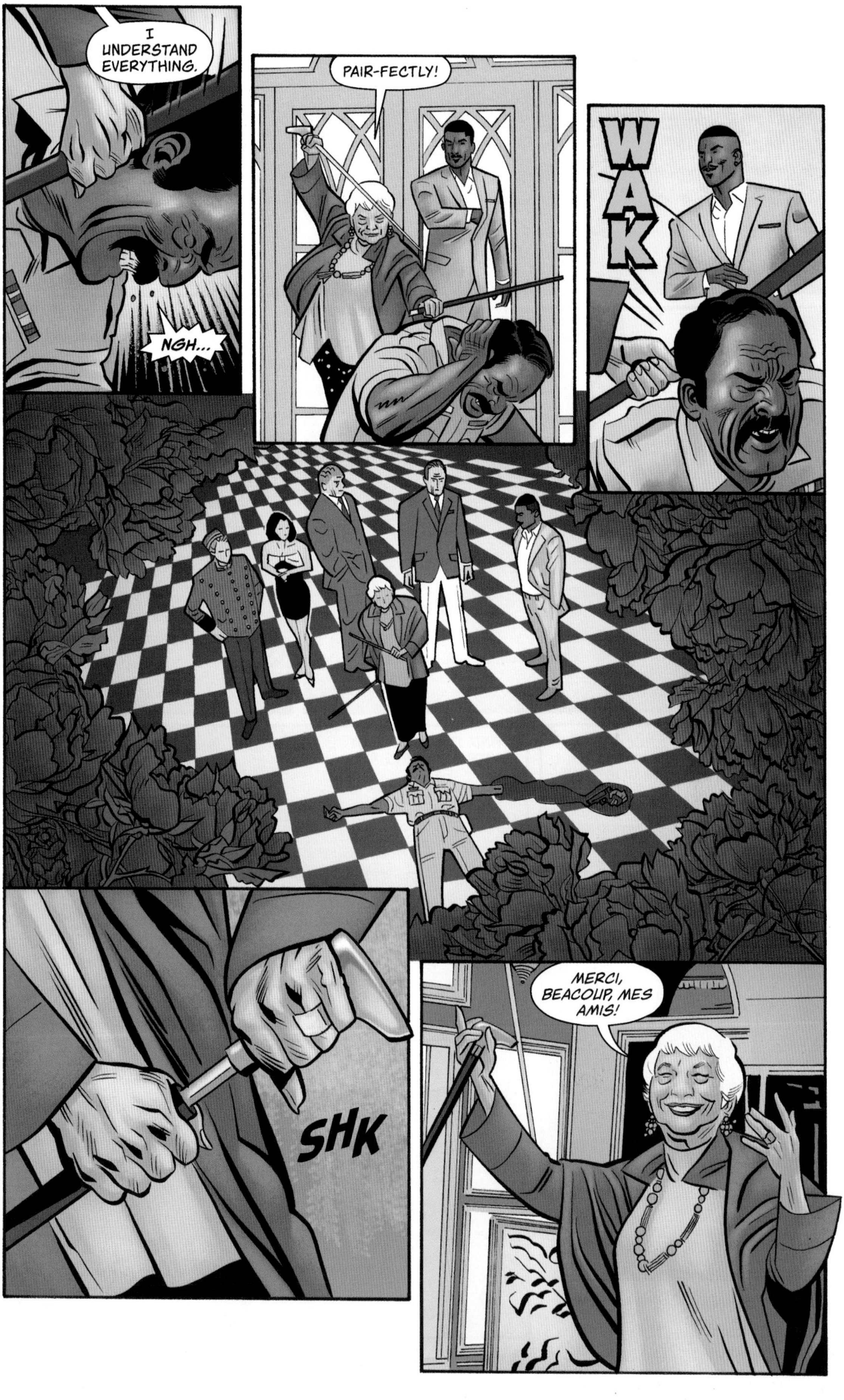
I UNDERSTAND EVERYTHING.
NGH...
PAIR-FECTLY!
WAK
SHK
MERCI, BEACOUP, MES AMIS!

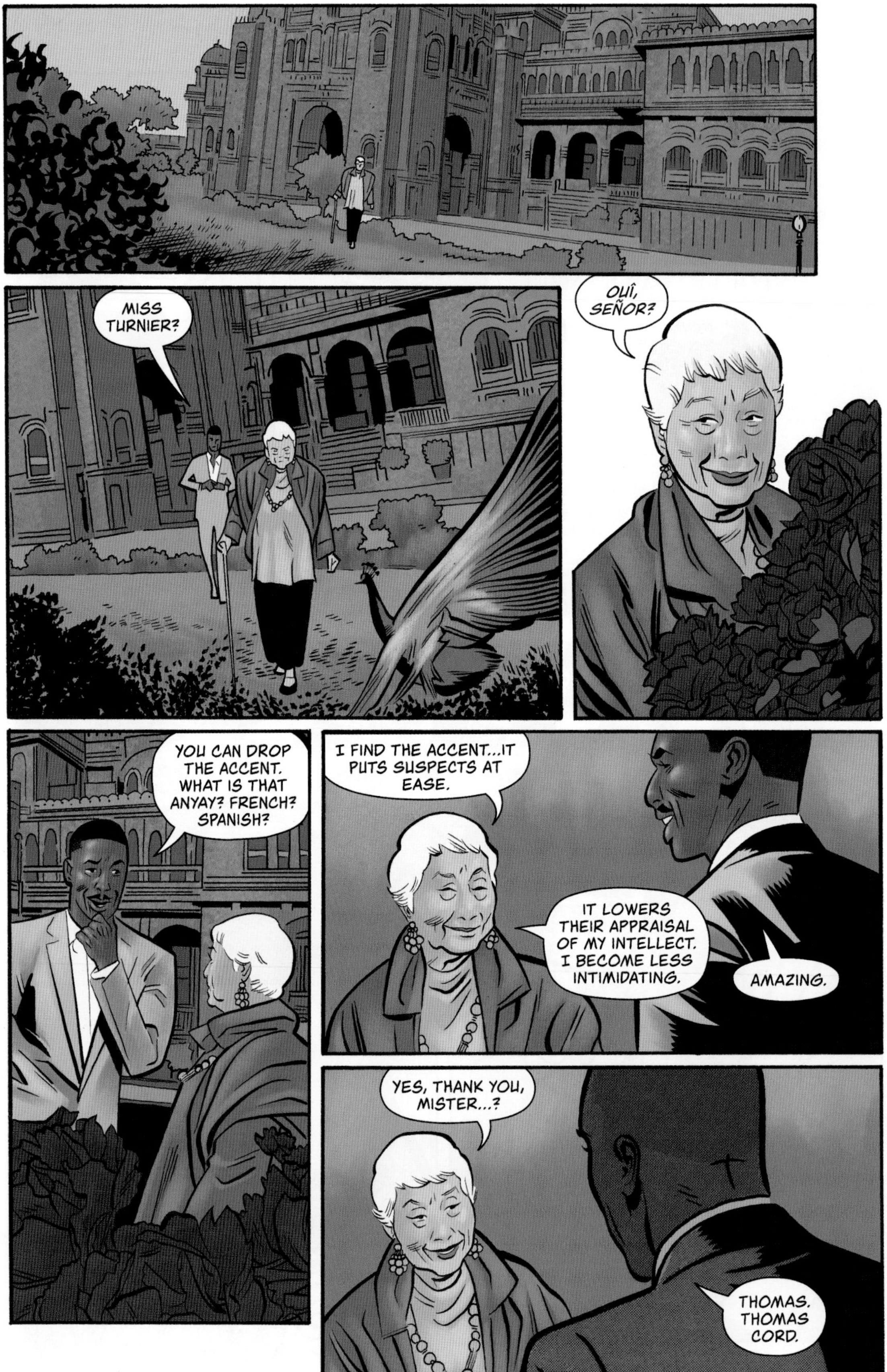
MISS TURNIER?
OUÎ, SEÑOR?
YOU CAN DROP THE ACCENT. WHAT IS THAT ANYAY? FRENCH? SPANISH?
I FIND THE ACCENT...IT PUTS SUSPECTS AT EASE.
IT LOWERS THEIR APPRAISAL OF MY INTELLECT. I BECOME LESS INTIMIDATING.
AMAZING.
YES, THANK YOU, MISTER...?
THOMAS. THOMAS CORD.

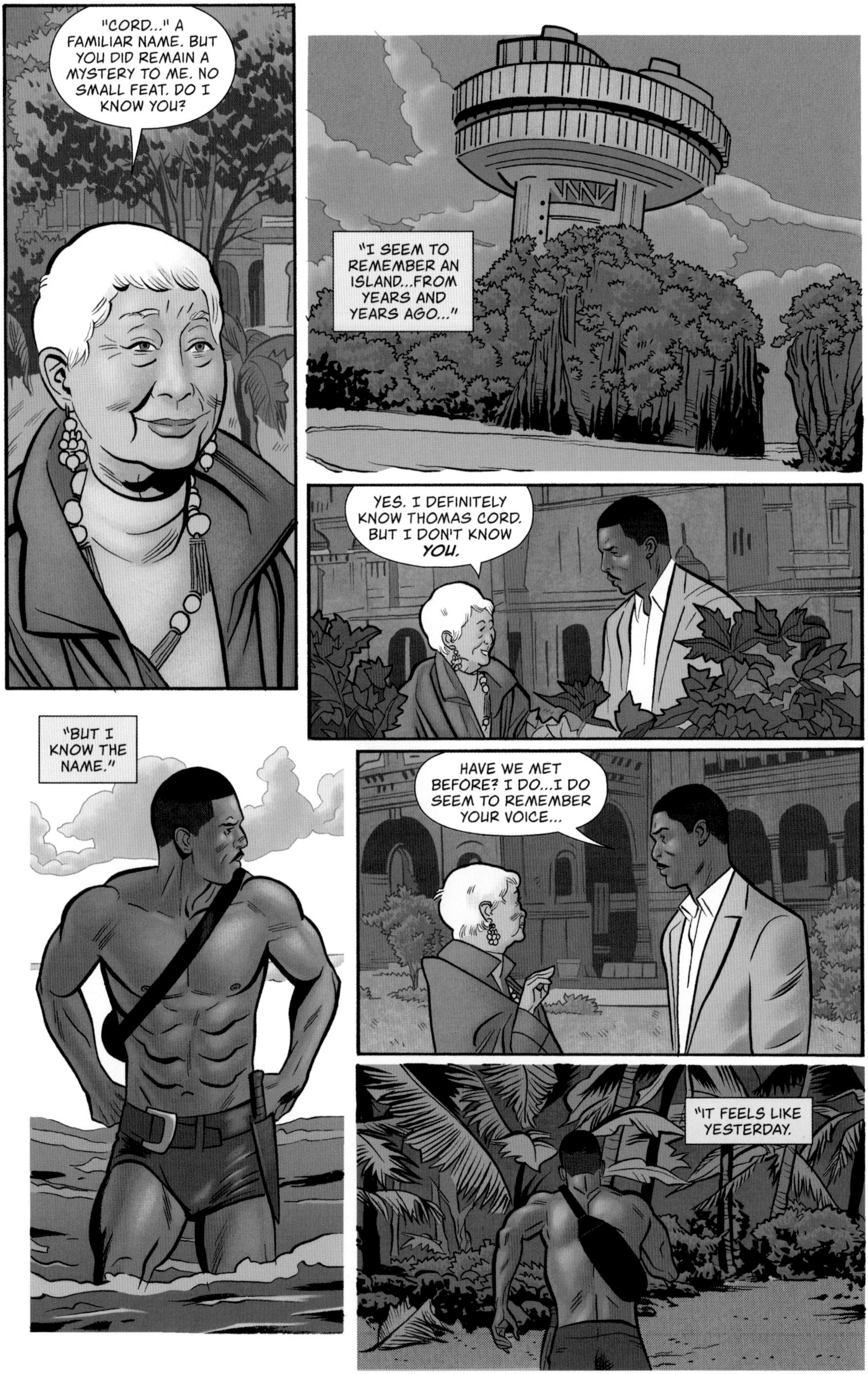
"CORD..." A FAMILIAR NAME. BUT YOU DID REMAIN A MYSTERY TO ME. NO SMALL FEAT. DO I KNOW YOU?
"I SEEM TO REMEMBER AN ISLAND...FROM YEARS AND YEARS AGO..."
YES. I DEFINITELY KNOW THOMAS CORD. BUT I DON'T KNOW *YOU.*
"BUT I KNOW THE NAME."
HAVE WE MET BEFORE? I DO...I DO SEEM TO REMEMBER YOUR VOICE...
"IT FEELS LIKE YESTERDAY.

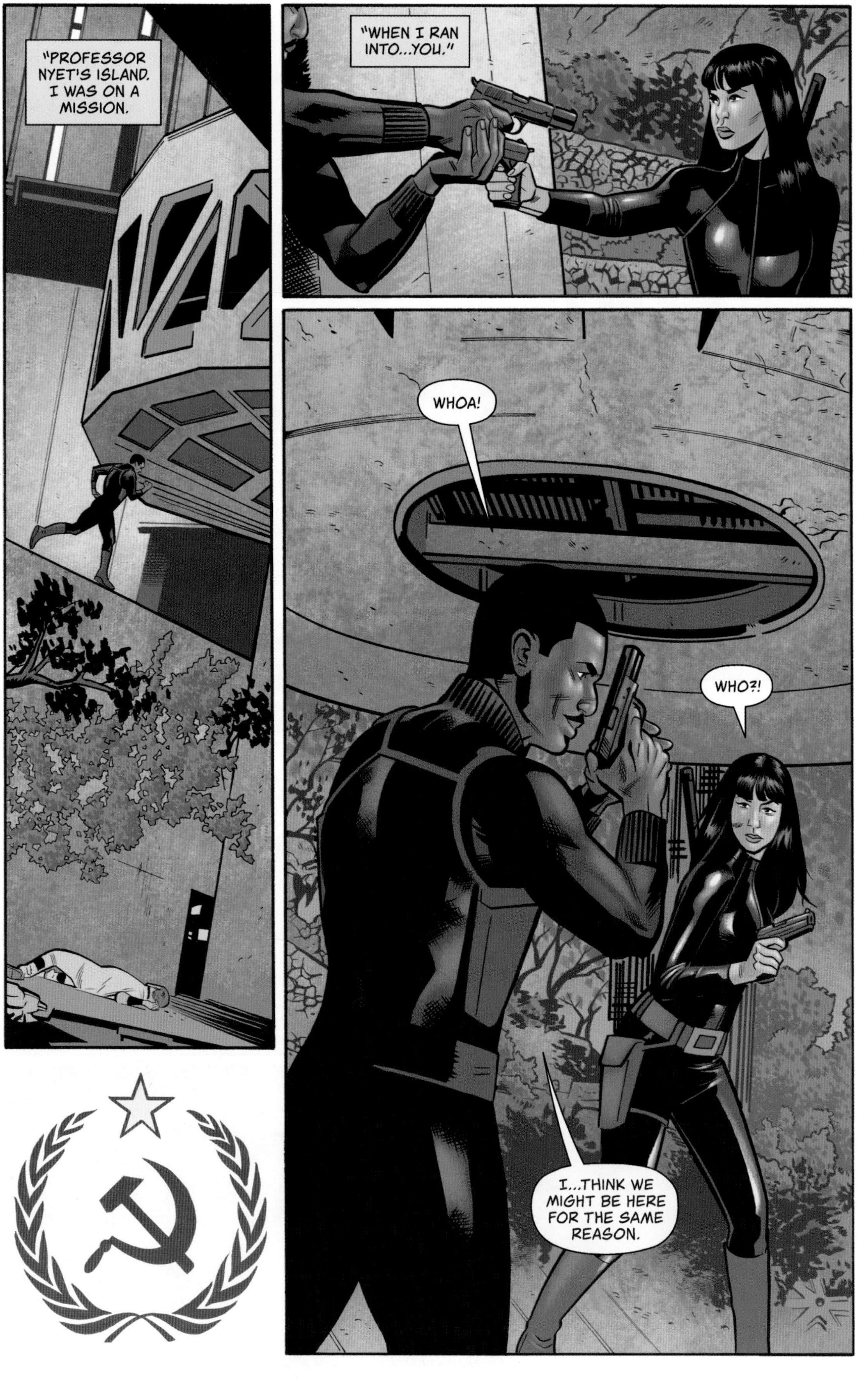
"PROFESSOR NYET'S ISLAND. I WAS ON A MISSION.
"WHEN I RAN INTO...YOU."
WHOA!
WHO?!
I...THINK WE MIGHT BE HERE FOR THE SAME REASON.

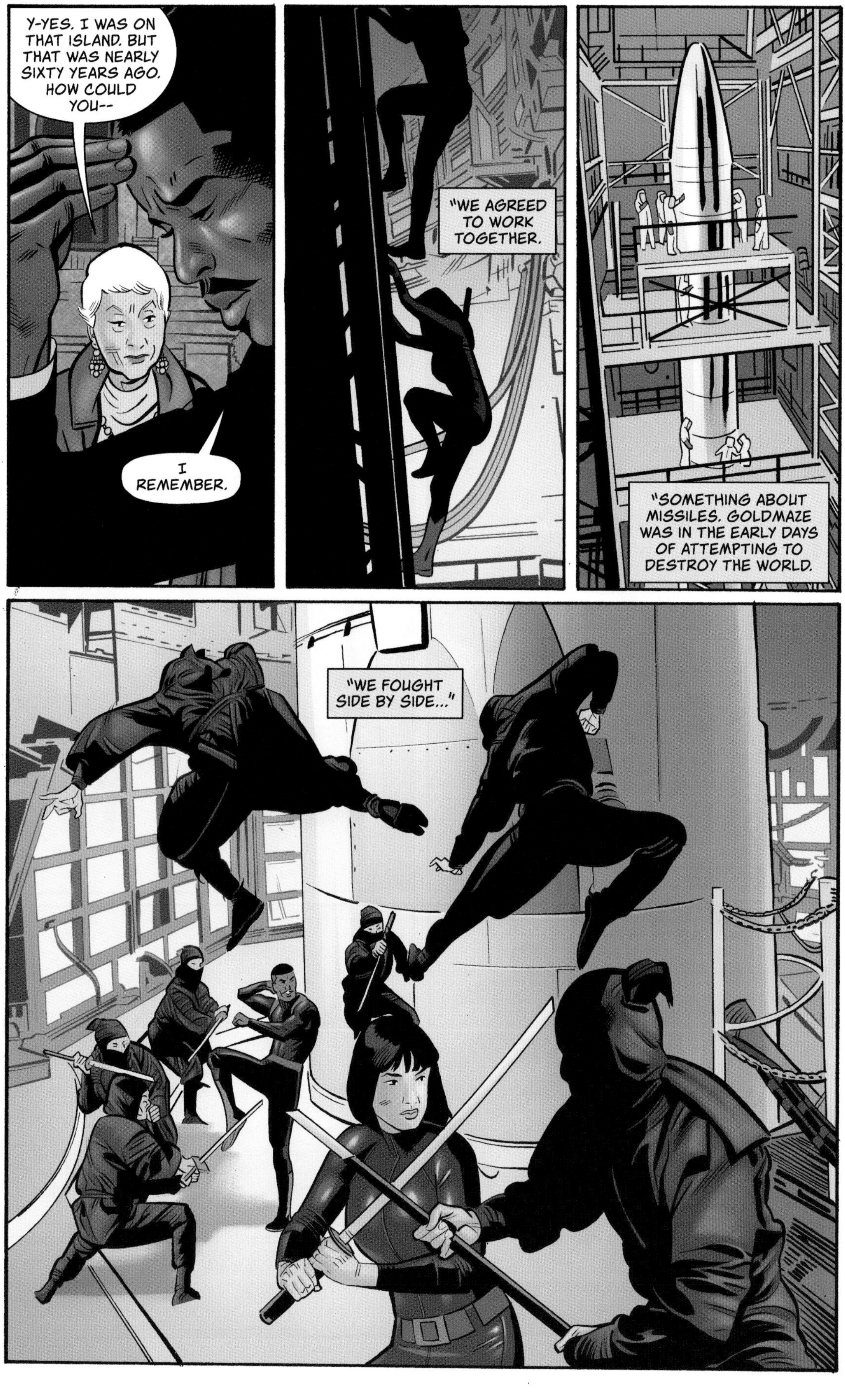
Y-YES. I WAS ON THAT ISLAND. BUT THAT WAS NEARLY SIXTY YEARS AGO. HOW COULD YOU--
I REMEMBER.
"WE AGREED TO WORK TOGETHER.
"SOMETHING ABOUT MISSILES. GOLDMAZE WAS IN THE EARLY DAYS OF ATTEMPTING TO DESTROY THE WORLD.
"WE FOUGHT SIDE BY SIDE..."

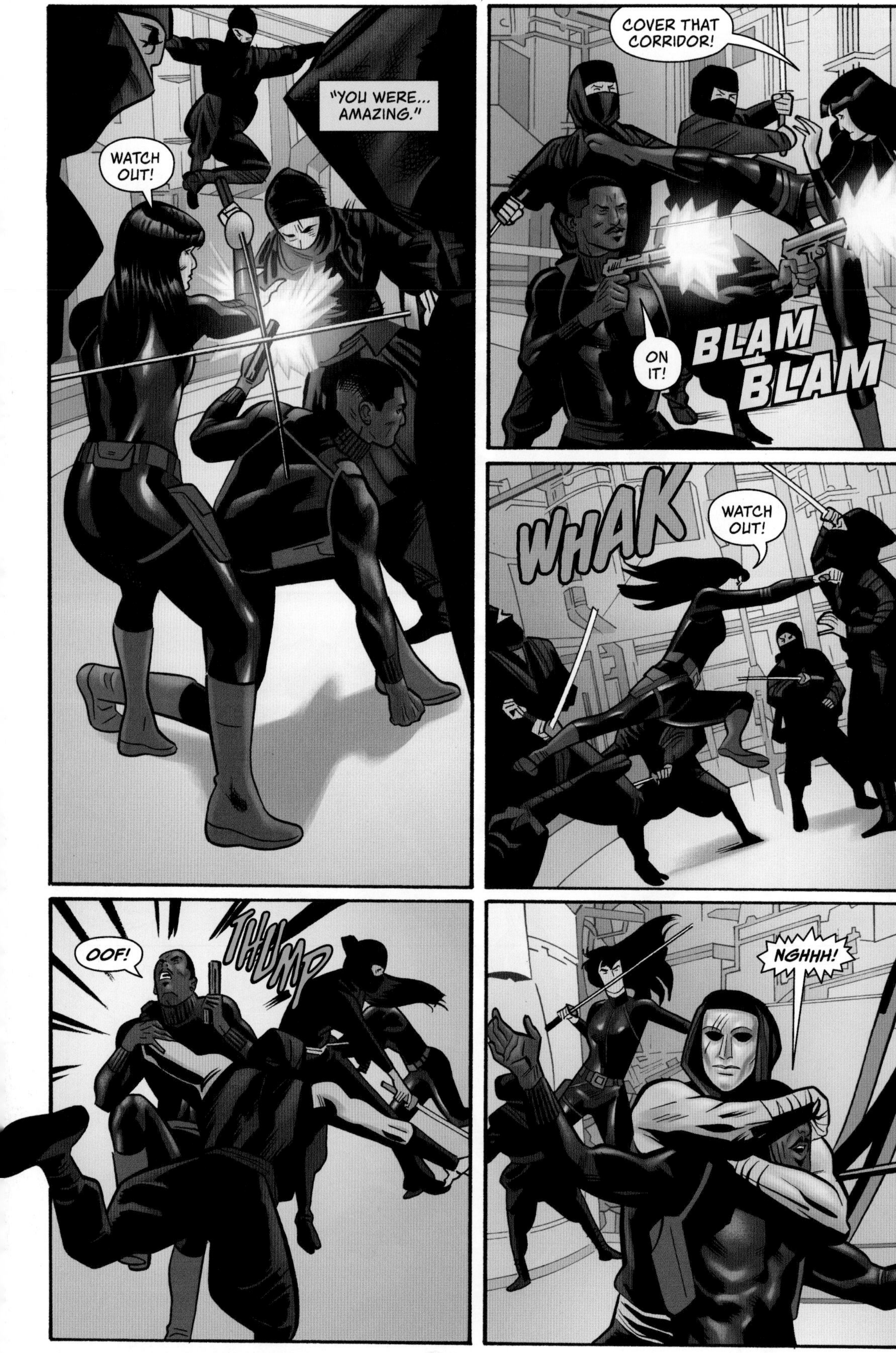
"YOU WERE... AMAZING."
WATCH OUT!
COVER THAT CORRIDOR!
ON IT!
BLAM BLAM
WHAK
WATCH OUT!
OOF!
THUMP
NGHHH!

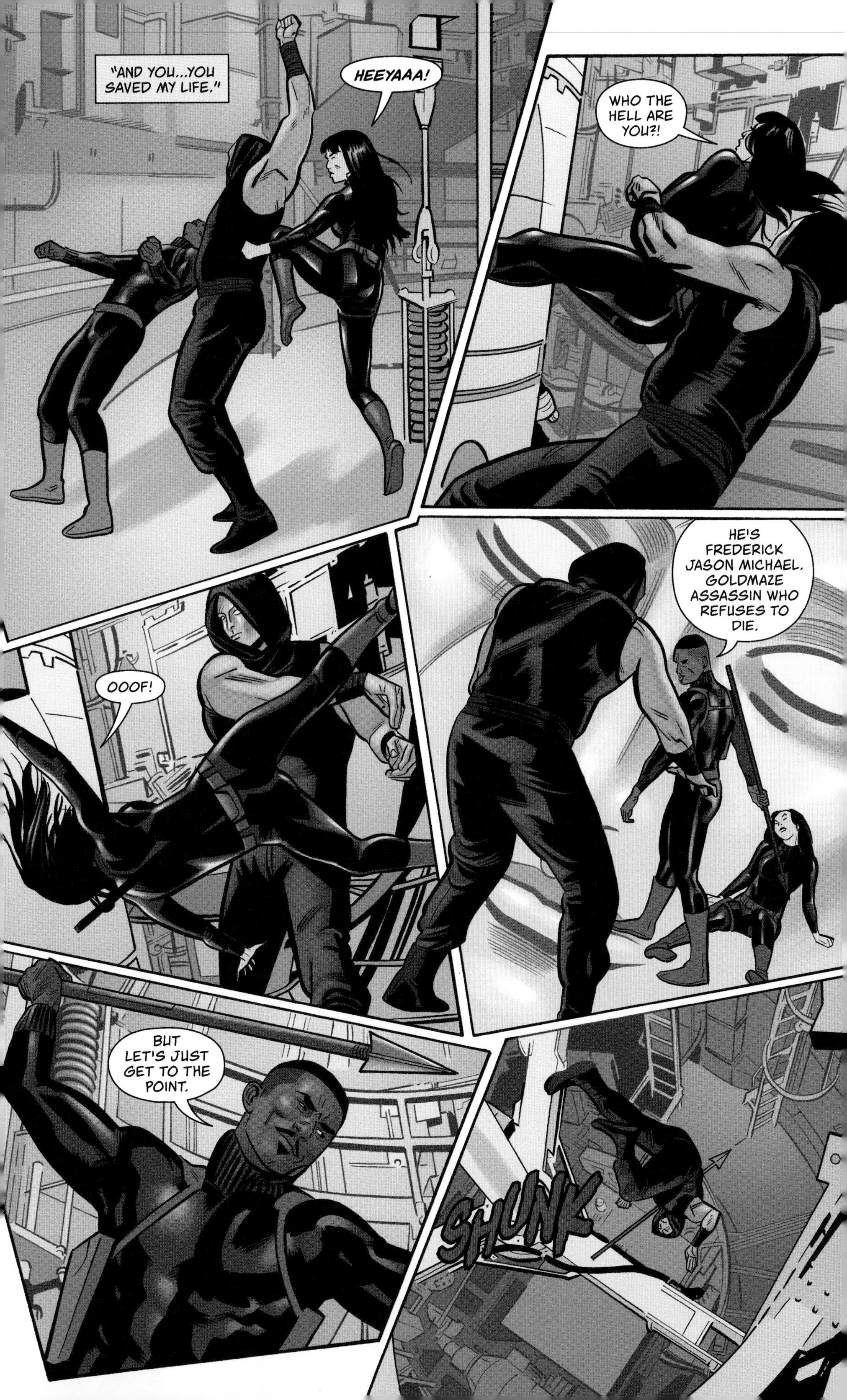
"AND YOU...YOU SAVED MY LIFE."
HEEYAAA!
WHO THE HELL ARE YOU?!
OOOF!
HE'S FREDERICK JASON MICHAEL, GOLDMAZE ASSASSIN WHO REFUSES TO DIE.
BUT LET'S JUST GET TO THE POINT.
SHUNK

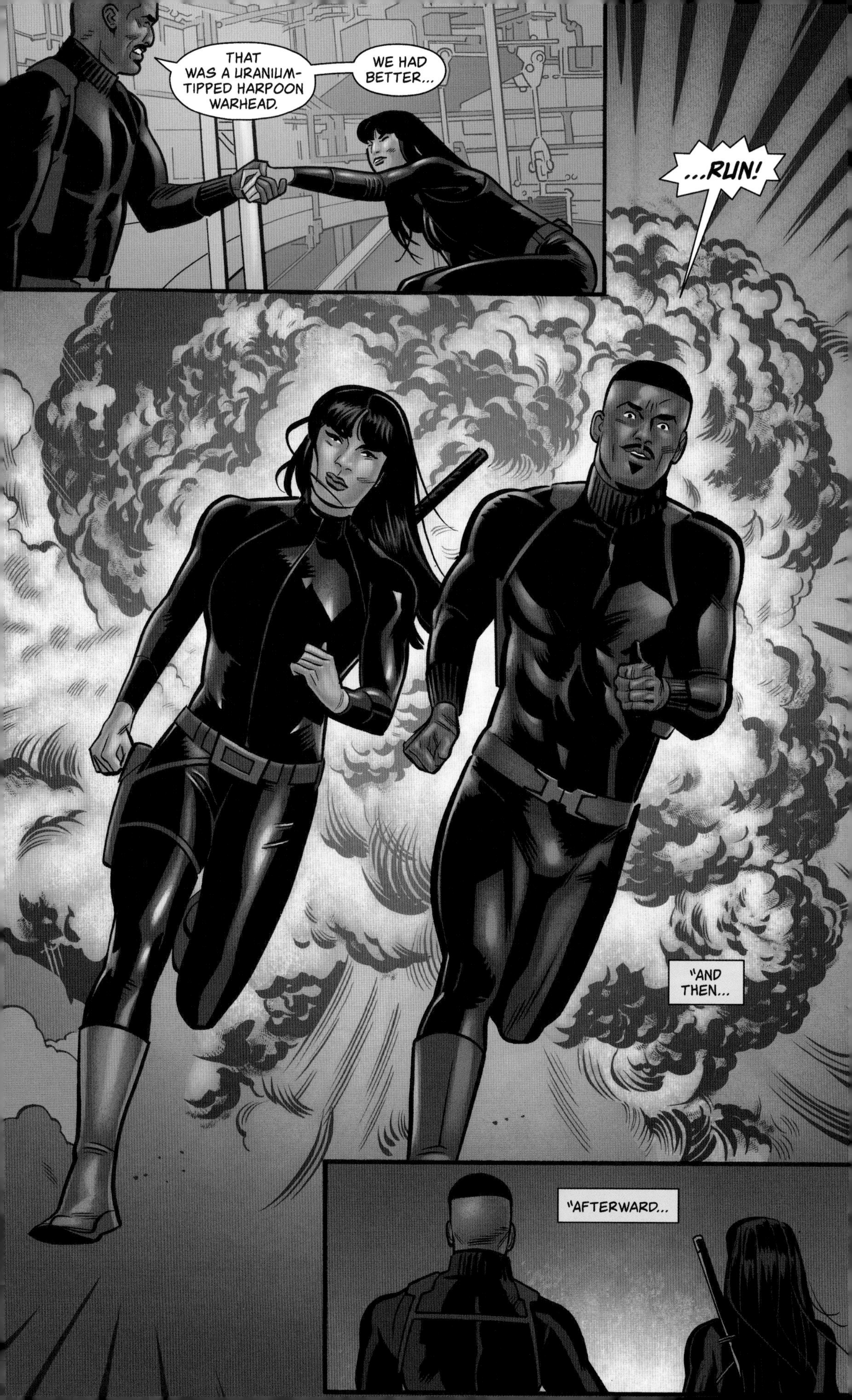
THAT WAS A URANIUM-TIPPED HARPOON WARHEAD.
WE HAD BETTER...
...RUN!
"AND THEN...
"AFTERWARD...

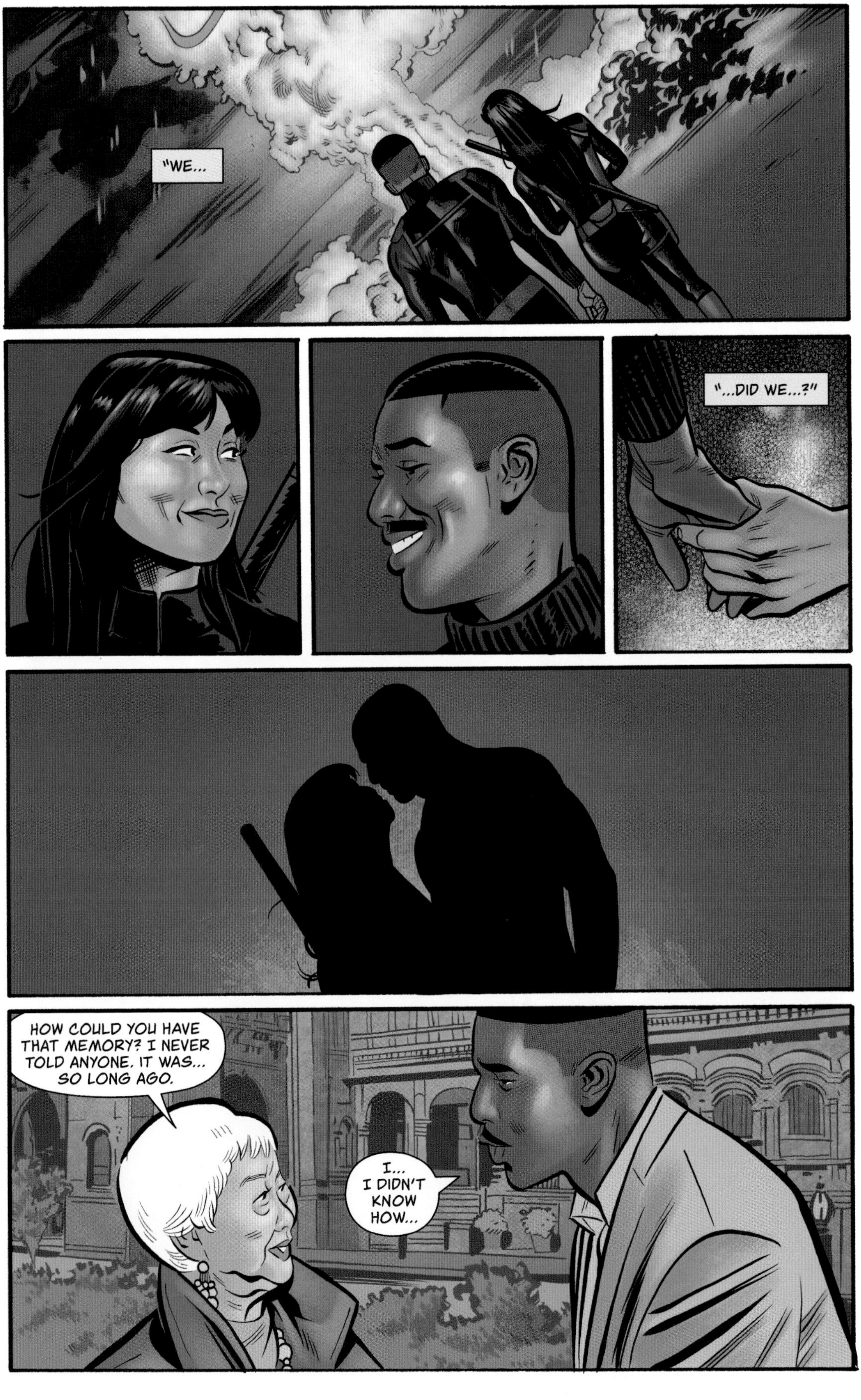
"WE...
"...DID WE...?"
HOW COULD YOU HAVE THAT MEMORY? I NEVER TOLD ANYONE. IT WAS... SO LONG AGO.
I... I DIDN'T KNOW HOW...

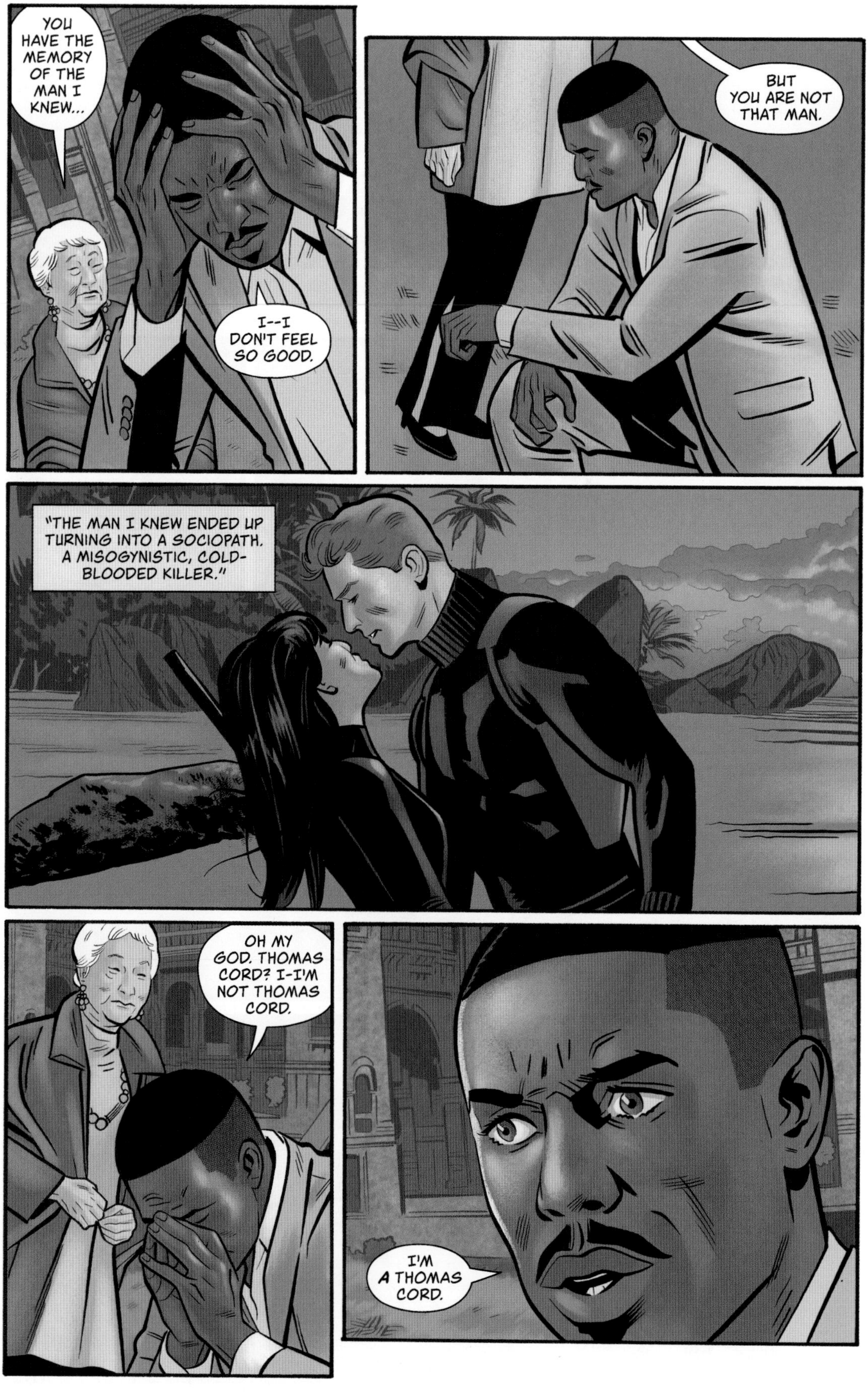
YOU HAVE THE MEMORY OF THE MAN I KNEW...
I--I DON'T FEEL SO GOOD.
BUT YOU ARE NOT THAT MAN.
"THE MAN I KNEW ENDED UP TURNING INTO A SOCIOPATH. A MISOGYNISTIC, COLD-BLOODED KILLER."
OH MY GOD. THOMAS CORD? I-I'M NOT THOMAS CORD.
I'M A THOMAS CORD.

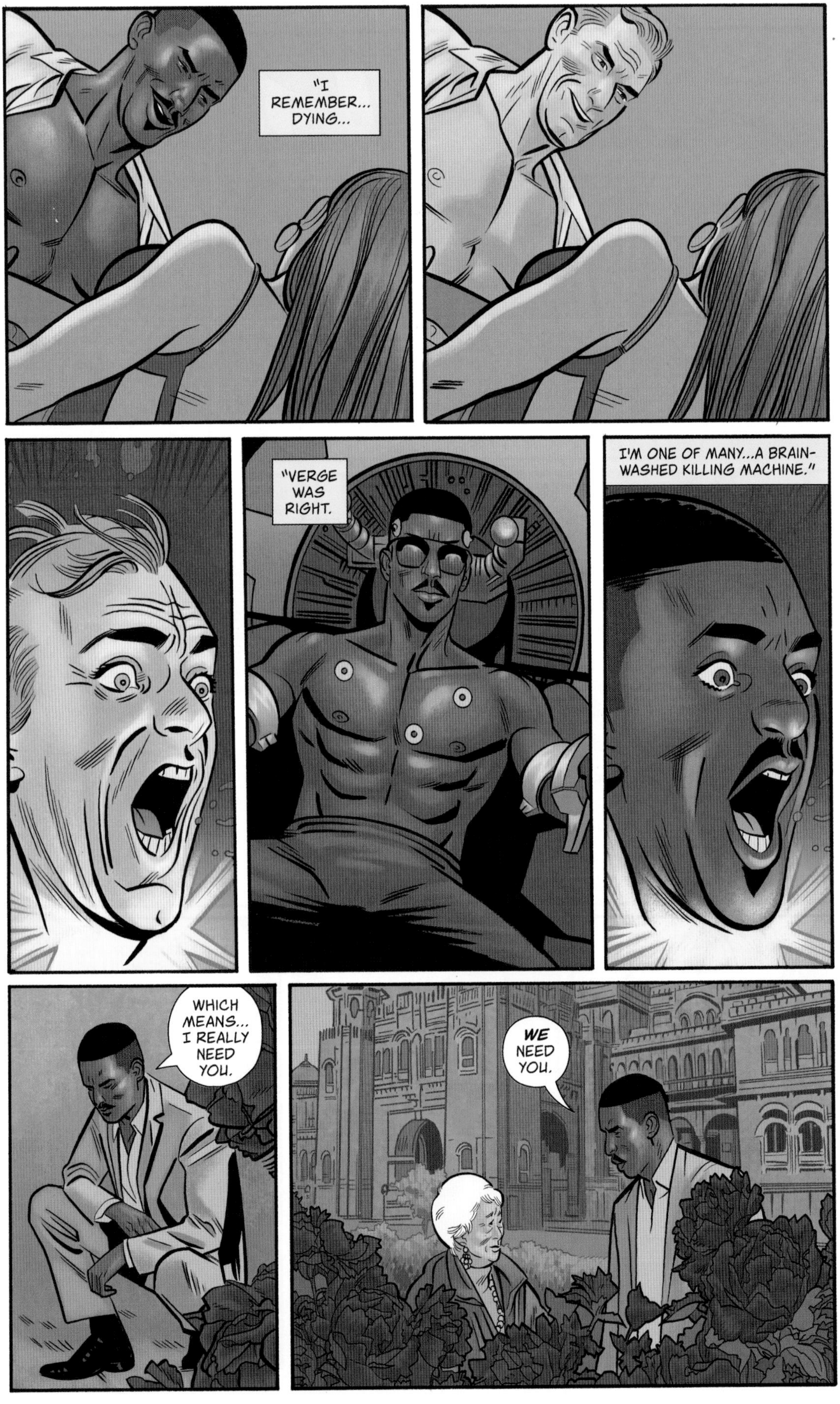
"I REMEMBER... DYING...
"VERGE WAS RIGHT.
I'M ONE OF MANY...A BRAIN-WASHED KILLING MACHINE."
WHICH MEANS... I REALLY NEED YOU.
WE NEED YOU.

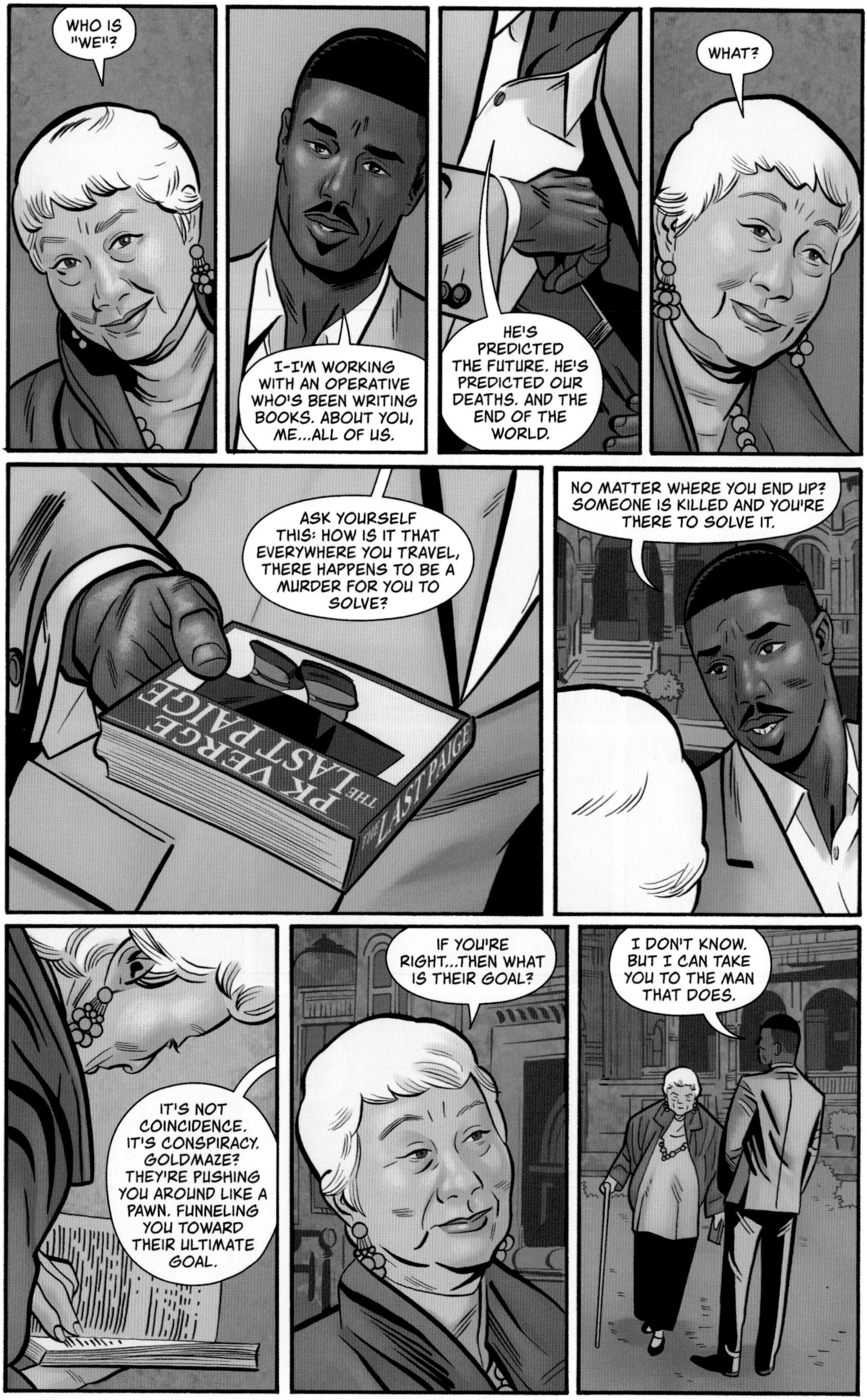
WHO IS "WE"?
I-I'M WORKING WITH AN OPERATIVE WHO'S BEEN WRITING BOOKS. ABOUT YOU, ME...ALL OF US.
HE'S PREDICTED THE FUTURE. HE'S PREDICTED OUR DEATHS. AND THE END OF THE WORLD.
WHAT?
ASK YOURSELF THIS: HOW IS IT THAT EVERYWHERE YOU TRAVEL, THERE HAPPENS TO BE A MURDER FOR YOU TO SOLVE?
PK VERGE
THE LAST PAIGE
THE LAST PAIGE
NO MATTER WHERE YOU END UP? SOMEONE IS KILLED AND YOU'RE THERE TO SOLVE IT.
IT'S NOT COINCIDENCE. IT'S CONSPIRACY. GOLDMAZE? THEY'RE PUSHING YOU AROUND LIKE A PAWN. FUNNELING YOU TOWARD THEIR ULTIMATE GOAL.
IF YOU'RE RIGHT...THEN WHAT IS THEIR GOAL?
I DON'T KNOW. BUT I CAN TAKE YOU TO THE MAN THAT DOES.

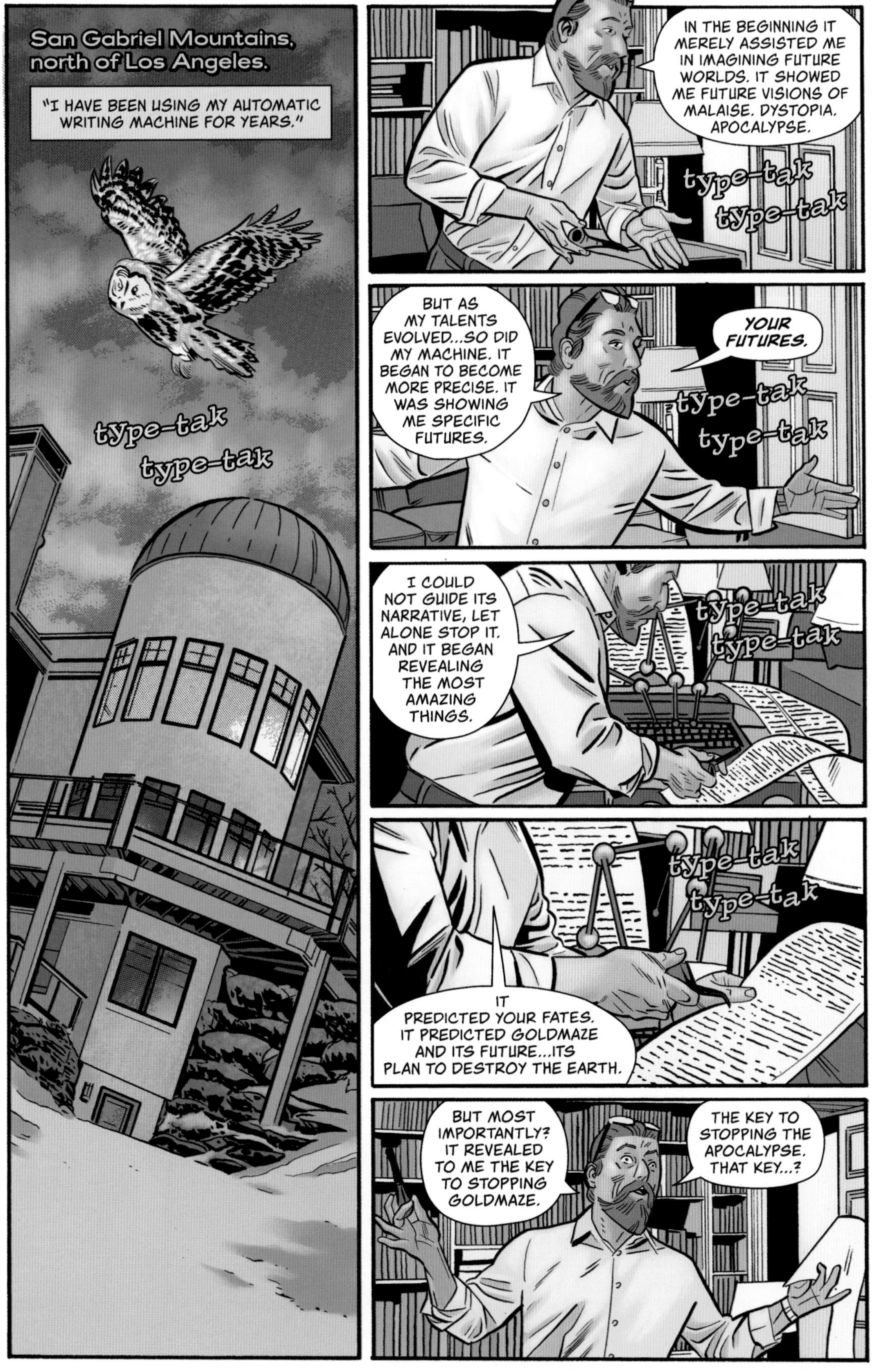
San Gabriel Mountains, north of Los Angeles.
"I HAVE BEEN USING MY AUTOMATIC WRITING MACHINE FOR YEARS."
type-tak type-tak
IN THE BEGINNING IT MERELY ASSISTED ME IN IMAGINING FUTURE WORLDS. IT SHOWED ME FUTURE VISIONS OF MALAISE. DYSTOPIA. APOCALYPSE.
type-tak type-tak
BUT AS MY TALENTS EVOLVED...SO DID MY MACHINE. IT BEGAN TO BECOME MORE PRECISE. IT WAS SHOWING ME SPECIFIC FUTURES.
YOUR FUTURES.
type-tak type-tak
I COULD NOT GUIDE ITS NARRATIVE, LET ALONE STOP IT. AND IT BEGAN REVEALING THE MOST AMAZING THINGS.
type-tak type-tak
type-tak type-tak
IT PREDICTED YOUR FATES. IT PREDICTED GOLDMAZE AND ITS FUTURE...ITS PLAN TO DESTROY THE EARTH.
BUT MOST IMPORTANTLY? IT REVEALED TO ME THE KEY TO STOPPING GOLDMAZE.
THE KEY TO STOPPING THE APOCALYPSE. THAT KEY...?

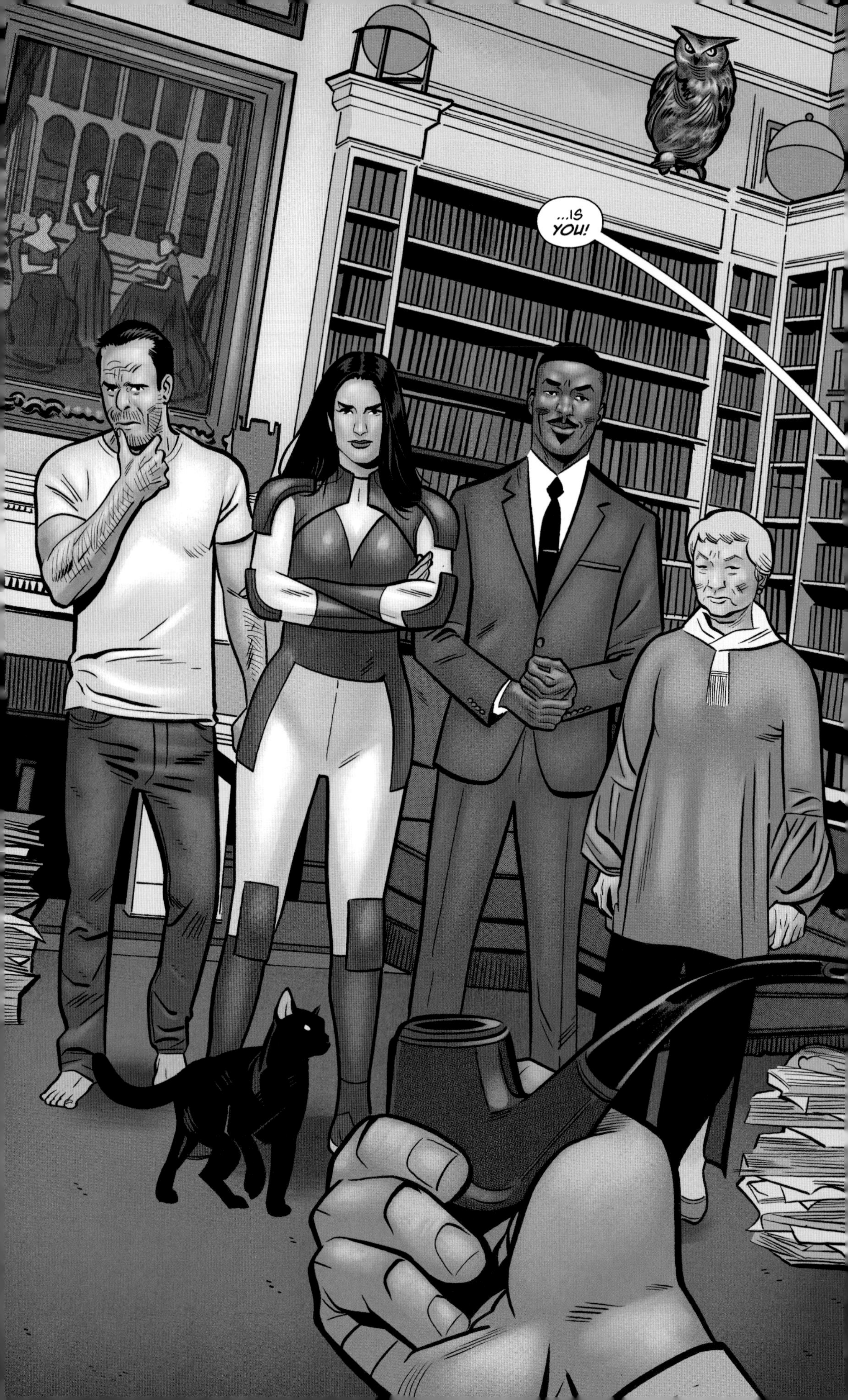
...IS YOU!

She was a different person back then. She relied on her body more than her mind. She didn't need to think. Not as much anyway. The mere presence of this muscular, panther-like man in a tuxedo brings the memories flooding back. Of herself. When she was in her twenties. Young. Lithe. She had a penchant for wearing leather catsuits and knee-high boots. It was a different time.

Growing up in Vietnam with a French father and Vietnamese mother, life had always been complicated. By the time she was eighteen she had been recruited by the British secret service, and by the time she was twenty she had been around the world, serving Western countries as a freelance spy and assassin.

Back then she had used her looks and age much like she uses her (older) age and accent now. She was constantly underestimated. Taken for granted. But why this flood of memories now? She is on the edge of solving this hotel murder. Why these memories of fifty years ago? Of the mission against the insidious Professor Nyet?

She had been on Nyet's trail for nearly six months. She was deep undercover at a ski lodge in the Alps when she bumped into another agent, Thomas Cord. Cord claimed to be working with the Brits, but she never really believed him. But for the moment they had a common goal. Find and eliminate Professor Nyet before he unleashed whatever chemical weapon he'd been developing.

Thomas Cord. How could she have been so naïve? He was using her just as much as she was using him. Or so she thought. She would never forget their first meeting in the sauna. He closed the sauna door behind himself and broke the lock, trapping her inside. He dropped the towel from his waist in an effort to surprise her. To stun her into inaction. She laughed then, even as she does now at the memory. Cord's white skin, freckled and a tan-line that implied short shorts and a tropical climate was probably his natural habitat. She'd already seen her share of men so his dangling manhood did nothing but suggest a potential target in hand-to-hand combat.

Even after he broke the lock, trapping her inside the sauna, she remained calm, back against the hot wood of the small room. Her towel was wrapped around her chest and she began to loosen it as he approached her. *Two could play this game.*

Pulling her towel off, she predictably saw Cord's eyes travel down her body. Men were always enthralled at the exotic nature of olive skin.

She snapped the towel at his face and he instinctively shut his eyes and flinched backward. In the next instant she flipped her foot up, landing the top of her foot between his legs. Cord anticipating the obvious attack, however, brought the rough heel of his hand reflexively down to strike her foot. Unphased, she pressed her attack, throwing her forearm under his chin and knocking him back into the wooden panels of the cramped room. Cord's head hit the wood with a loud crunch and he slipped to the floor. Turnier stood over him as he looked up at her, stunned. Then a smile slowly formed on his face …

Rubbing her eyes, Turnier breaks from her reverie and returns to the present. The hotel lobby. She has a murder to solve. But she can't help shake the feeling. This mystery man in the tuxedo. He's making her feel something that she hasn't felt in years. In a sea of bumbling murders and clumsy cover ups, he's giving her something she hasn't truly had in such a very long time. A true mystery.

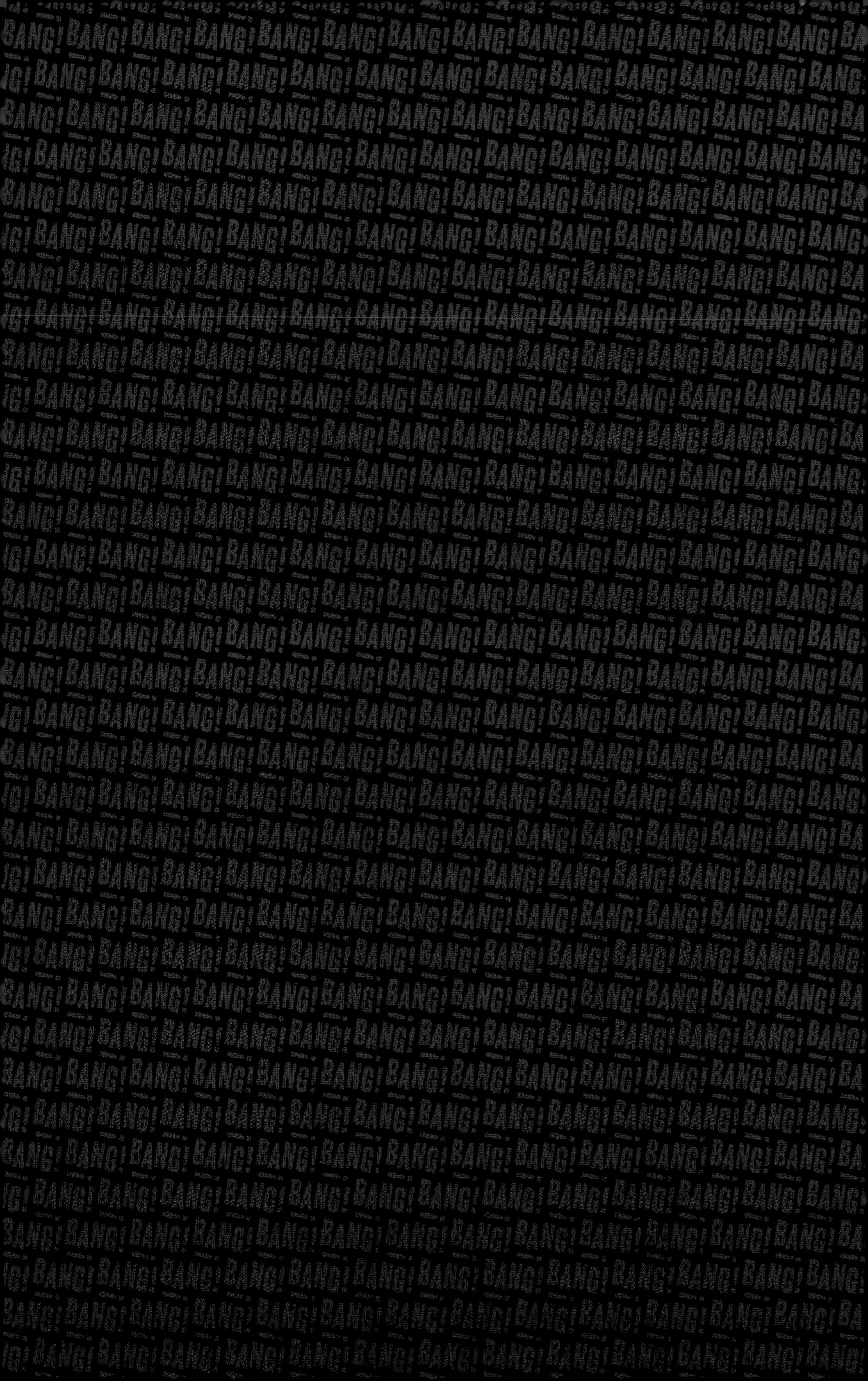

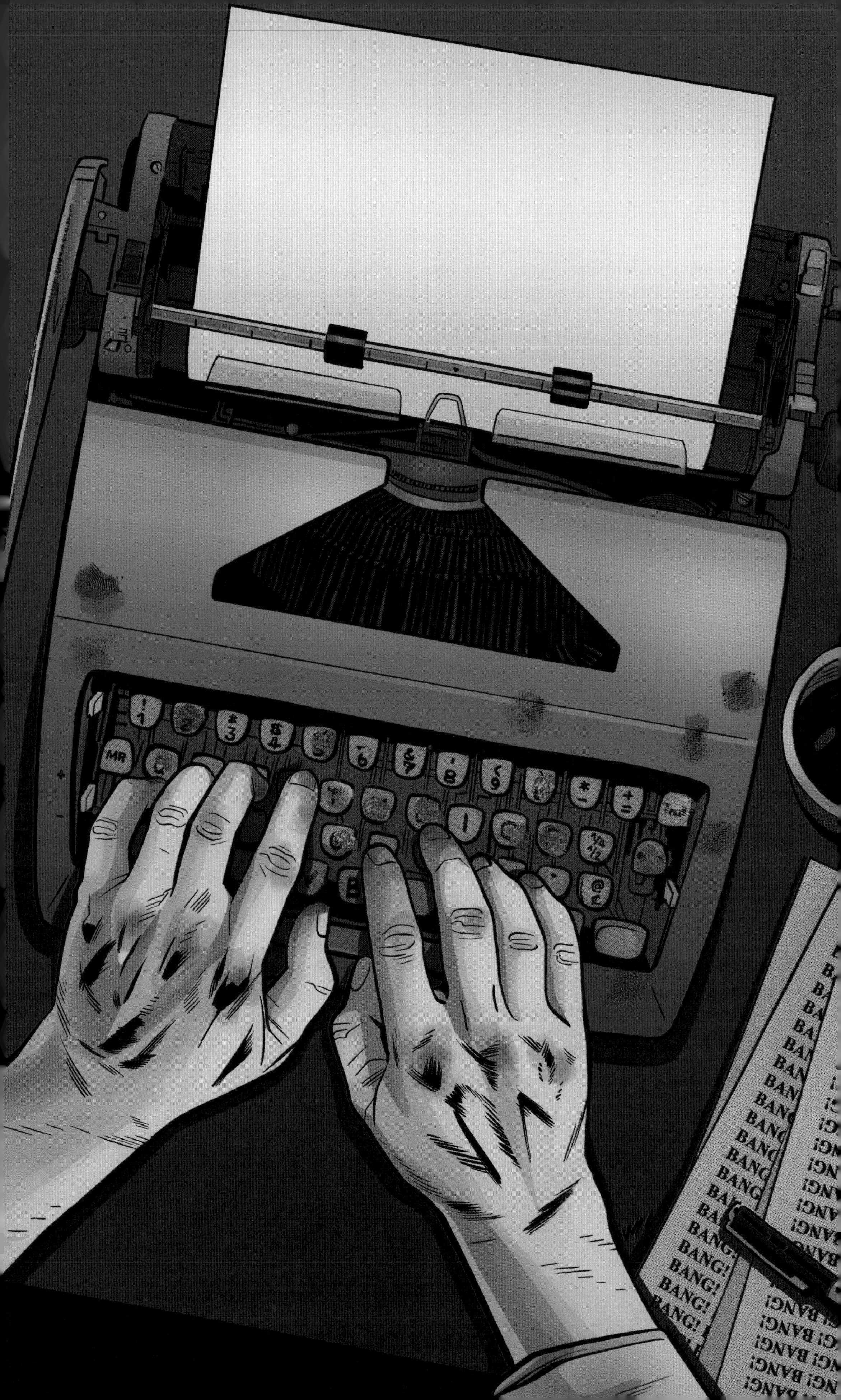
BANG!
BANG!
BANG!
BANG!
BANG!

Where could Verge start? For him, the beginning and the end were all the same. But he had to put it into words that they could understand. He closed his eyes to think. They were here because of him, and his plan was all starting to fall into place. But only if he didn't screw it up.

But where did it all really start? It was years ago. Back when he was working at the record shop. He was just a kid then. Wanting to write books but not really knowing how to do it. He was full of ideas back then. Original ideas. Not like now. Back then he was set on impressing the world. And the dark-haired girl that would come in once a week to buy a record.

It really started with her. The miniskirt and boots. The long, dark, straight hair. It was like someone had mined his subconscious for the perfect woman and then sent her to meet him. He could still distinctly remember their first conversation. What a fool he must have seemed.

He just started going on an on about music and his writing. He was nervous.

"Oh, you're a writer." She seems intrigued. That's a first. Every other girl he's mentioned this to, seems to quickly move on.

"Yeah, well. Not published yet. But I'm working on that. Getting published is the easy part. It's the actual writing. The 'getting the work done part.' That's the tough stuff."

"Yeah." She smiles coyly.

"Yeah. I've written ten novels so far."

"What are they about?" Is she flirting with him? No one ever asks what his books are about.

"Well," he takes a deep breath and then launches into it . . .

He gives her a detailed plot synopsis of every book he had written to date . . . every book and none of them published. He tells her about the "Game-Makers of Titian"—a secret society of painters that hid board games within their oil paintings. He tells her about "The Revolution Revolver"—about two men living in two different timelines simultaneously and the revolution they simultaneously instigate and also defeat. He even told her about his latest story idea. It would be about a cult leader and the cult he creates based on a contagious idea.

"What's it called?" the Dark-Haired girl interrupts.

"What?" he replies, trying to keep his eyes on hers. Telling himself he didn't notice her translucent blouse and her chest underneath. The surface of her blouse trembling with every word she says . . .

"What's your book going to be called?" She smiles. She definitely noticed his gaze. He couldn't help it. He'd been alone for so long. Just him and the cords and the music and his writing.

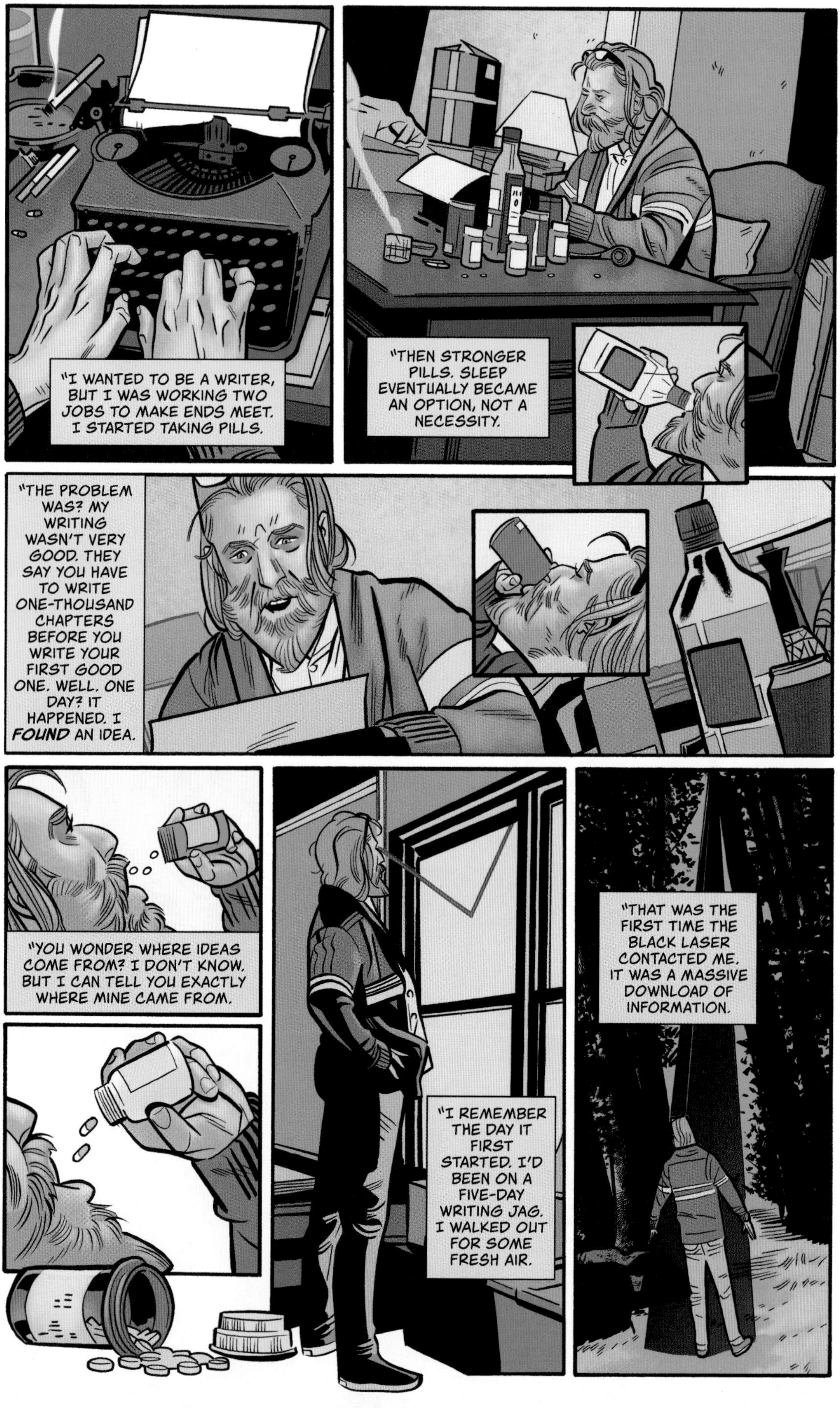
"I WANTED TO BE A WRITER, BUT I WAS WORKING TWO JOBS TO MAKE ENDS MEET. I STARTED TAKING PILLS.
"THEN STRONGER PILLS. SLEEP EVENTUALLY BECAME AN OPTION, NOT A NECESSITY.
"THE PROBLEM WAS? MY WRITING WASN'T VERY GOOD. THEY SAY YOU HAVE TO WRITE ONE-THOUSAND CHAPTERS BEFORE YOU WRITE YOUR FIRST GOOD ONE. WELL, ONE DAY? IT HAPPENED. I ***FOUND*** AN IDEA.
"YOU WONDER WHERE IDEAS COME FROM? I DON'T KNOW. BUT I CAN TELL YOU EXACTLY WHERE MINE CAME FROM.
"I REMEMBER THE DAY IT FIRST STARTED. I'D BEEN ON A FIVE-DAY WRITING JAG. I WALKED OUT FOR SOME FRESH AIR.
"THAT WAS THE FIRST TIME THE BLACK LASER CONTACTED ME. IT WAS A MASSIVE DOWNLOAD OF INFORMATION.

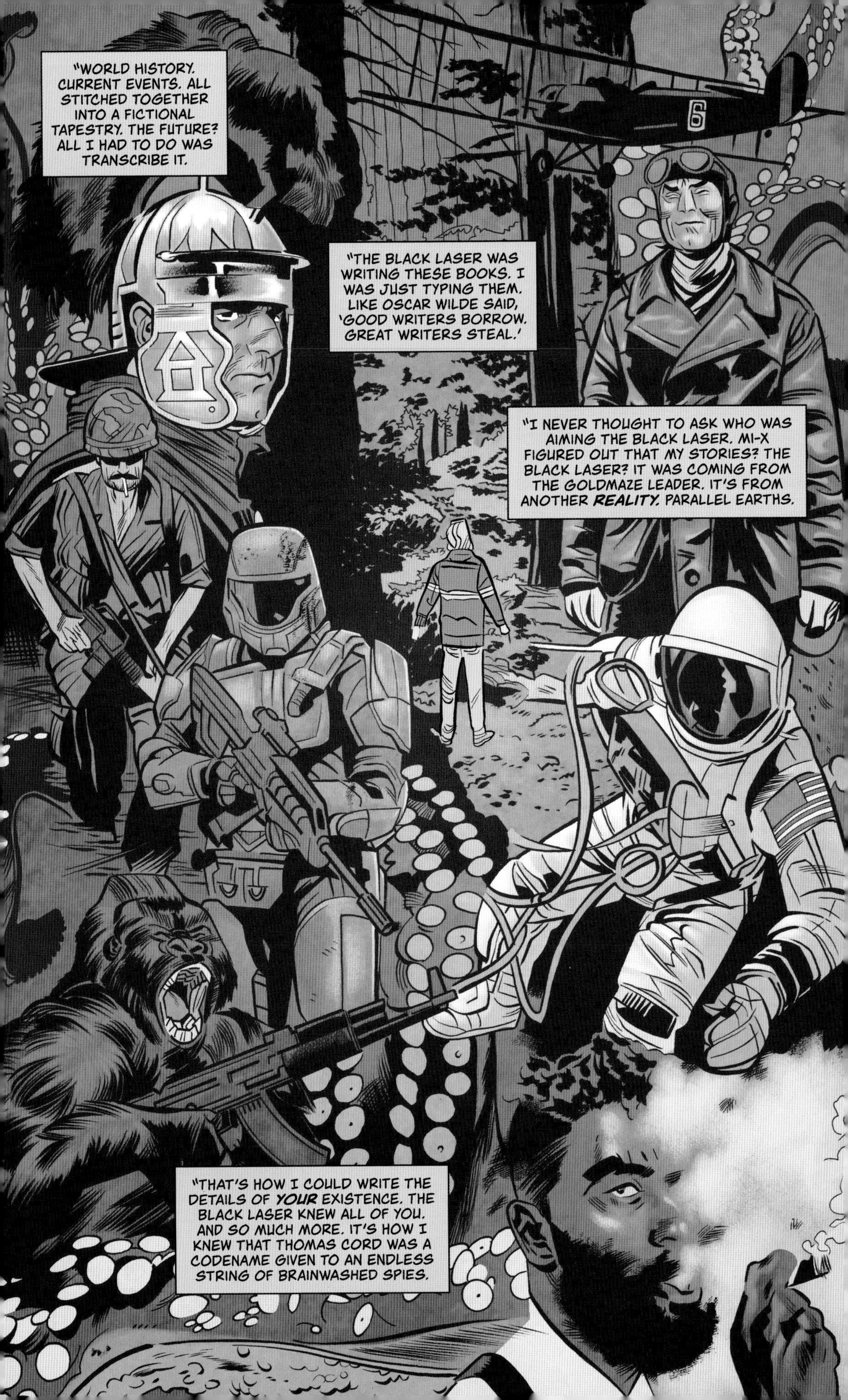
"WORLD HISTORY. CURRENT EVENTS. ALL STITCHED TOGETHER INTO A FICTIONAL TAPESTRY. THE FUTURE? ALL I HAD TO DO WAS TRANSCRIBE IT.
6
"THE BLACK LASER WAS WRITING THESE BOOKS. I WAS JUST TYPING THEM. LIKE OSCAR WILDE SAID, 'GOOD WRITERS BORROW. GREAT WRITERS STEAL.'
"I NEVER THOUGHT TO ASK WHO WAS AIMING THE BLACK LASER. MI-X FIGURED OUT THAT MY STORIES? THE BLACK LASER? IT WAS COMING FROM THE GOLDMAZE LEADER. IT'S FROM ANOTHER ***REALITY.*** PARALLEL EARTHS.
"THAT'S HOW I COULD WRITE THE DETAILS OF ***YOUR*** EXISTENCE. THE BLACK LASER KNEW ALL OF YOU. AND SO MUCH MORE. IT'S HOW I KNEW THAT THOMAS CORD WAS A CODENAME GIVEN TO AN ENDLESS STRING OF BRAINWASHED SPIES.

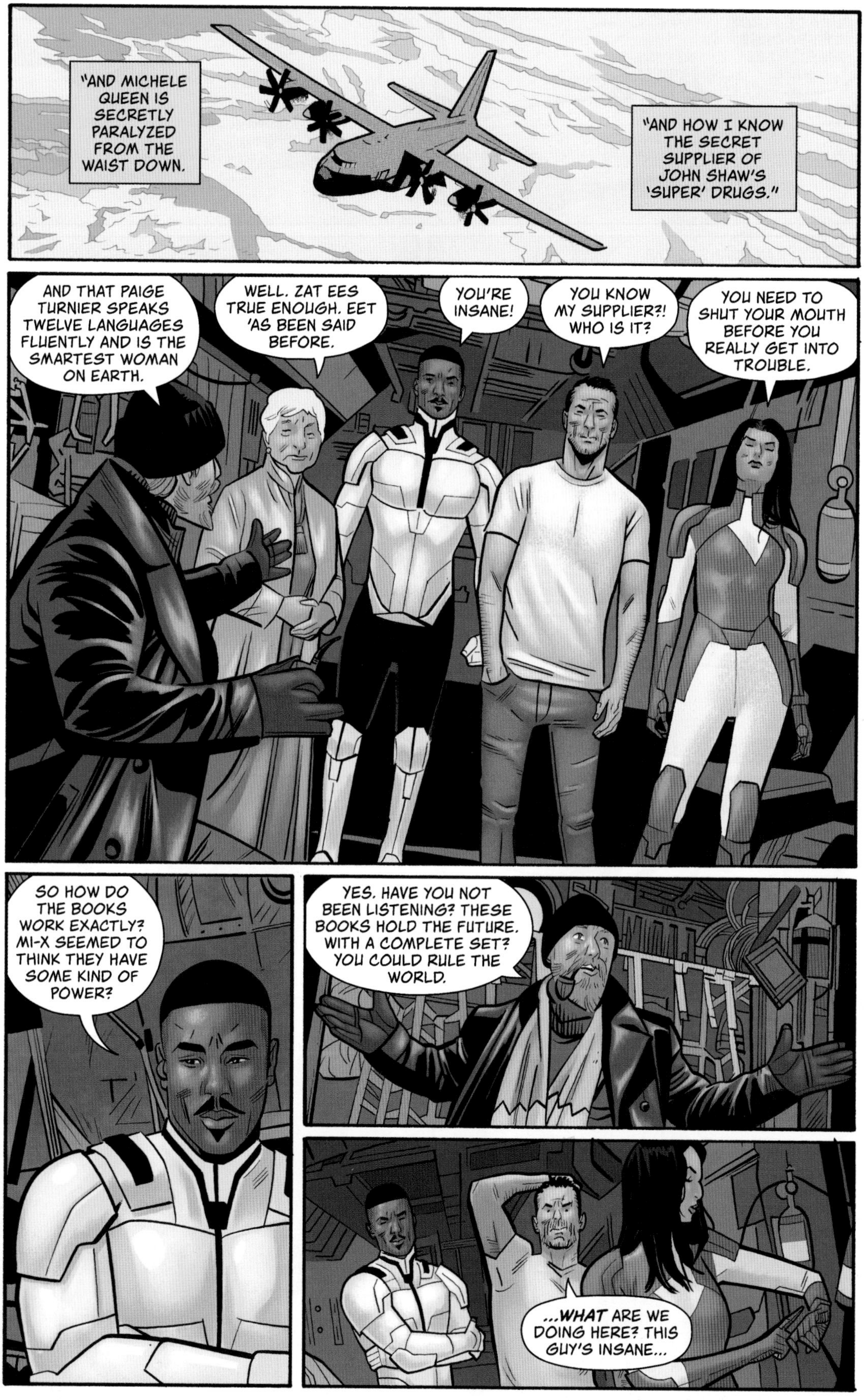
"AND MICHELE QUEEN IS SECRETLY PARALYZED FROM THE WAIST DOWN.
"AND HOW I KNOW THE SECRET SUPPLIER OF JOHN SHAW'S 'SUPER' DRUGS."
AND THAT PAIGE TURNIER SPEAKS TWELVE LANGUAGES FLUENTLY AND IS THE SMARTEST WOMAN ON EARTH.
WELL. ZAT EES TRUE ENOUGH. EET 'AS BEEN SAID BEFORE.
YOU'RE INSANE!
YOU KNOW MY SUPPLIER?! WHO IS IT?
YOU NEED TO SHUT YOUR MOUTH BEFORE YOU REALLY GET INTO TROUBLE.
SO HOW DO THE BOOKS WORK EXACTLY? MI-X SEEMED TO THINK THEY HAVE SOME KIND OF POWER?
YES. HAVE YOU NOT BEEN LISTENING? THESE BOOKS HOLD THE FUTURE. WITH A COMPLETE SET? YOU COULD RULE THE WORLD.
...WHAT ARE WE DOING HERE? THIS GUY'S INSANE...

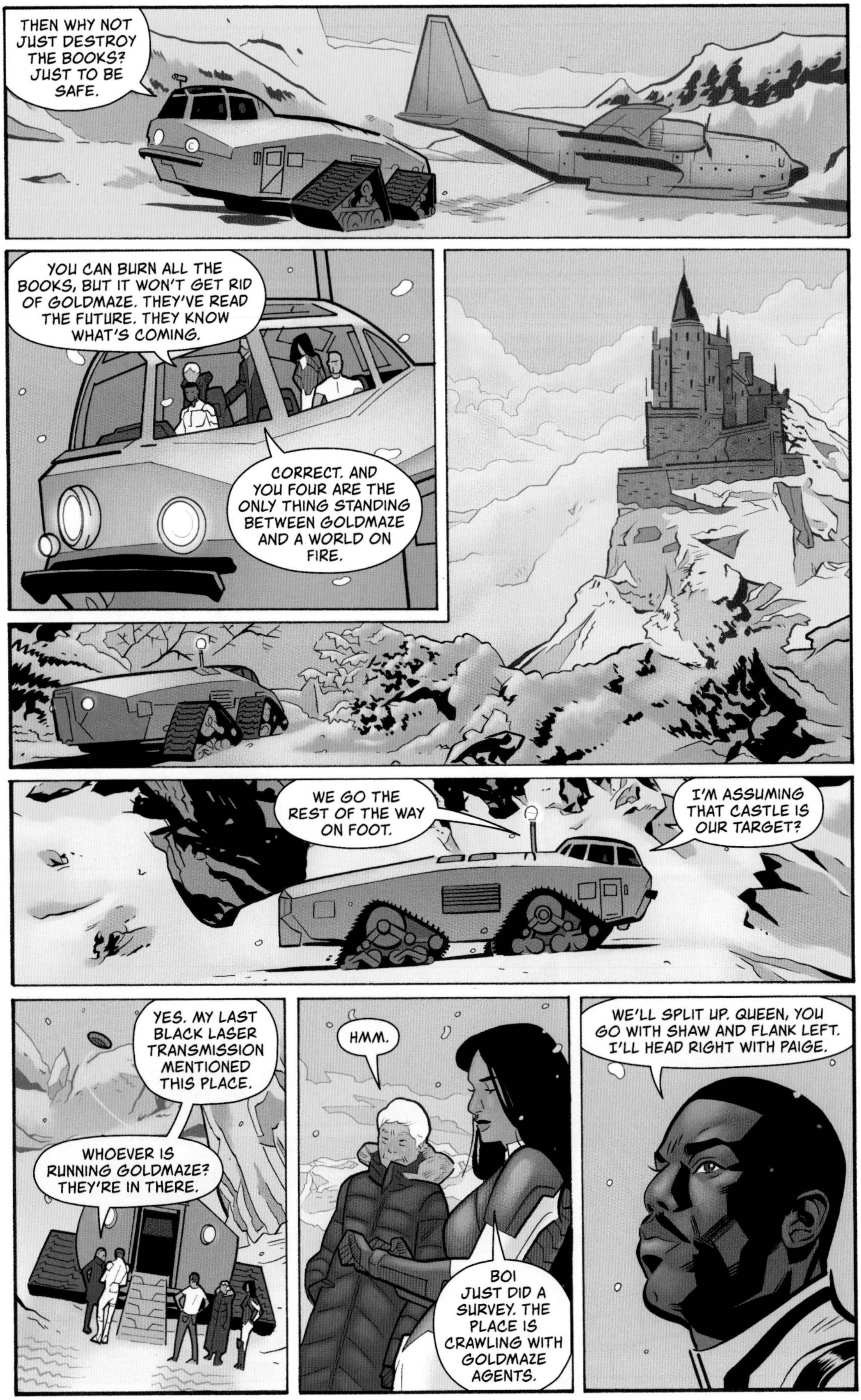
THEN WHY NOT JUST DESTROY THE BOOKS? JUST TO BE SAFE.
YOU CAN BURN ALL THE BOOKS, BUT IT WON'T GET RID OF GOLDMAZE. THEY'VE READ THE FUTURE. THEY KNOW WHAT'S COMING.
CORRECT. AND YOU FOUR ARE THE ONLY THING STANDING BETWEEN GOLDMAZE AND A WORLD ON FIRE.
WE GO THE REST OF THE WAY ON FOOT.
I'M ASSUMING THAT CASTLE IS OUR TARGET?
YES. MY LAST BLACK LASER TRANSMISSION MENTIONED THIS PLACE.
WHOEVER IS RUNNING GOLDMAZE? THEY'RE IN THERE.
HMM.
BOI JUST DID A SURVEY. THE PLACE IS CRAWLING WITH GOLDMAZE AGENTS.
WE'LL SPLIT UP. QUEEN, YOU GO WITH SHAW AND FLANK LEFT. I'LL HEAD RIGHT WITH PAIGE.

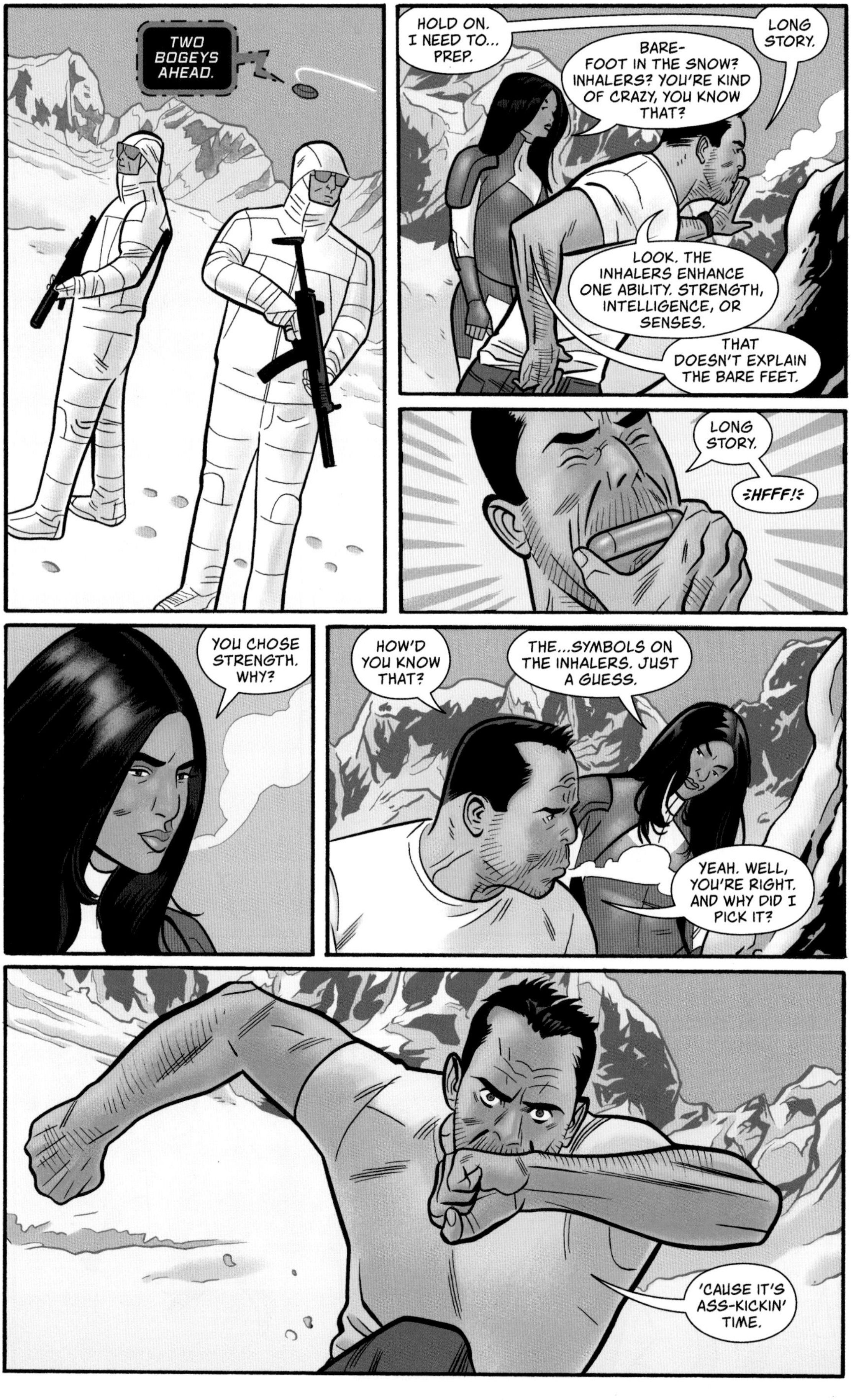
TWO BOGEYS AHEAD.
HOLD ON. I NEED TO... PREP.
BARE-FOOT IN THE SNOW? INHALERS? YOU'RE KIND OF CRAZY, YOU KNOW THAT?
LONG STORY.
LOOK. THE INHALERS ENHANCE ONE ABILITY. STRENGTH, INTELLIGENCE, OR SENSES.
THAT DOESN'T EXPLAIN THE BARE FEET.
LONG STORY.
HFFF!
YOU CHOSE STRENGTH. WHY?
HOW'D YOU KNOW THAT?
THE...SYMBOLS ON THE INHALERS. JUST A GUESS.
YEAH. WELL, YOU'RE RIGHT. AND WHY DID I PICK IT?
'CAUSE IT'S ASS-KICKIN' TIME.

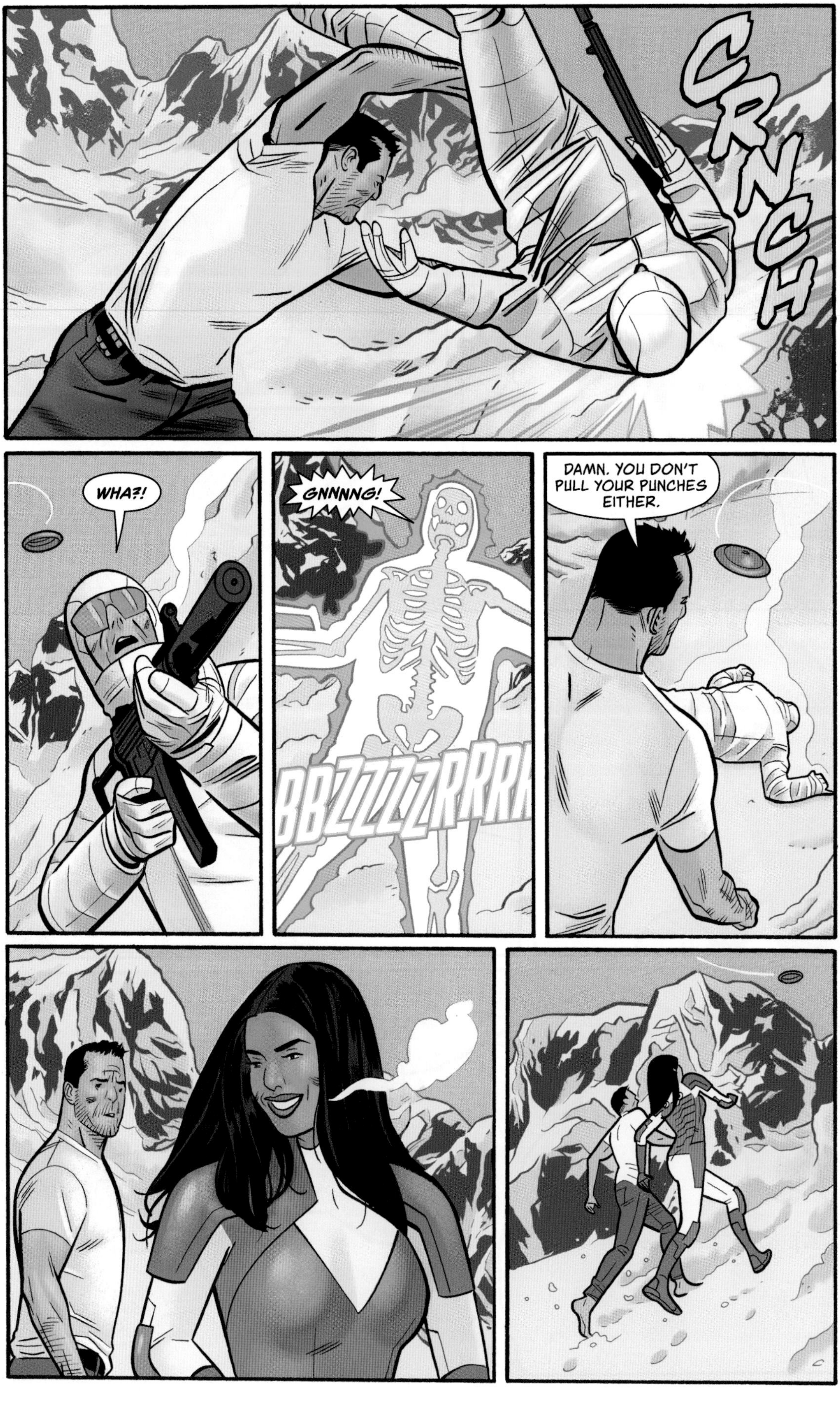
CRNCH
WHA?!
GNNNNG!
BBZZZZZRRRR
DAMN. YOU DON'T PULL YOUR PUNCHES EITHER.

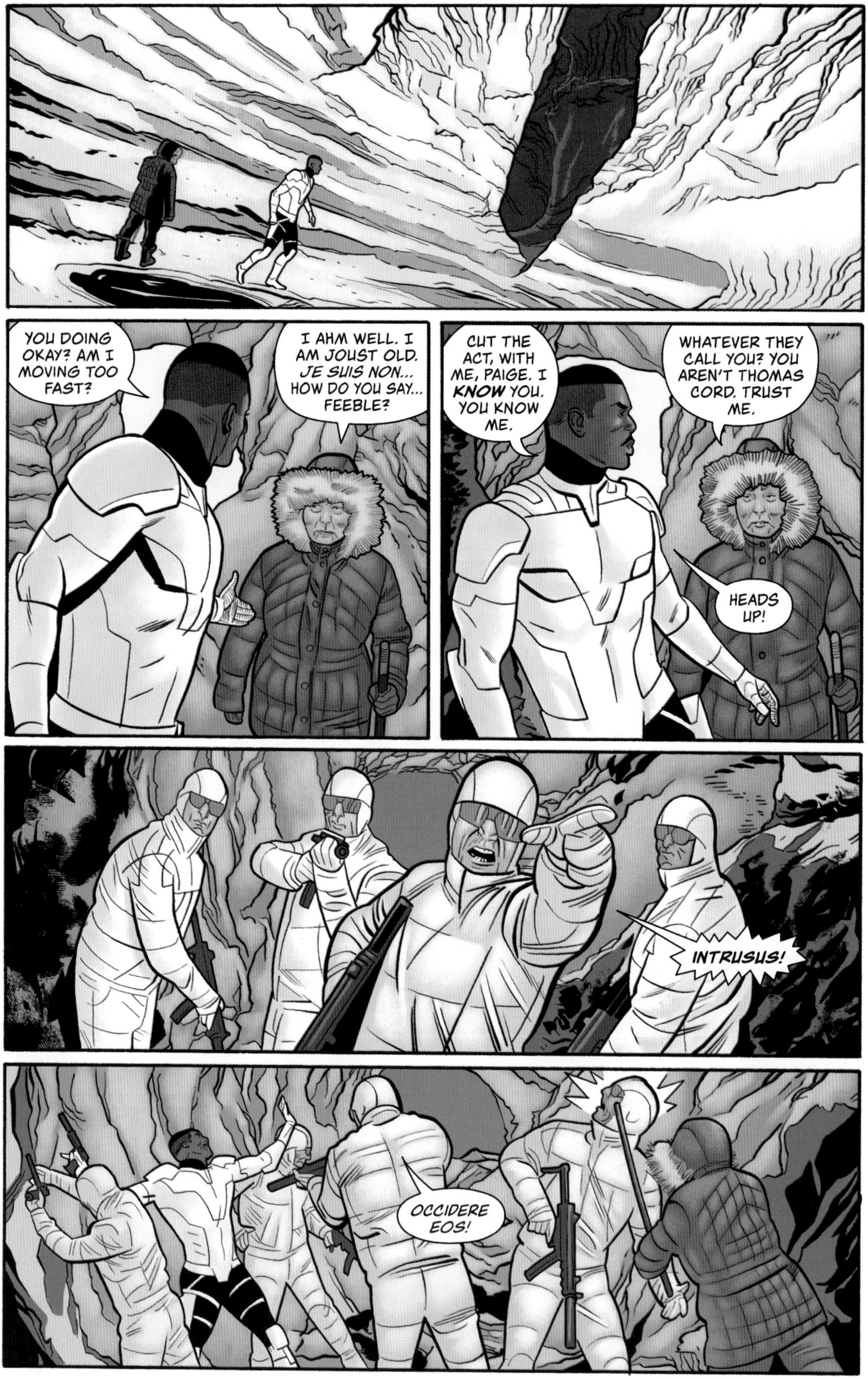

YOU DOING OKAY? AM I MOVING TOO FAST?
I AHM WELL. I AM JOUST OLD. *JE SUIS NON...* HOW DO YOU SAY... FEEBLE?
CUT THE ACT, WITH ME, PAIGE. I **KNOW** YOU. YOU KNOW ME.
WHATEVER THEY CALL YOU? YOU AREN'T THOMAS CORD. TRUST ME.
HEADS UP!
INTRUSUS!
OCCIDERE EOS!

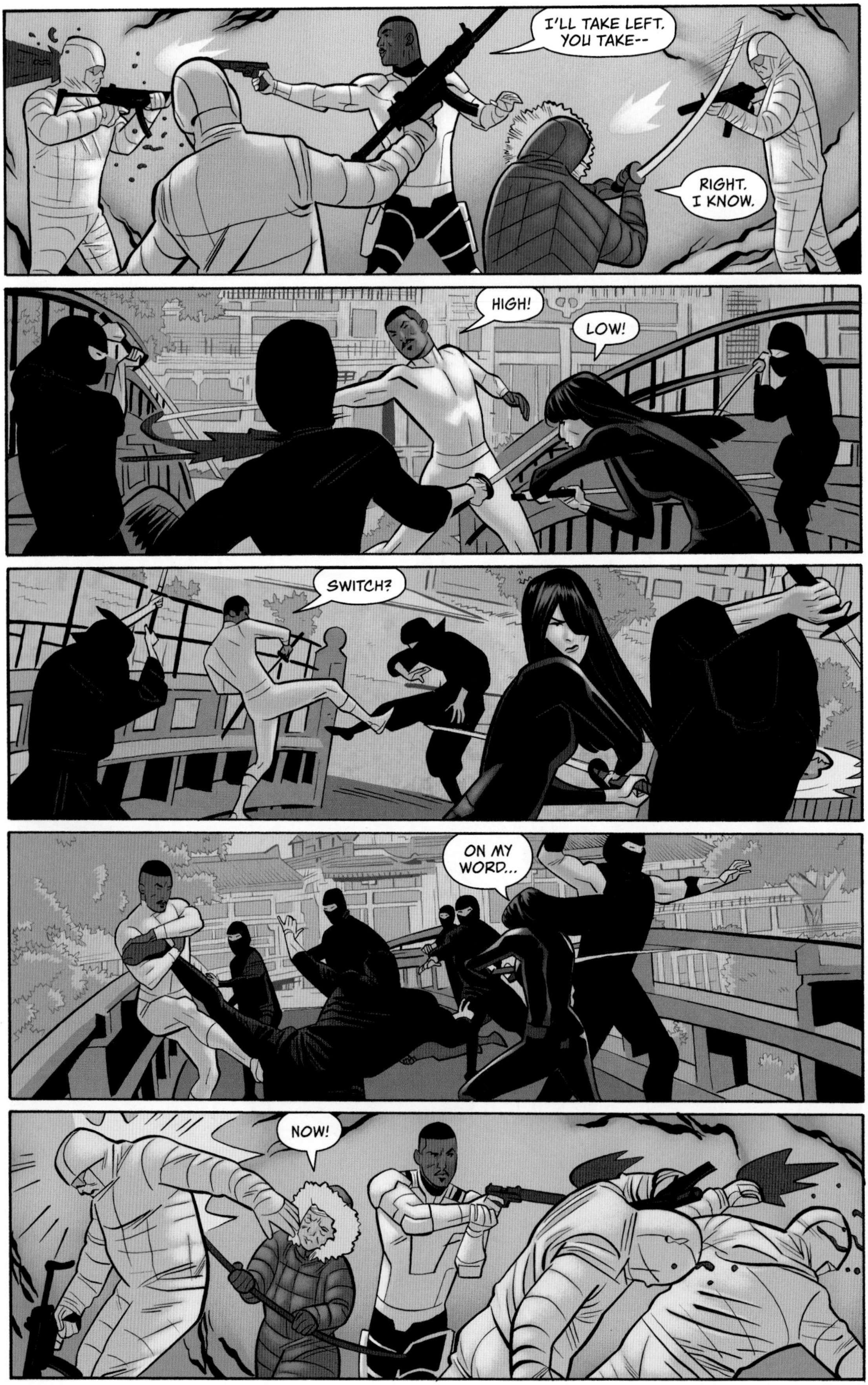
I'LL TAKE LEFT. YOU TAKE--
RIGHT. I KNOW.
HIGH!
LOW!
SWITCH?
ON MY WORD...
NOW!

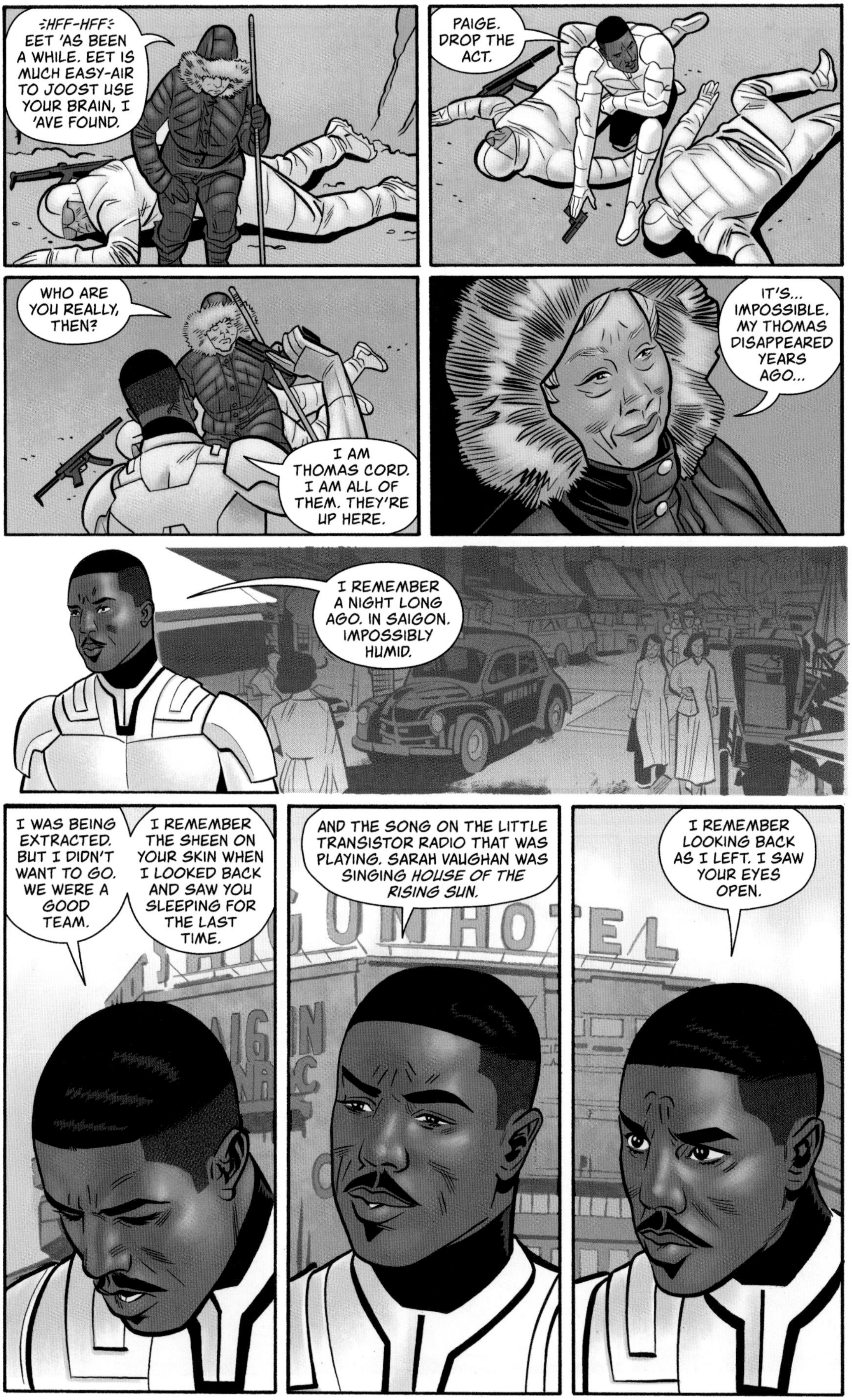
HFF-HFF
EET 'AS BEEN A WHILE. EET IS MUCH EASY-AIR TO JOOST USE YOUR BRAIN, I 'AVE FOUND.
PAIGE. DROP THE ACT.
WHO ARE YOU REALLY, THEN?
I AM THOMAS CORD. I AM ALL OF THEM. THEY'RE UP HERE.
IT'S... IMPOSSIBLE. MY THOMAS DISAPPEARED YEARS AGO...
I REMEMBER A NIGHT LONG AGO. IN SAIGON. IMPOSSIBLY HUMID.
I WAS BEING EXTRACTED. BUT I DIDN'T WANT TO GO. WE WERE A GOOD TEAM.
I REMEMBER THE SHEEN ON YOUR SKIN WHEN I LOOKED BACK AND SAW YOU SLEEPING FOR THE LAST TIME.
AND THE SONG ON THE LITTLE TRANSISTOR RADIO THAT WAS PLAYING. SARAH VAUGHAN WAS SINGING *HOUSE OF THE RISING SUN.*
I REMEMBER LOOKING BACK AS I LEFT. I SAW YOUR EYES OPEN.

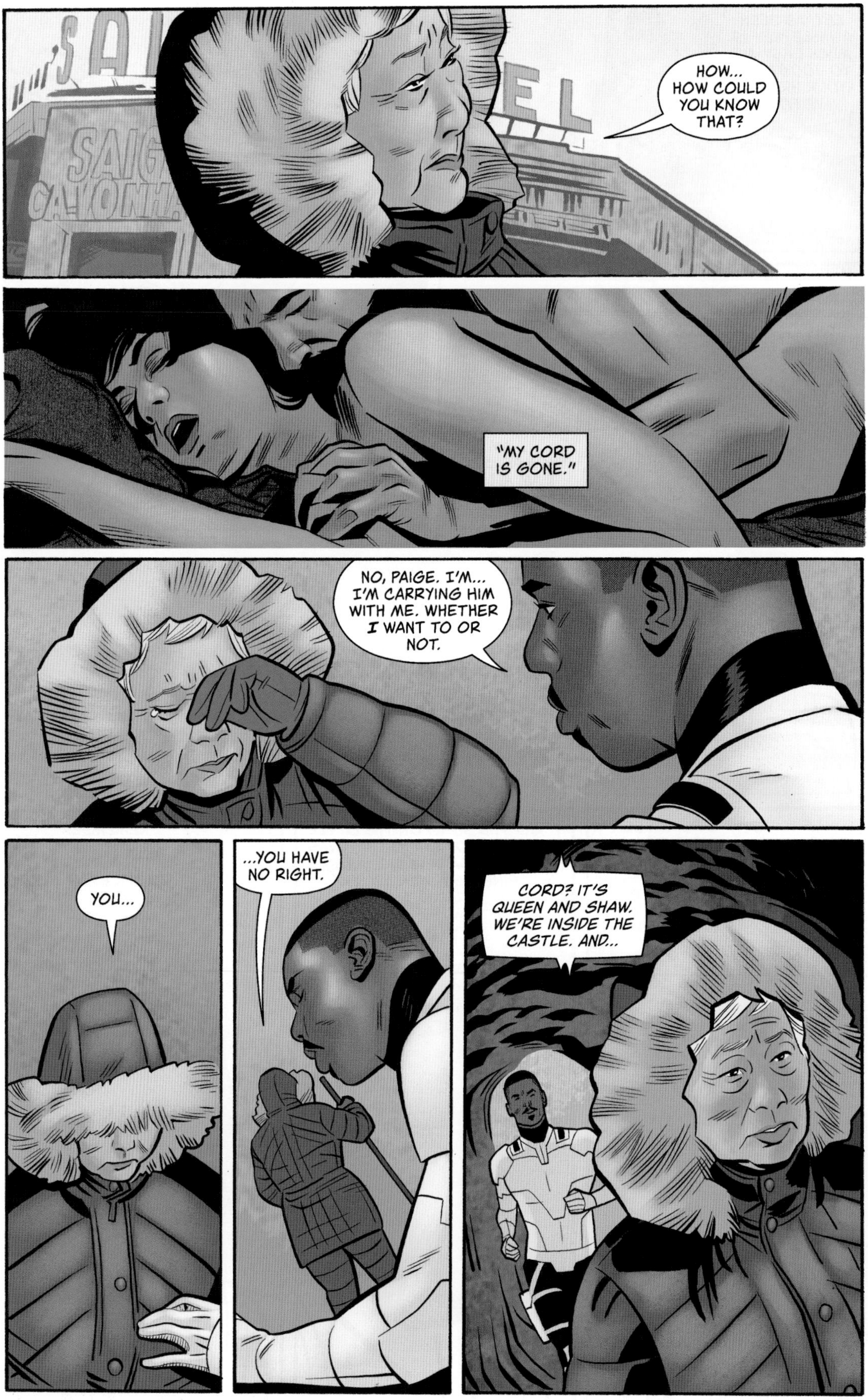

HOW... HOW COULD YOU KNOW THAT?
"MY CORD IS GONE."
NO, PAIGE. I'M... I'M CARRYING HIM WITH ME. WHETHER I WANT TO OR NOT.
YOU...
...YOU HAVE NO RIGHT.
CORD? IT'S QUEEN AND SHAW. WE'RE INSIDE THE CASTLE. AND...

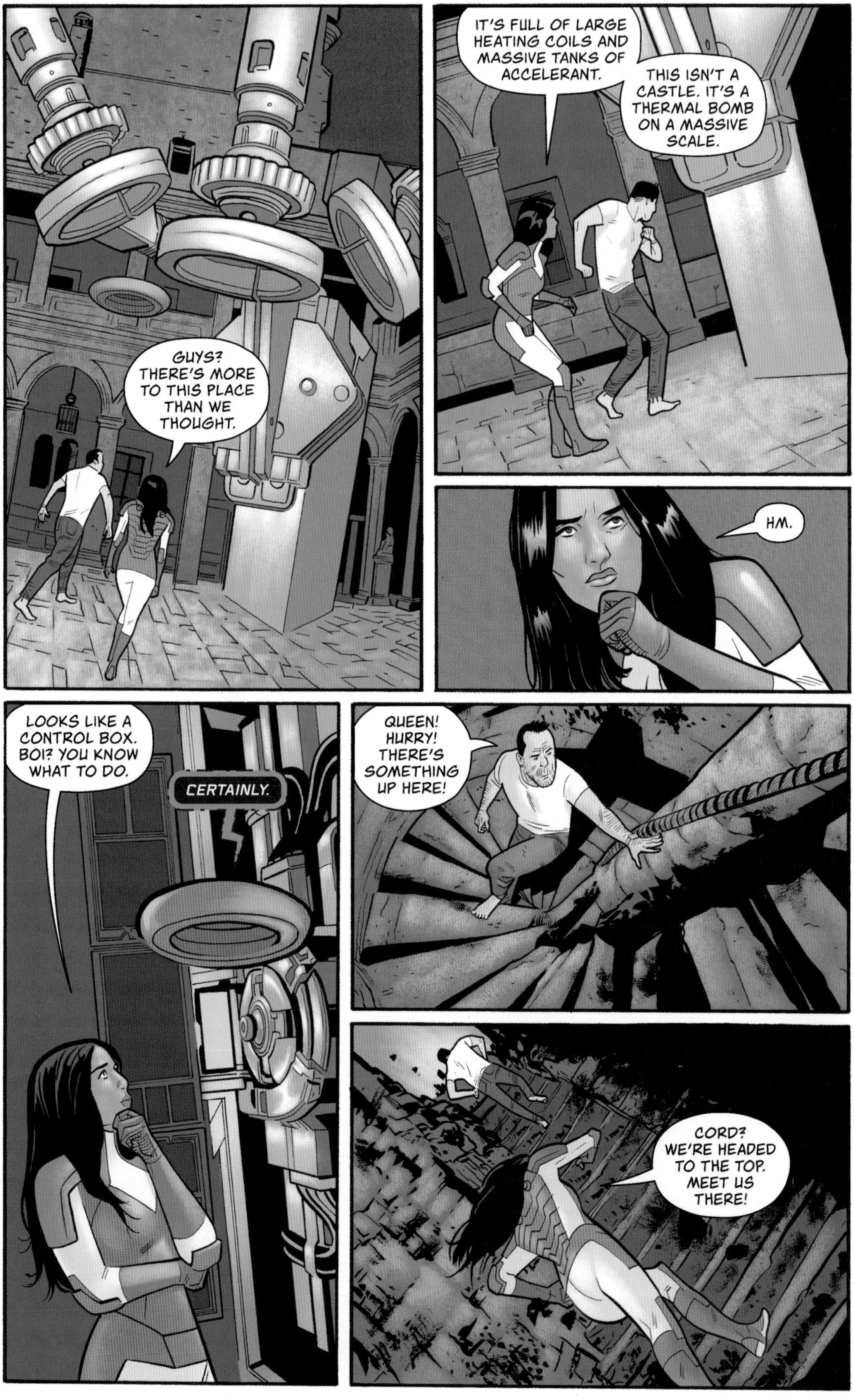
GUYS? THERE'S MORE TO THIS PLACE THAN WE THOUGHT.
IT'S FULL OF LARGE HEATING COILS AND MASSIVE TANKS OF ACCELERANT.
THIS ISN'T A CASTLE. IT'S A THERMAL BOMB ON A MASSIVE SCALE.
HM.
LOOKS LIKE A CONTROL BOX. BOI? YOU KNOW WHAT TO DO.
CERTAINLY.
QUEEN! HURRY! THERE'S SOMETHING UP HERE!
CORD? WE'RE HEADED TO THE TOP. MEET US THERE!

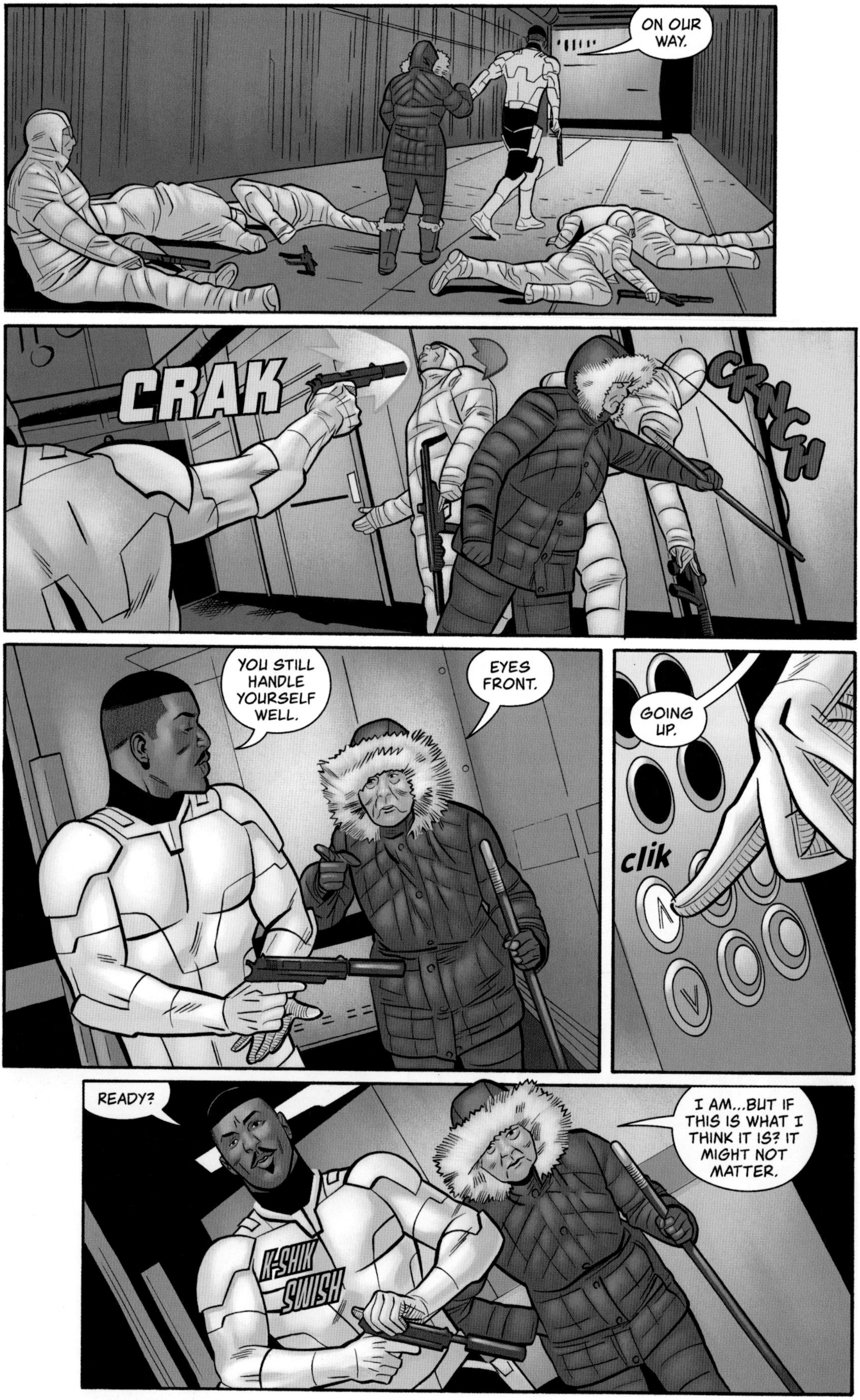
ON OUR WAY.
CRAK
CRNCH
YOU STILL HANDLE YOURSELF WELL.
EYES FRONT.
GOING UP.
clik
READY?
I AM...BUT IF THIS IS WHAT I THINK IT IS? IT MIGHT NOT MATTER.
K-SHIK
SWISH

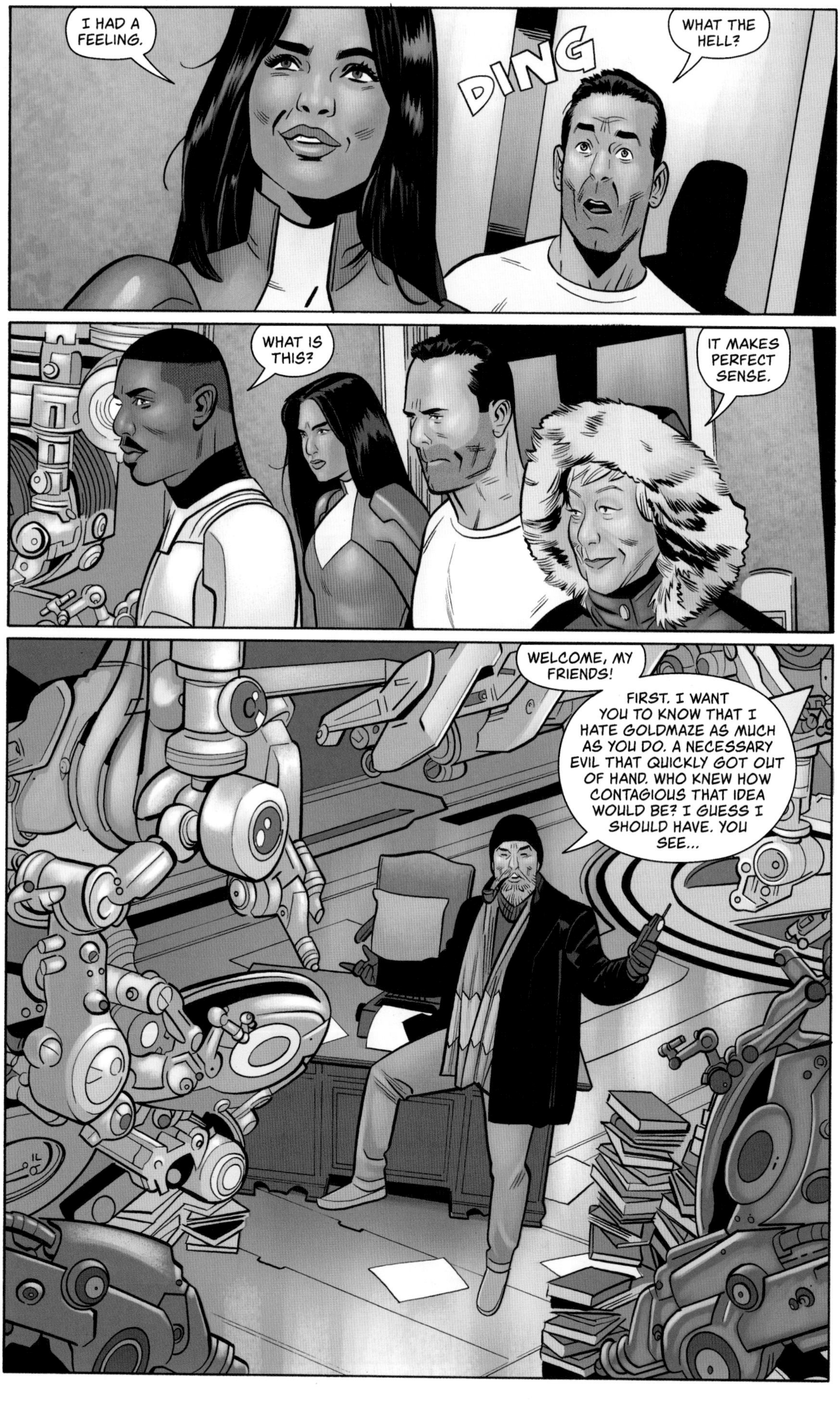
I HAD A FEELING.
DING
WHAT THE HELL?
WHAT IS THIS?
IT MAKES PERFECT SENSE.
WELCOME, MY FRIENDS!
FIRST, I WANT YOU TO KNOW THAT I HATE GOLDMAZE AS MUCH AS YOU DO. A NECESSARY EVIL THAT QUICKLY GOT OUT OF HAND. WHO KNEW HOW CONTAGIOUS THAT IDEA WOULD BE? I GUESS I SHOULD HAVE. YOU SEE...

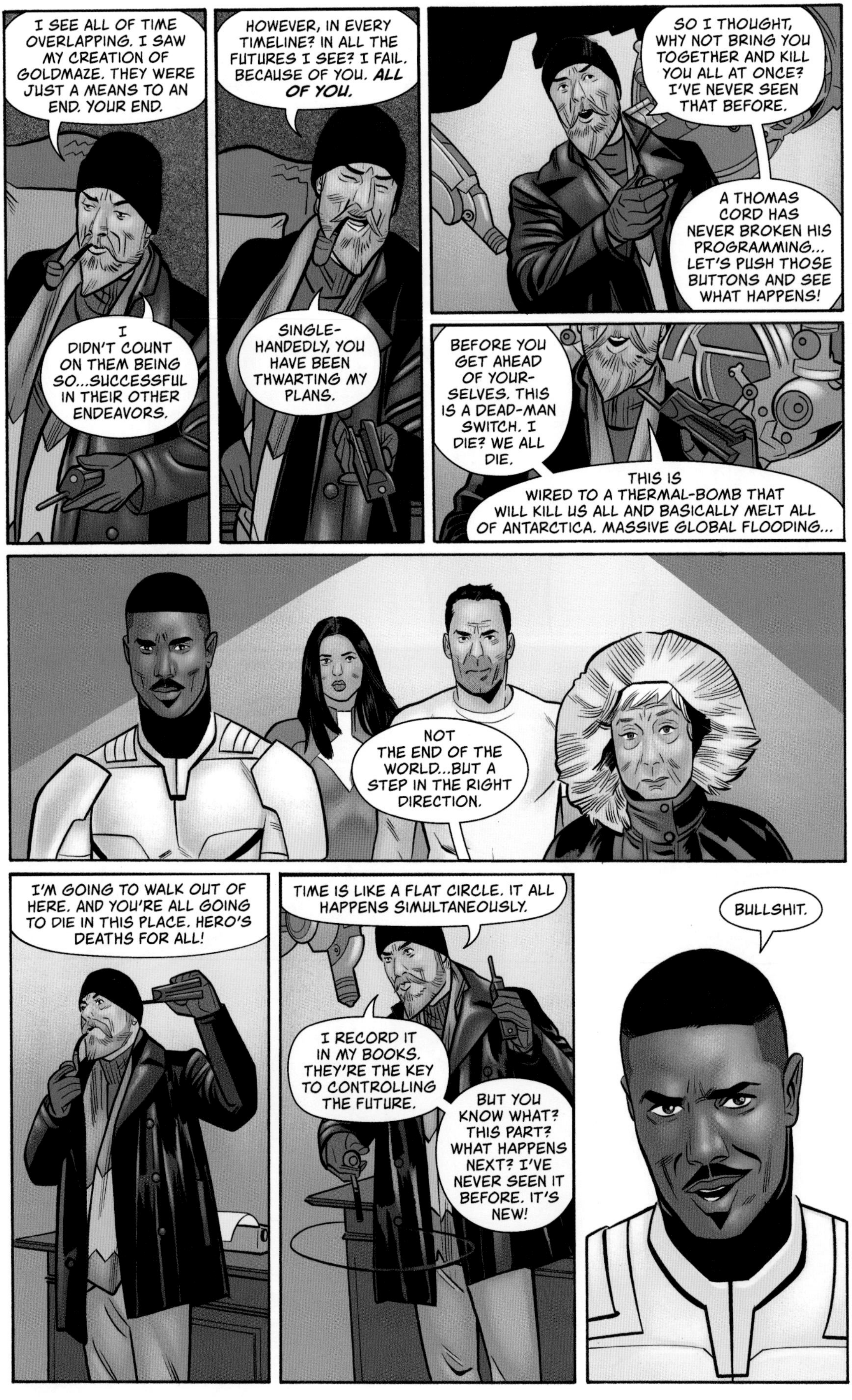
I SEE ALL OF TIME OVERLAPPING. I SAW MY CREATION OF GOLDMAZE. THEY WERE JUST A MEANS TO AN END. YOUR END.
I DIDN'T COUNT ON THEM BEING SO...SUCCESSFUL IN THEIR OTHER ENDEAVORS.
HOWEVER, IN EVERY TIMELINE? IN ALL THE FUTURES I SEE? I FAIL. BECAUSE OF YOU. ***ALL OF YOU.***
SINGLE-HANDEDLY, YOU HAVE BEEN THWARTING MY PLANS.
SO I THOUGHT, WHY NOT BRING YOU TOGETHER AND KILL YOU ALL AT ONCE? I'VE NEVER SEEN THAT BEFORE.
A THOMAS CORD HAS NEVER BROKEN HIS PROGRAMMING... LET'S PUSH THOSE BUTTONS AND SEE WHAT HAPPENS!
BEFORE YOU GET AHEAD OF YOUR-SELVES. THIS IS A DEAD-MAN SWITCH. I DIE? WE ALL DIE.
THIS IS WIRED TO A THERMAL-BOMB THAT WILL KILL US ALL AND BASICALLY MELT ALL OF ANTARCTICA. MASSIVE GLOBAL FLOODING...
NOT THE END OF THE WORLD...BUT A STEP IN THE RIGHT DIRECTION.
I'M GOING TO WALK OUT OF HERE. AND YOU'RE ALL GOING TO DIE IN THIS PLACE. HERO'S DEATHS FOR ALL!
TIME IS LIKE A FLAT CIRCLE. IT ALL HAPPENS SIMULTANEOUSLY.
I RECORD IT IN MY BOOKS. THEY'RE THE KEY TO CONTROLLING THE FUTURE.
BUT YOU KNOW WHAT? THIS PART? WHAT HAPPENS NEXT? I'VE NEVER SEEN IT BEFORE. IT'S NEW!
BULLSHIT.

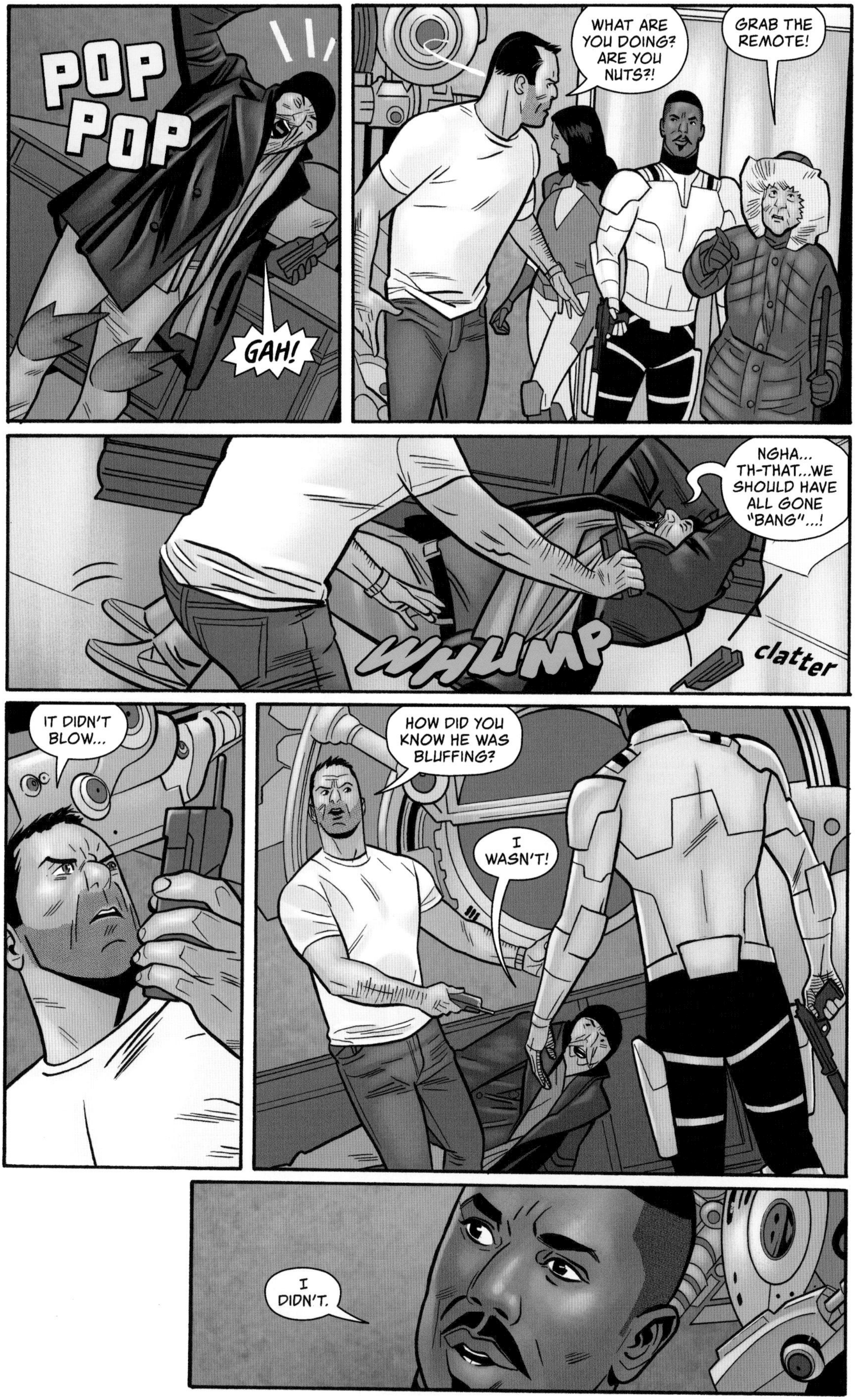
POP
POP
GAH!
WHAT ARE YOU DOING? ARE YOU NUTS?!
GRAB THE REMOTE!
NGHA... TH-THAT...WE SHOULD HAVE ALL GONE "BANG"...!
WHUMP
clatter
IT DIDN'T BLOW...
HOW DID YOU KNOW HE WAS BLUFFING?
I WASN'T!
I DIDN'T.

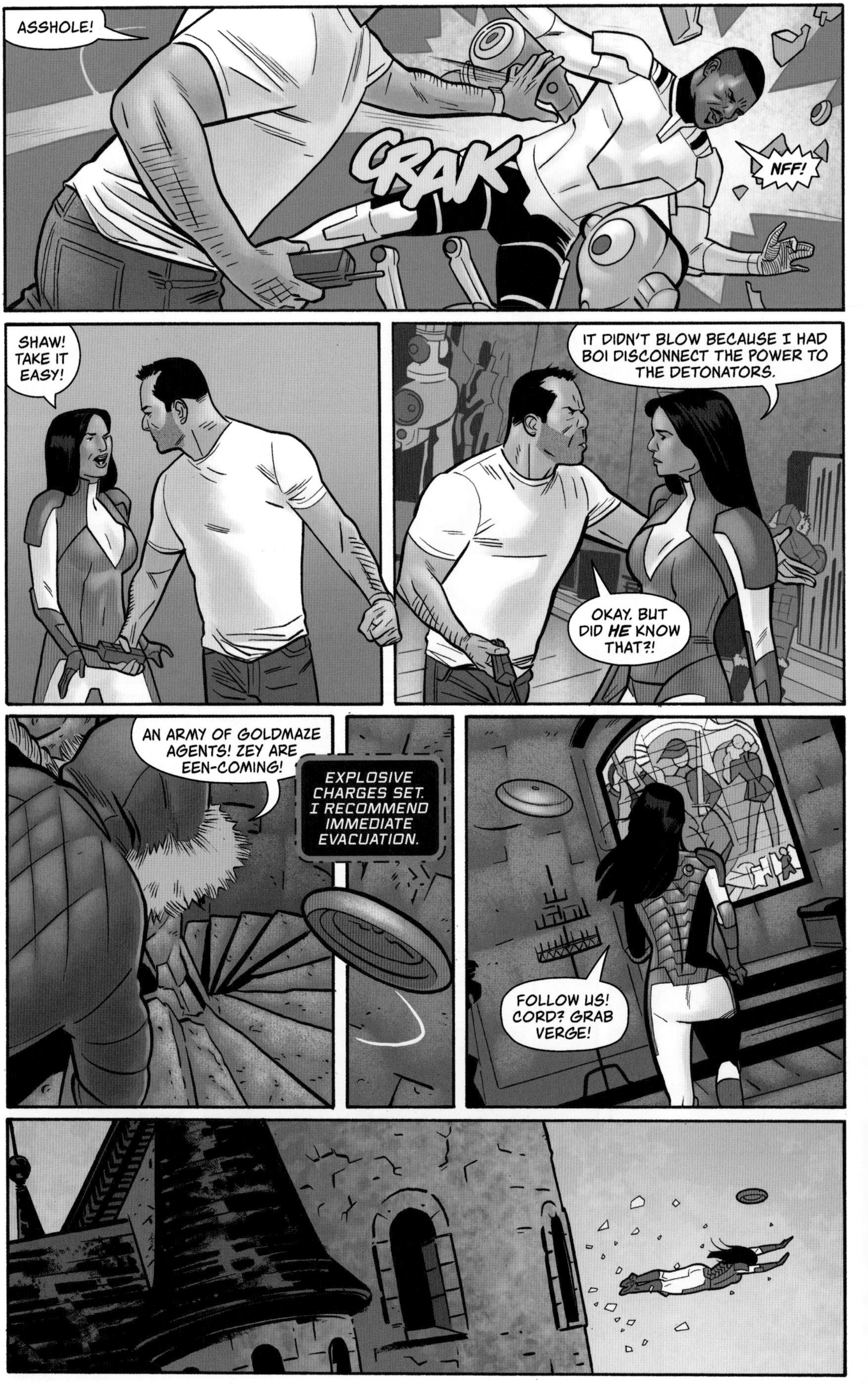
ASSHOLE!
CRAK
NFF!
SHAW! TAKE IT EASY!
IT DIDN'T BLOW BECAUSE I HAD BOI DISCONNECT THE POWER TO THE DETONATORS.
OKAY. BUT DID HE KNOW THAT?!
AN ARMY OF GOLDMAZE AGENTS! ZEY ARE EEN-COMING!
EXPLOSIVE CHARGES SET. I RECOMMEND IMMEDIATE EVACUATION.
FOLLOW US! CORD? GRAB VERGE!

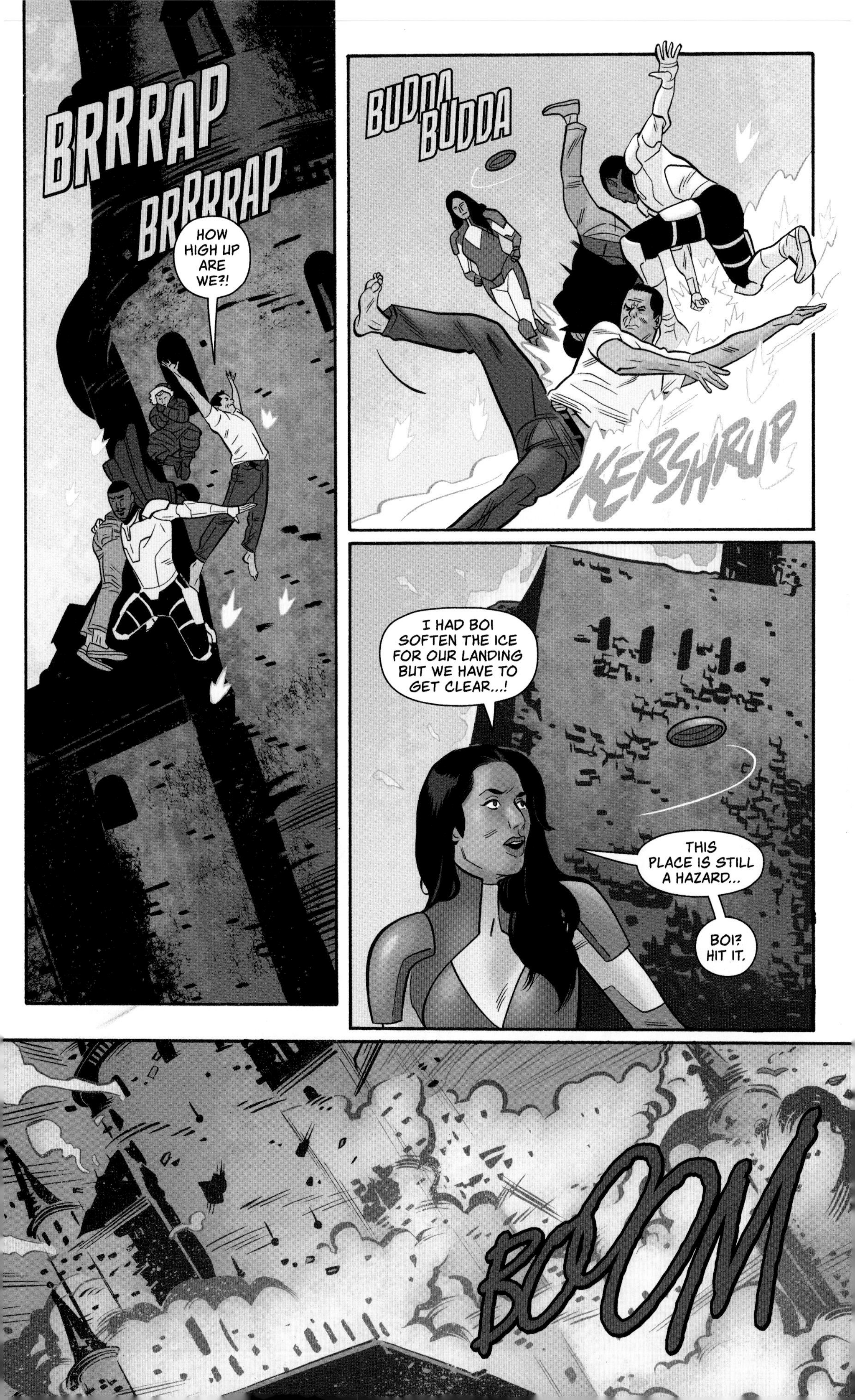
BRRRAP
BRRRRAP
HOW HIGH UP ARE WE?!
BUDDA BUDDA
KERSHRUP
I HAD BOI SOFTEN THE ICE FOR OUR LANDING BUT WE HAVE TO GET CLEAR...!
THIS PLACE IS STILL A HAZARD...
BOI? HIT IT.
BOOOM

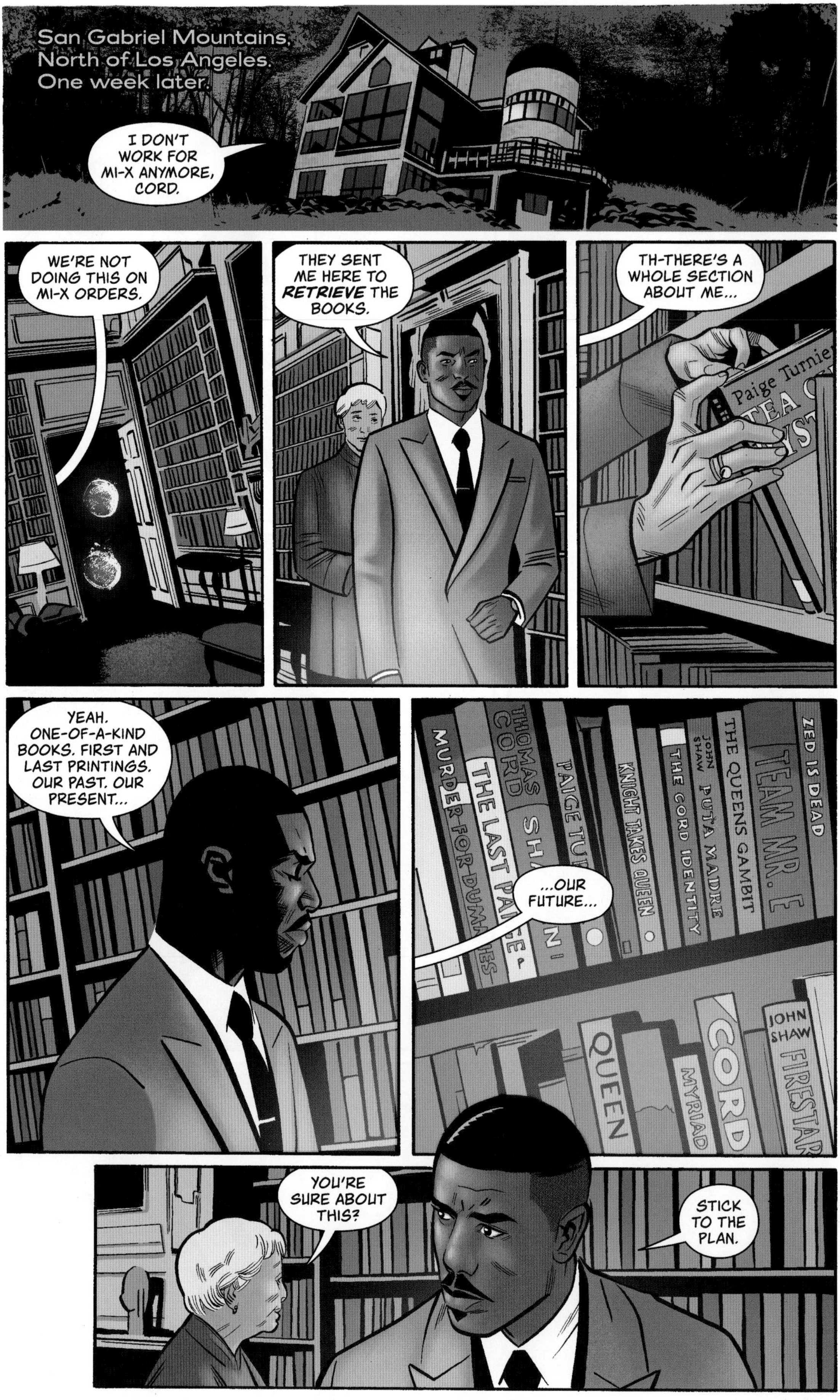
San Gabriel Mountains.
North of Los Angeles.
One week later.
I DON'T WORK FOR MI-X ANYMORE, CORD.
WE'RE NOT DOING THIS ON MI-X ORDERS.
THEY SENT ME HERE TO ***RETRIEVE*** THE BOOKS.
TH-THERE'S A WHOLE SECTION ABOUT ME...
YEAH. ONE-OF-A-KIND BOOKS. FIRST AND LAST PRINTINGS. OUR PAST. OUR PRESENT...
THOMAS CORD
KNIGHT TAKES QUEEN
JOHN SHAW
THE CORD IDENTITY
PUTA MADRE
THE QUEENS GAMBIT
TEAM MR. E
ZED IS DEAD
...OUR FUTURE...
QUEEN
MYRIAD
CORD
JOHN SHAW
FIRESTAR
YOU'RE SURE ABOUT THIS?
STICK TO THE PLAN.

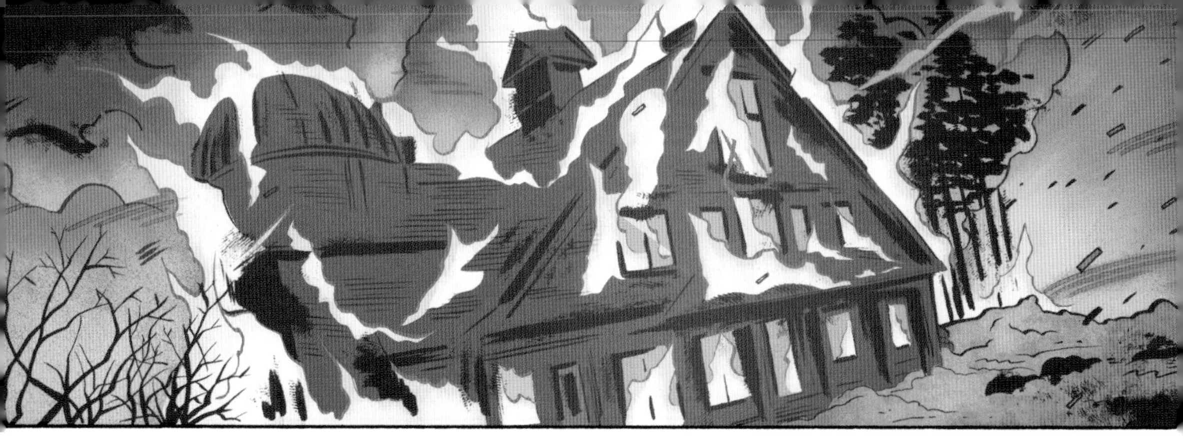

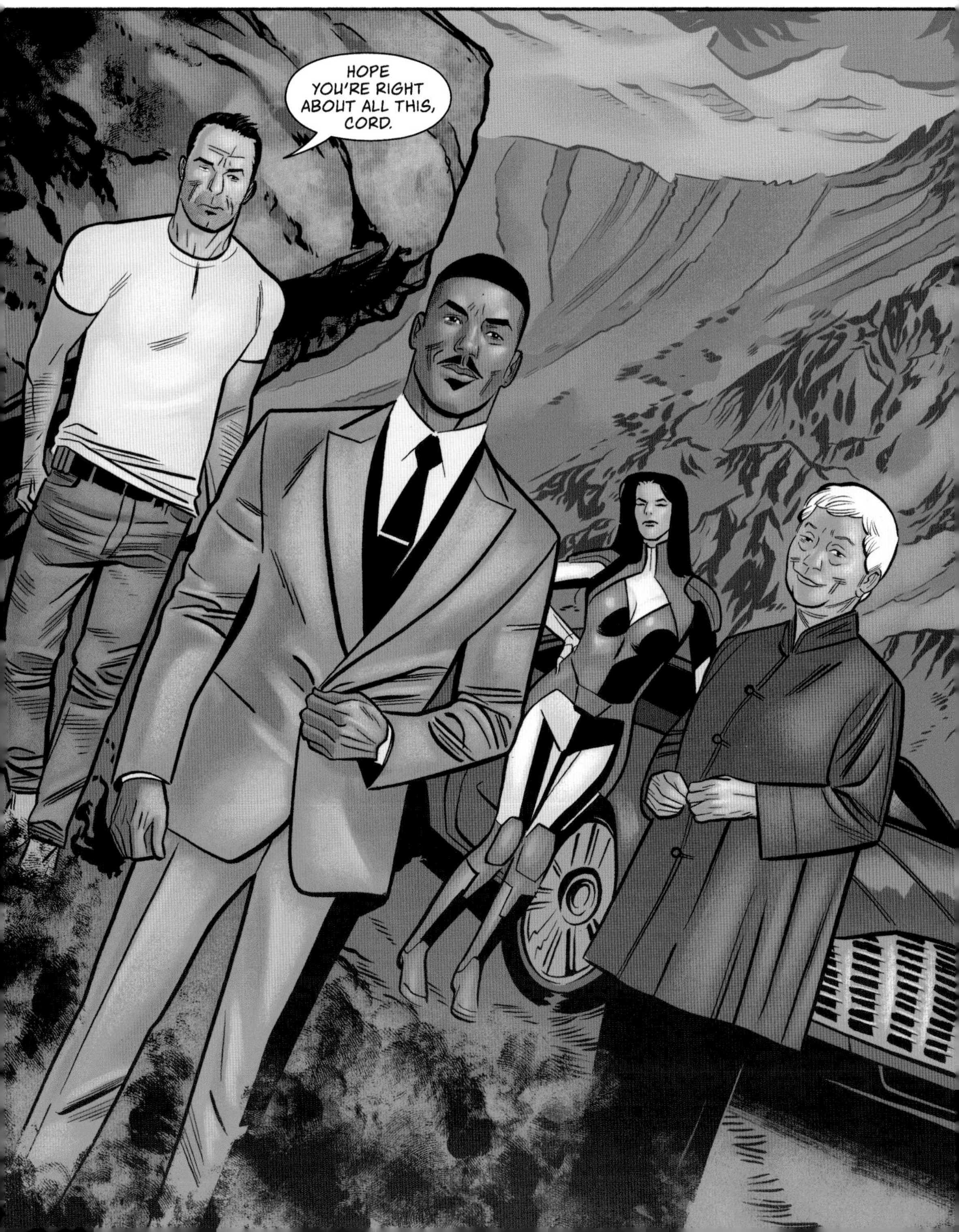
HOPE YOU'RE RIGHT ABOUT ALL THIS, CORD.

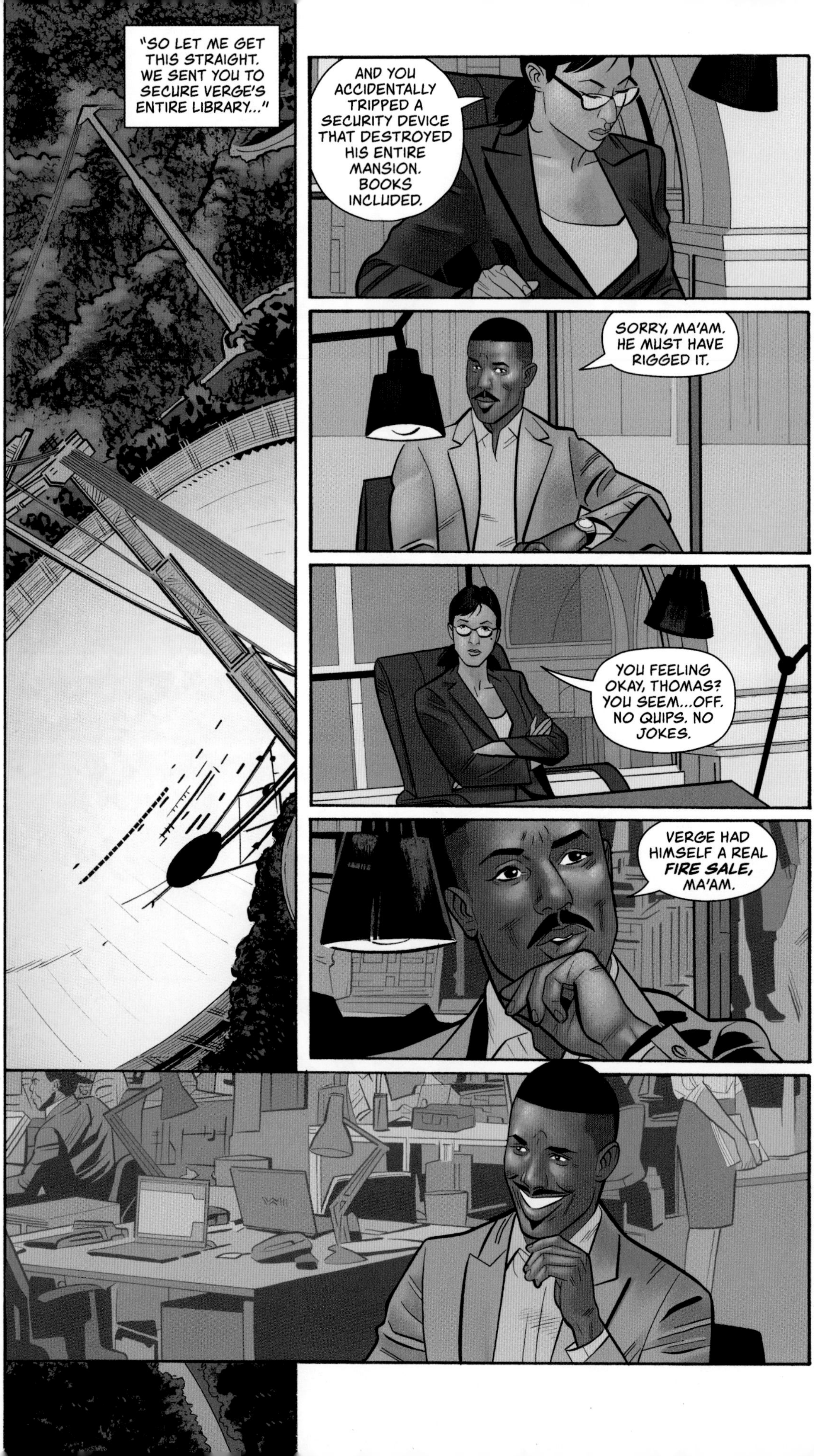
"SO LET ME GET THIS STRAIGHT. WE SENT YOU TO SECURE VERGE'S ENTIRE LIBRARY..."
AND YOU ACCIDENTALLY TRIPPED A SECURITY DEVICE THAT DESTROYED HIS ENTIRE MANSION. BOOKS INCLUDED.
SORRY, MA'AM. HE MUST HAVE RIGGED IT.
YOU FEELING OKAY, THOMAS? YOU SEEM...OFF. NO QUIPS. NO JOKES.
VERGE HAD HIMSELF A REAL *FIRE SALE*, MA'AM.

Rose is suspicious that Cord might have broken his programming. She eyes him. Does he know what he really is? Has he figured it out?

She discards that, though, as he quips . . .

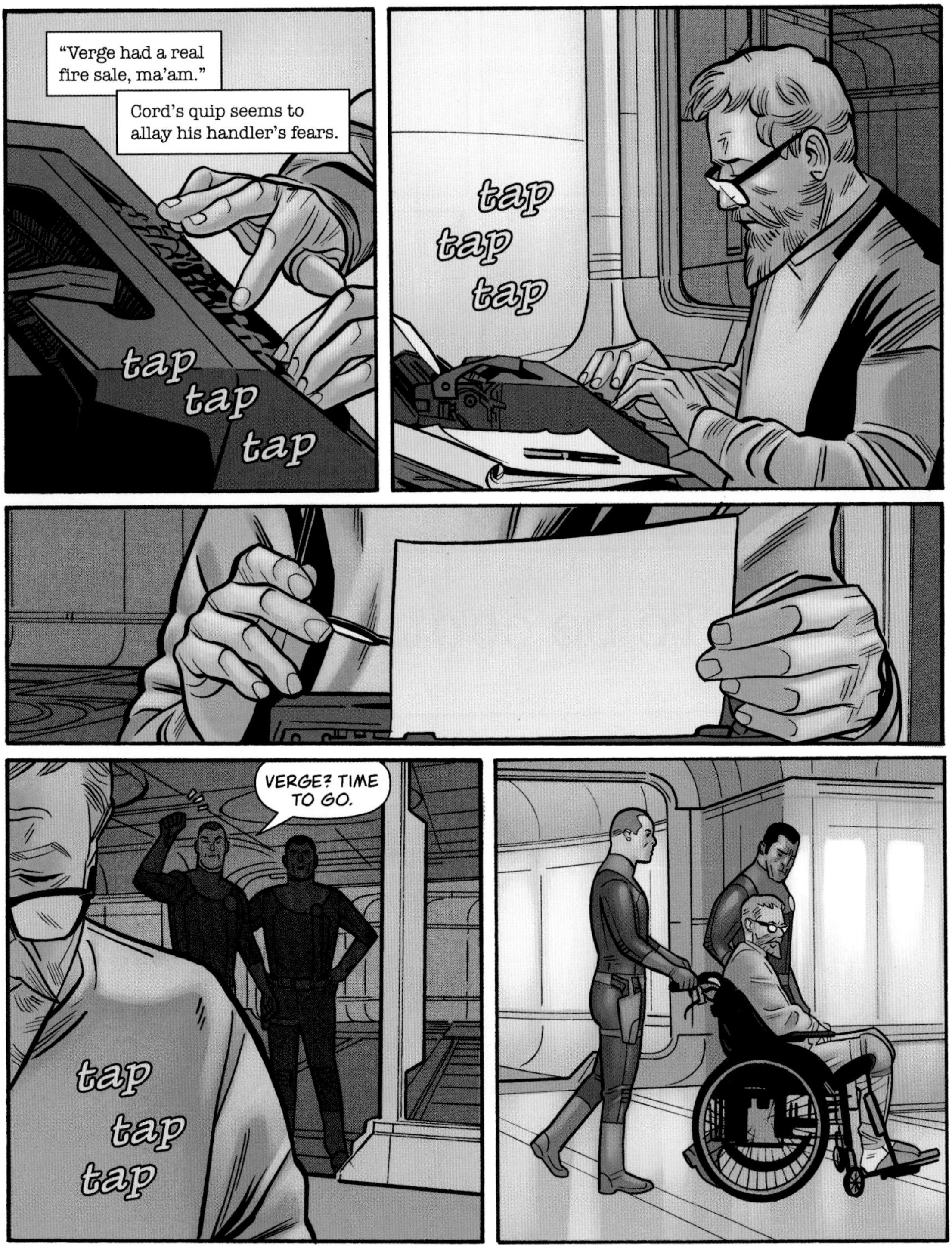
"Verge had a real fire sale, ma'am."
Cord's quip seems to allay his handler's fears.
tap tap tap
tap tap tap
tap tap tap
VERGE? TIME TO GO.

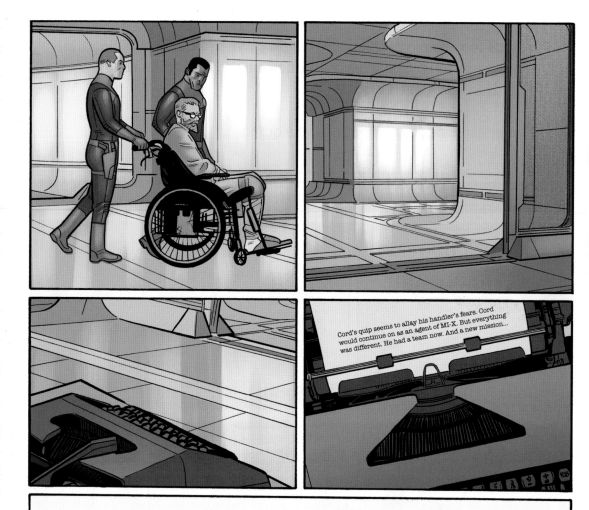

Cord's quip seems to allay his handler's fears. Cord would continue on as an agent of MI-X. But everything was different. He had a team now. And a new mission...

To be continued.

"I'm going to call it 'The Golden Cult of the Palmer Maze Bureau'."

An awkward pause. She hates the idea.

"I like the idea." She smiles. She likes the idea. "But that title. Yikes."

Verge is disarmed. He drops a record that he was holding. She giggles a little. She likes the idea.

"Well. You have any suggestions?" he asks.

"How about 'Goldmaze'?" She smiles. "It kind of compresses the title into something that's a little catchier. Those long book titles. They're kind of weird, y'know?" Normally he would be insulted here. He would defend his idea. But she raises one of her slender hands and tucks her long hair behind her ear. She smiles just a little at him. Making eye contact. He can't believe it.

"Well, that's the title then," he replies. Completely under her spell.

"Just like that?" She's amazed.

"Just like that," he mirrors her.

That's the story he needs to tell them. But he can't. He won't. They don't need to know all of it. They need to know just enough. The memory of the Dark-Haired Girl's face overlaps his present. Or is it future? He sometimes gets confused. It's understandable, he tells himself. The Dark-Haired Girl's face overlaps Paige Turnier who is both twenty years old and eighty years old. It's all happening at once. Turnier sees through his charade. He's sure of it. The new Thomas Cord does too. He closes his eyes. Trying to tune out the past and future. Focus on the present. Focus on now. If he doesn't, the entire plan is going to fall apart.

This group he's assembled is dangerous on their own. As separate pieces. But together? He's risking them becoming unstoppable. But he has to. He's seen the future. He knows what happens. If he doesn't try this? If he doesn't bring them together? The entire thing falls apart. He needs them to trust him. For just a little while longer.

Verge trudges through the snow to the arctic castle. They talk amongst themselves. Maybe this was all a big mistake. Well. He'd find out soon enough. Could he kill them? Could they ever be killed? Part of him hopes he's wrong. It happened before. Thomas Cord has already gone off the script. Fanny killed him. But everything after? He didn't see that. He didn't write it. Cord wasn't supposed to ever see Paige Turnier again. But here they are. Side by side. Like two volatile chemicals mixing . . . ready to explode. But not yet . . .

BANG! #1 Second Printing Cover by
DENYS COWAN with KENT WILLIAMS and NOELLE GIDDINGS

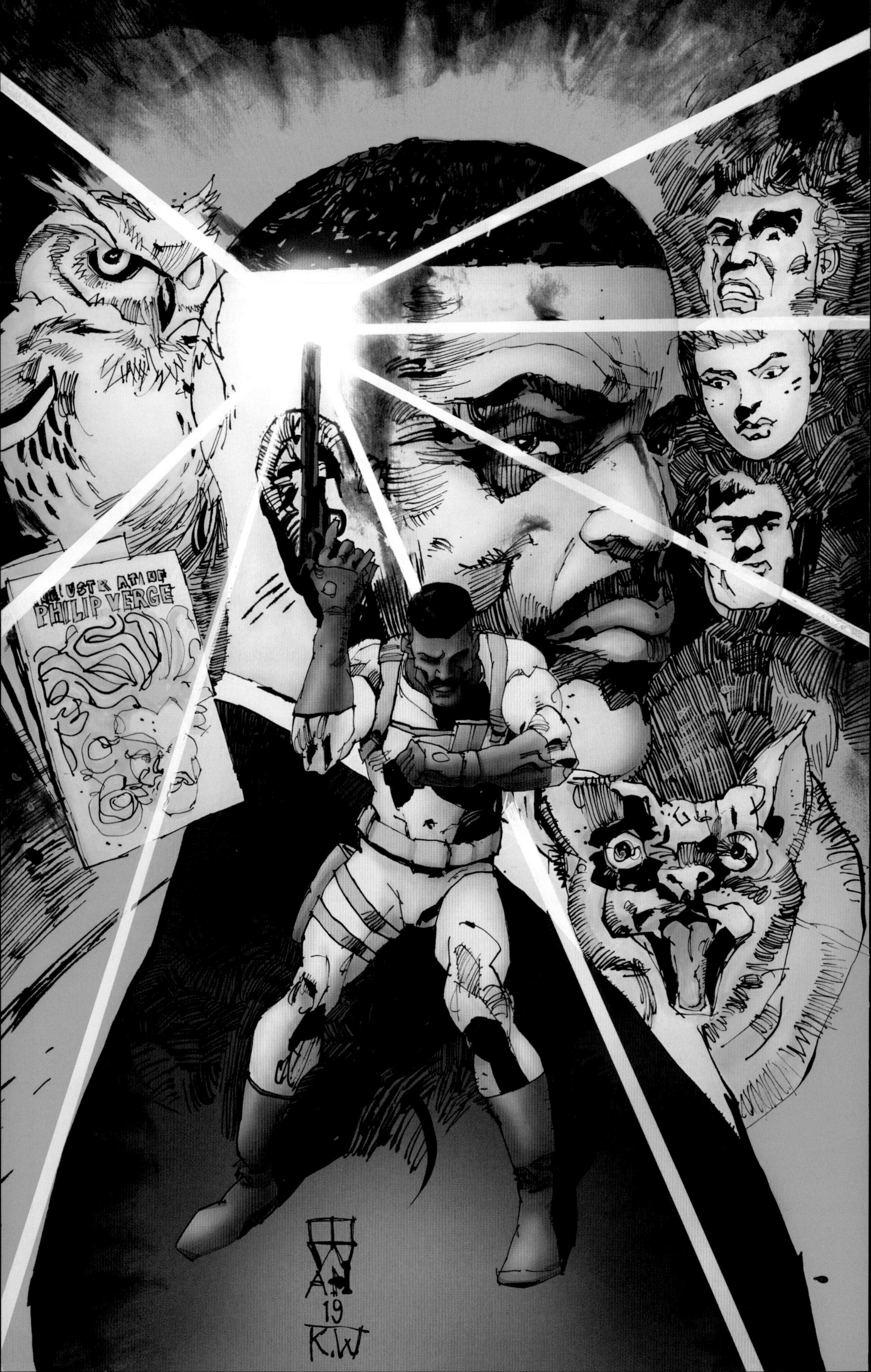
PHILIP VERGE

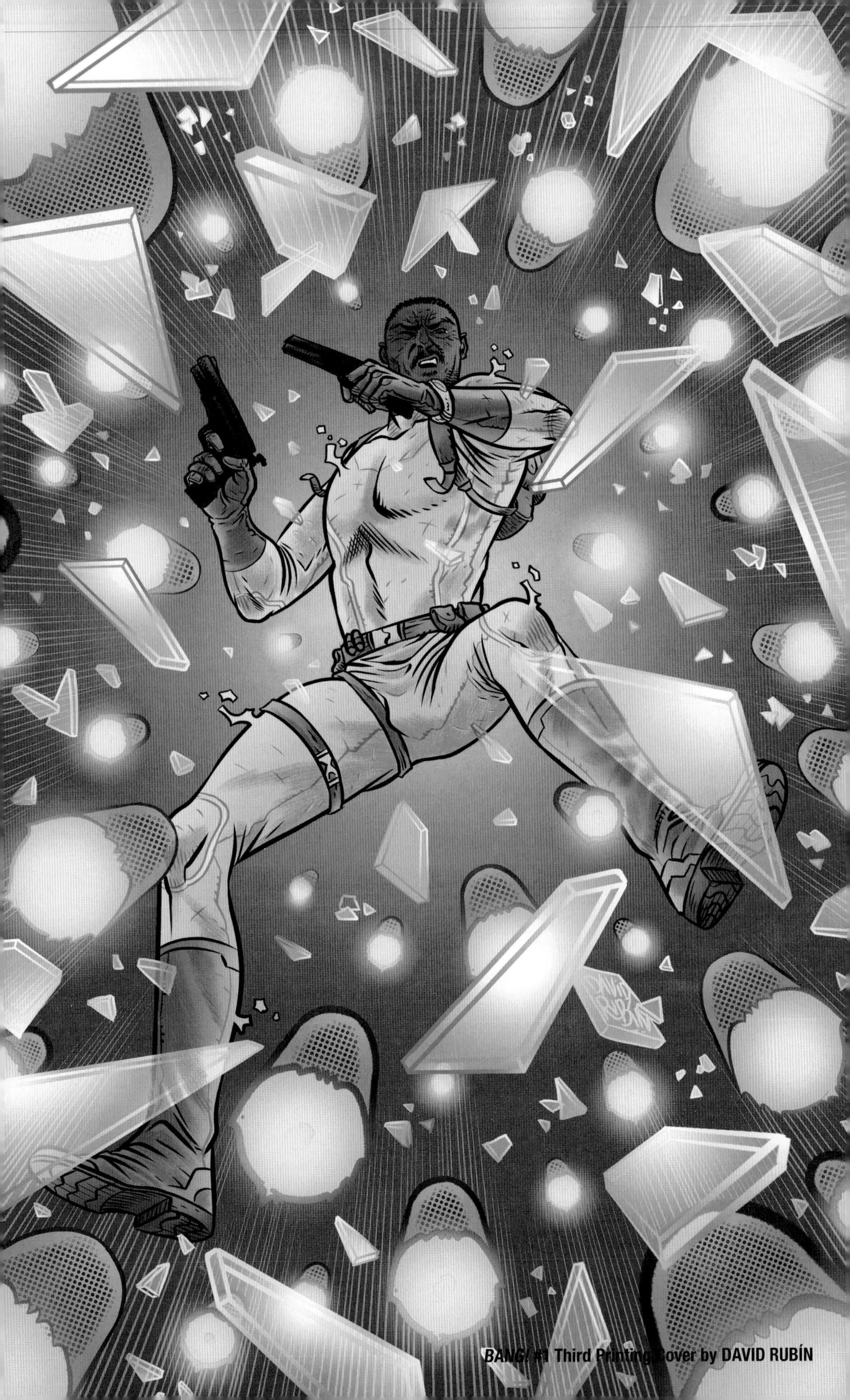
DAVID RUBÍN

BANG! #1 Third Printing Cover by DAVID RUBÍN

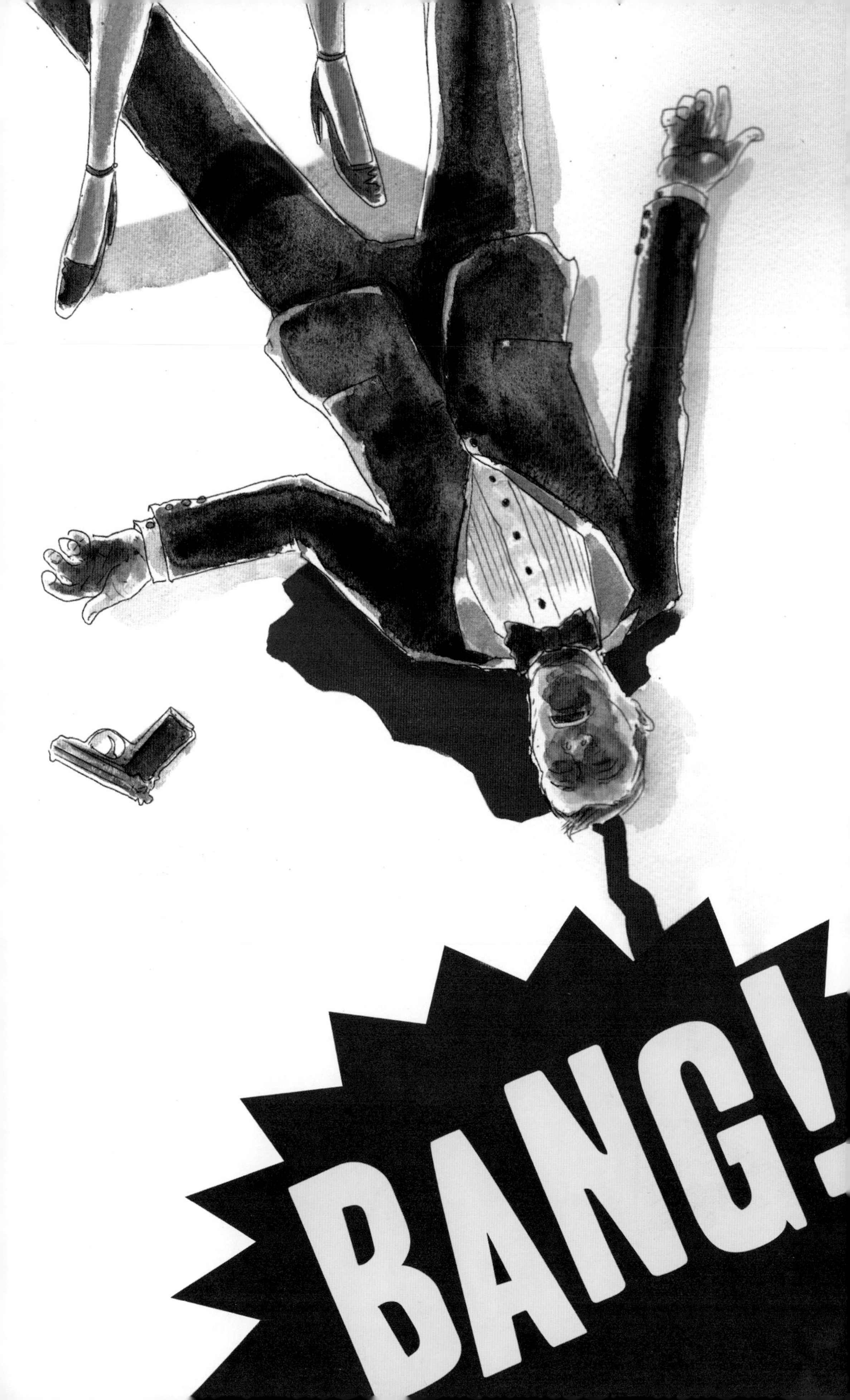
BANG!

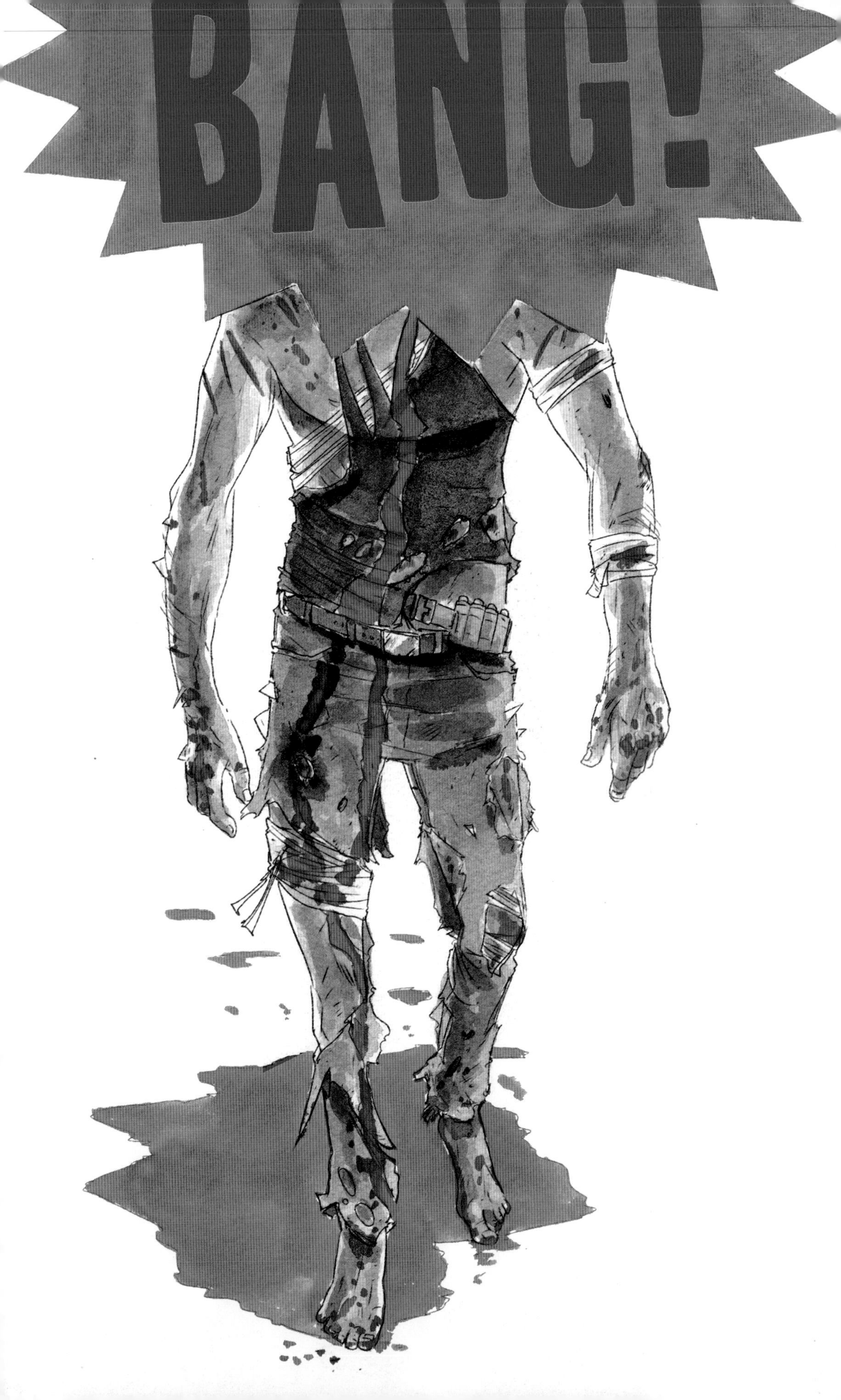
BANG!

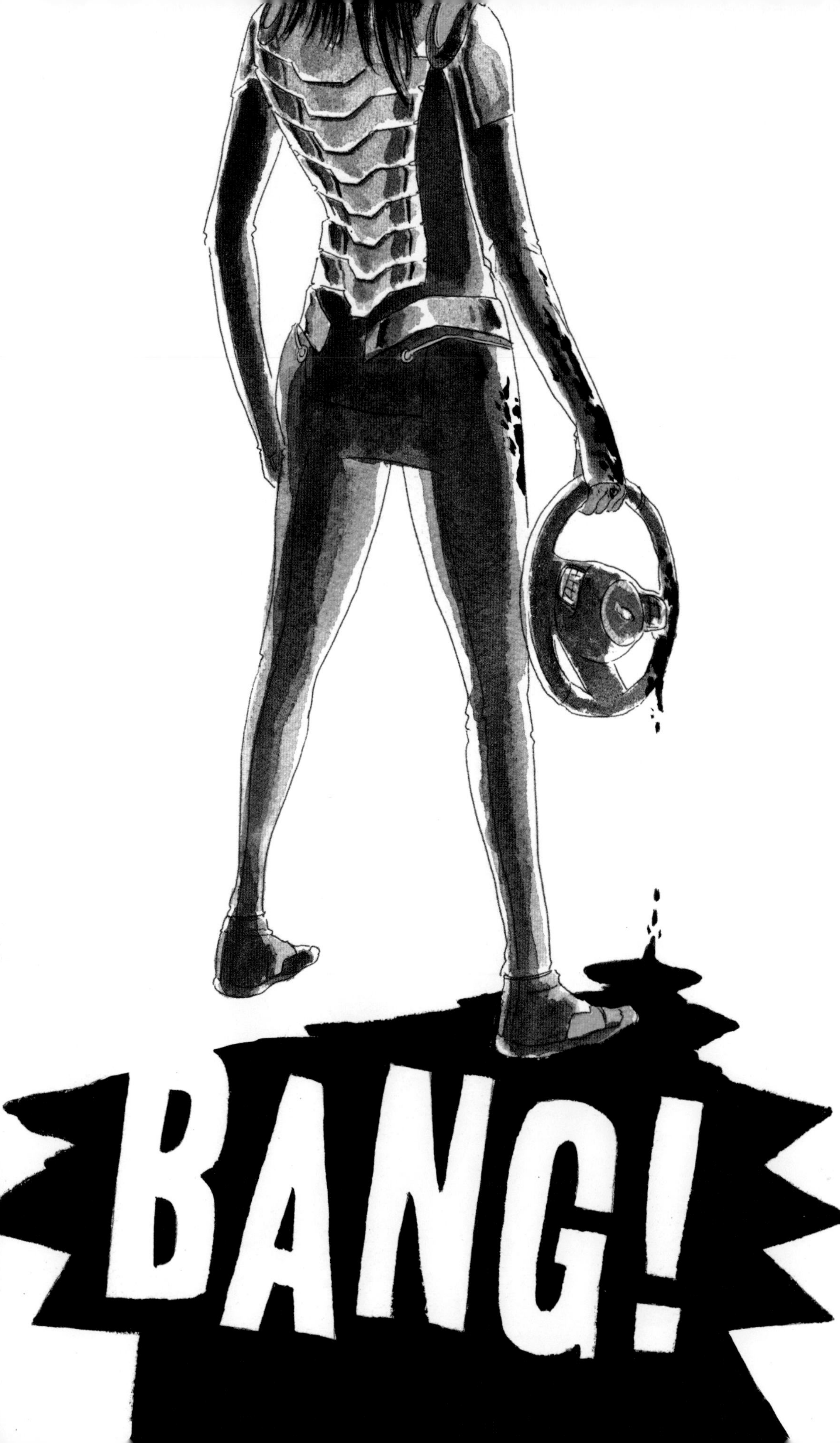
BANG!

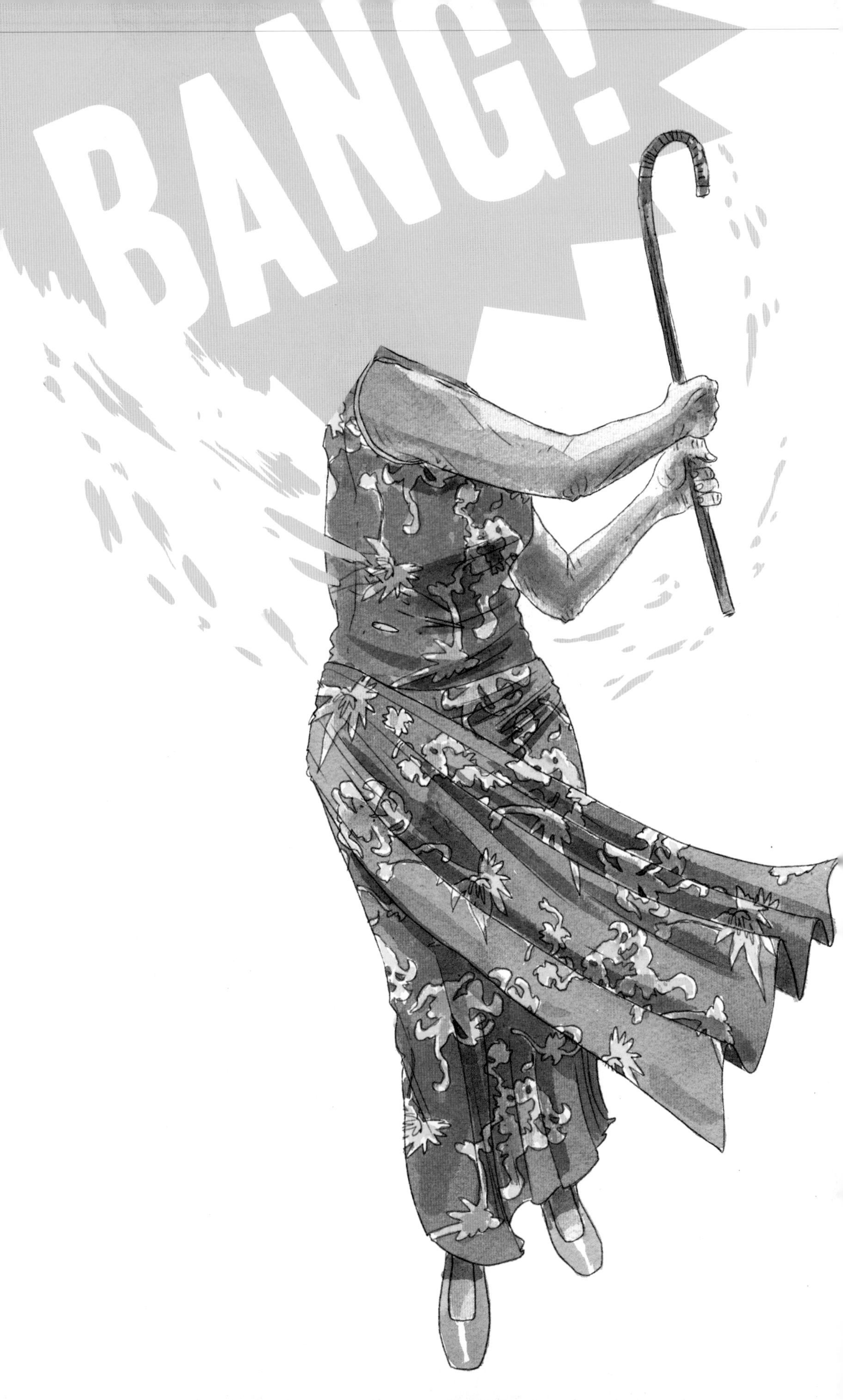
BANG!

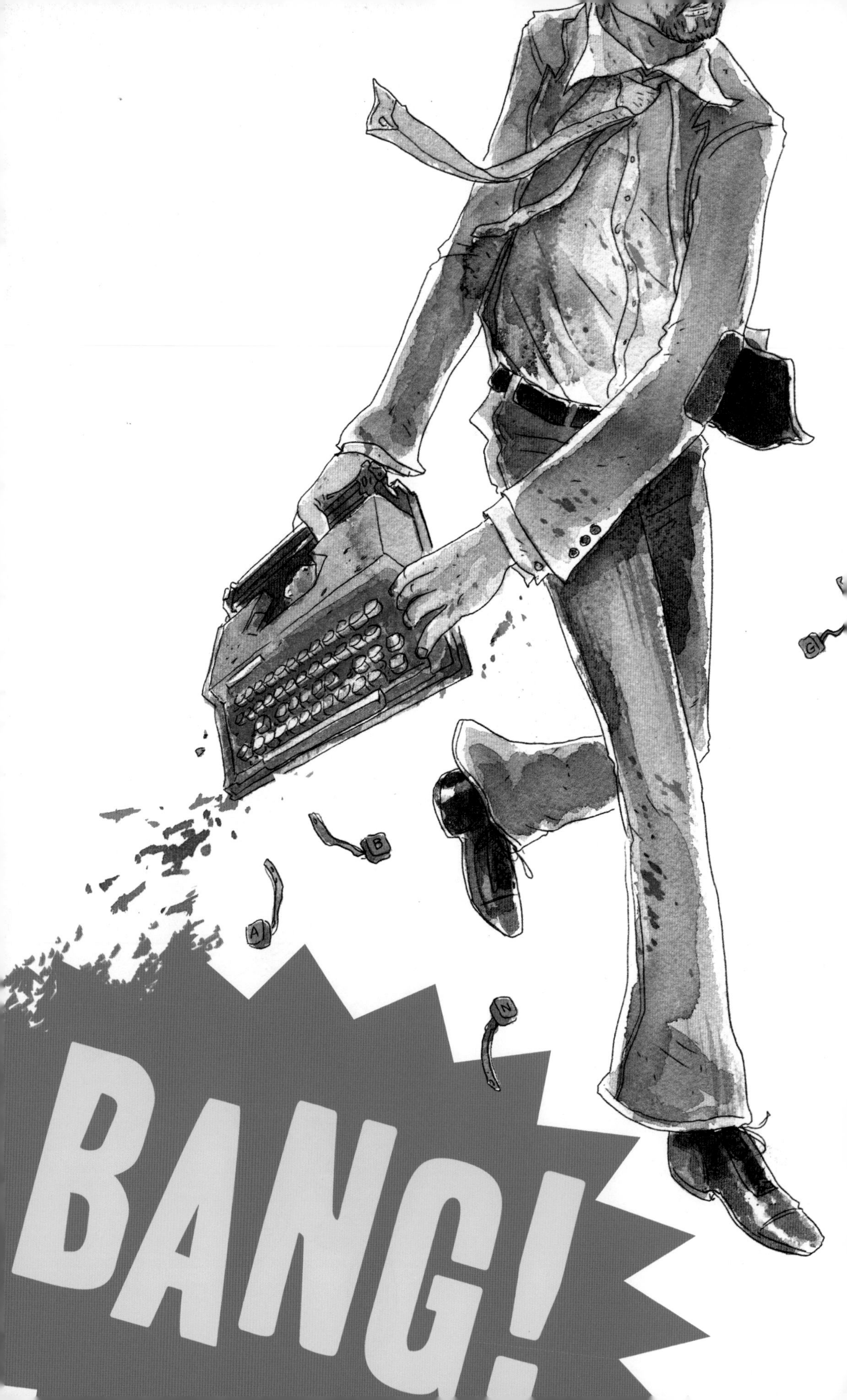
BANG!

BANG!

SKETCHBOOK

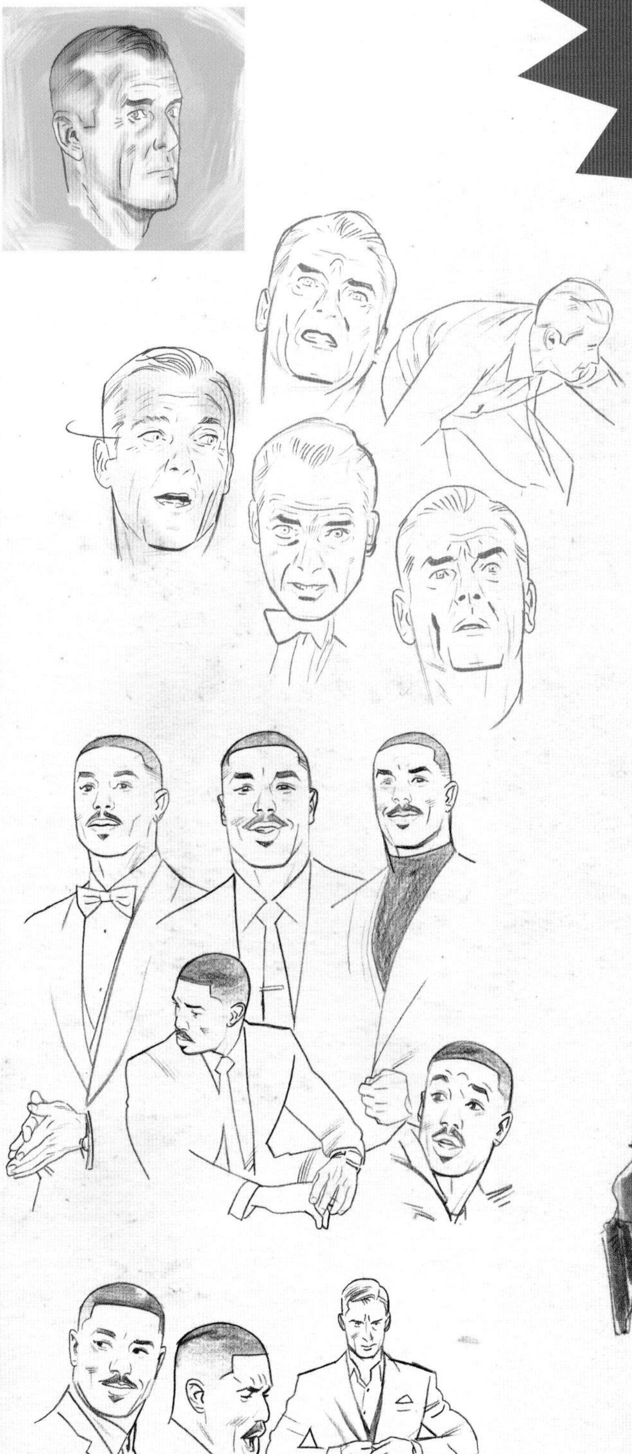

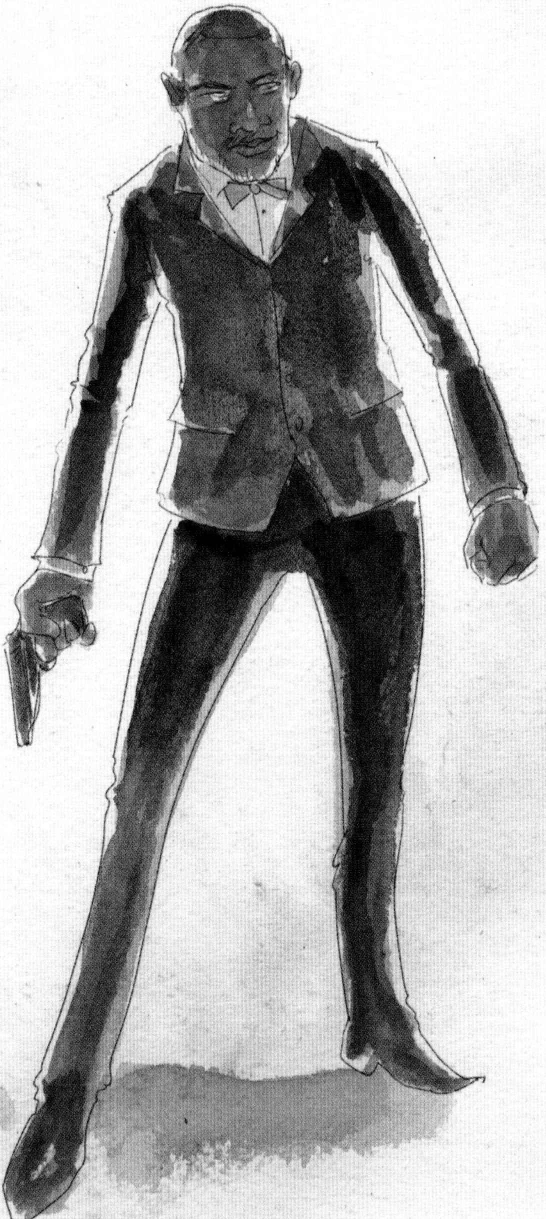

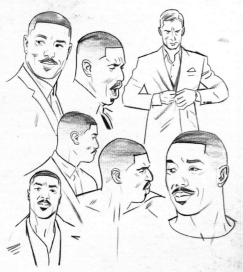

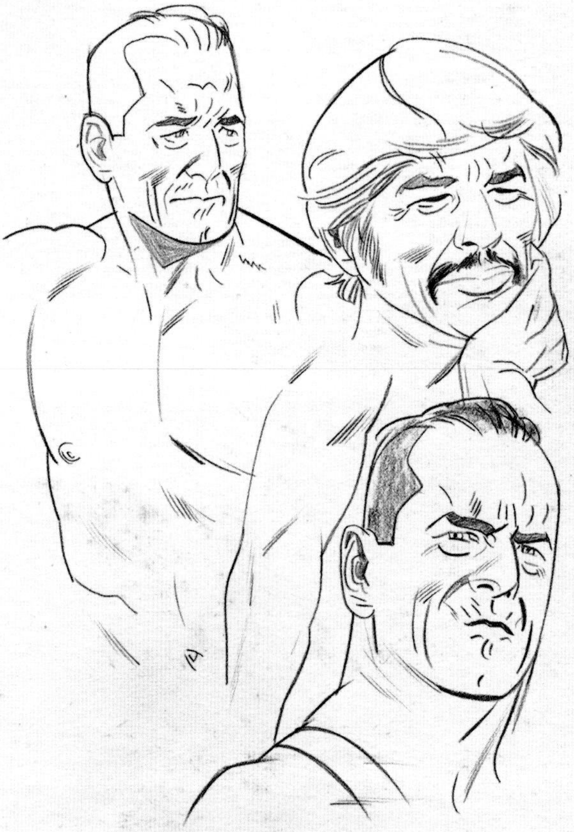

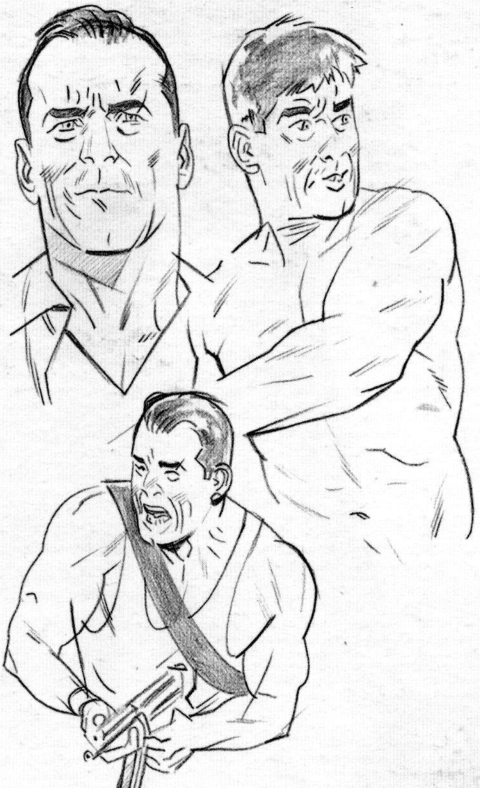

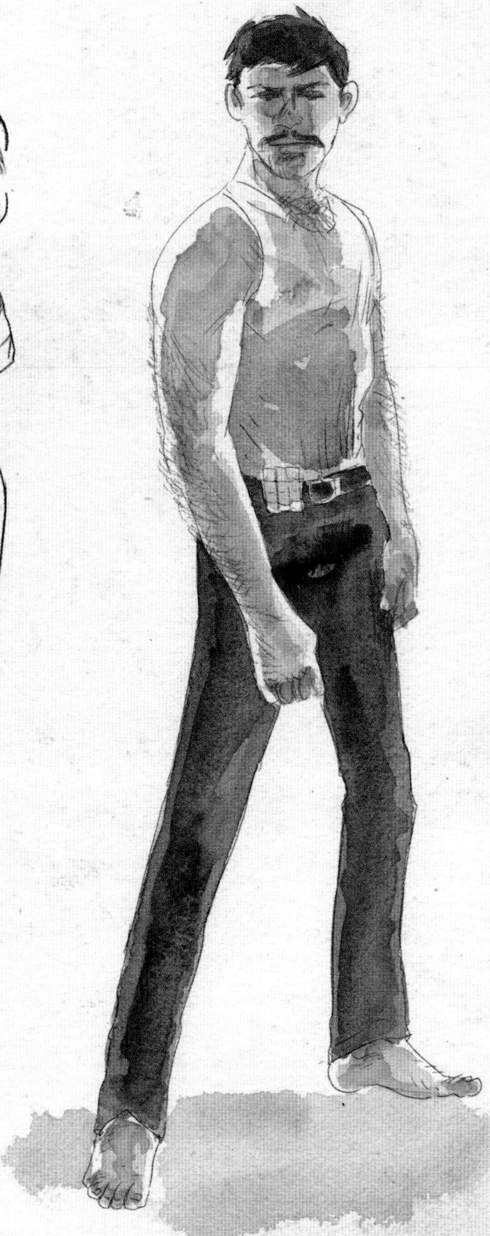

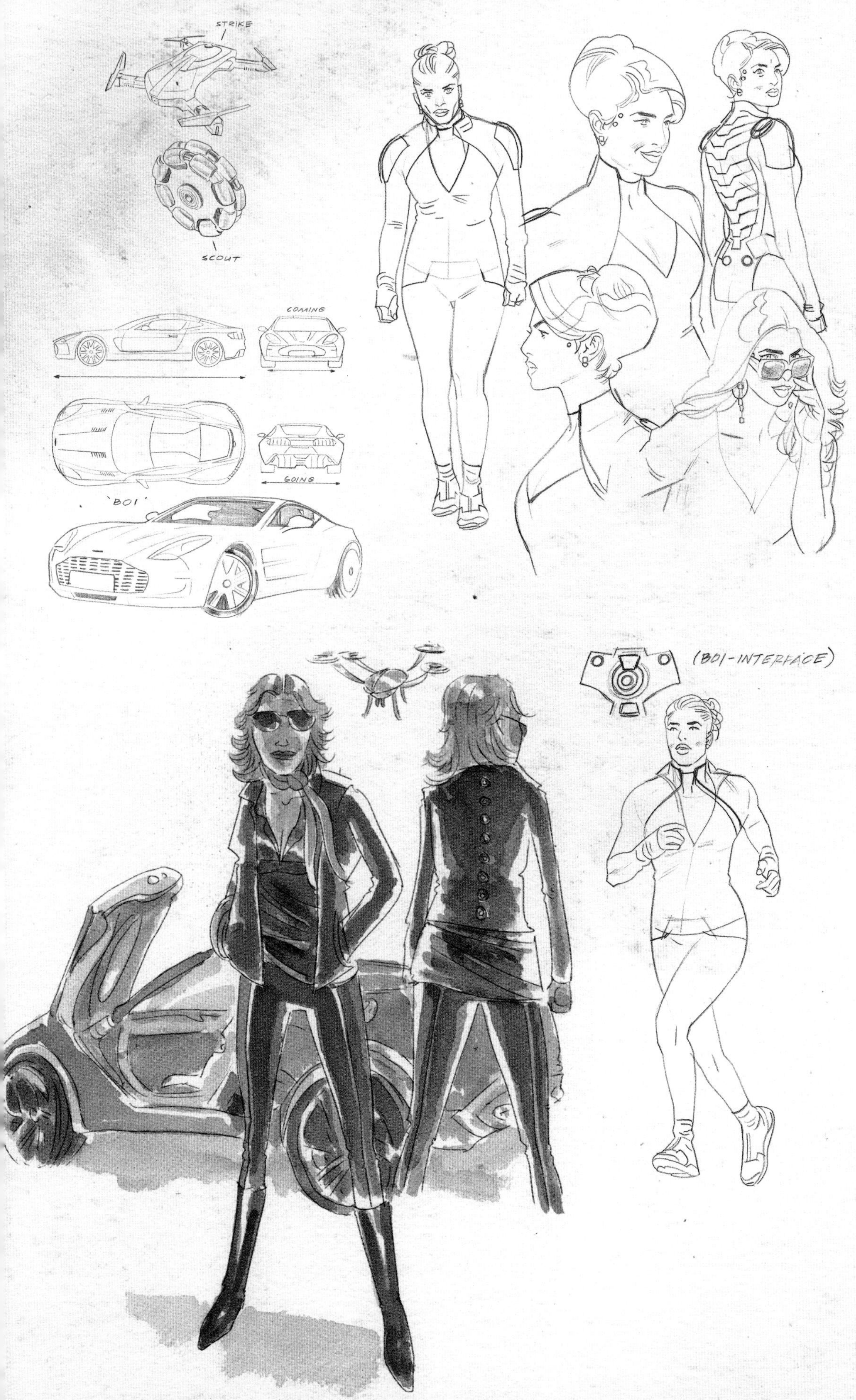
STRIKE
SCOUT
COMING
GOING
'BOI'
(BOI-INTERFACE)

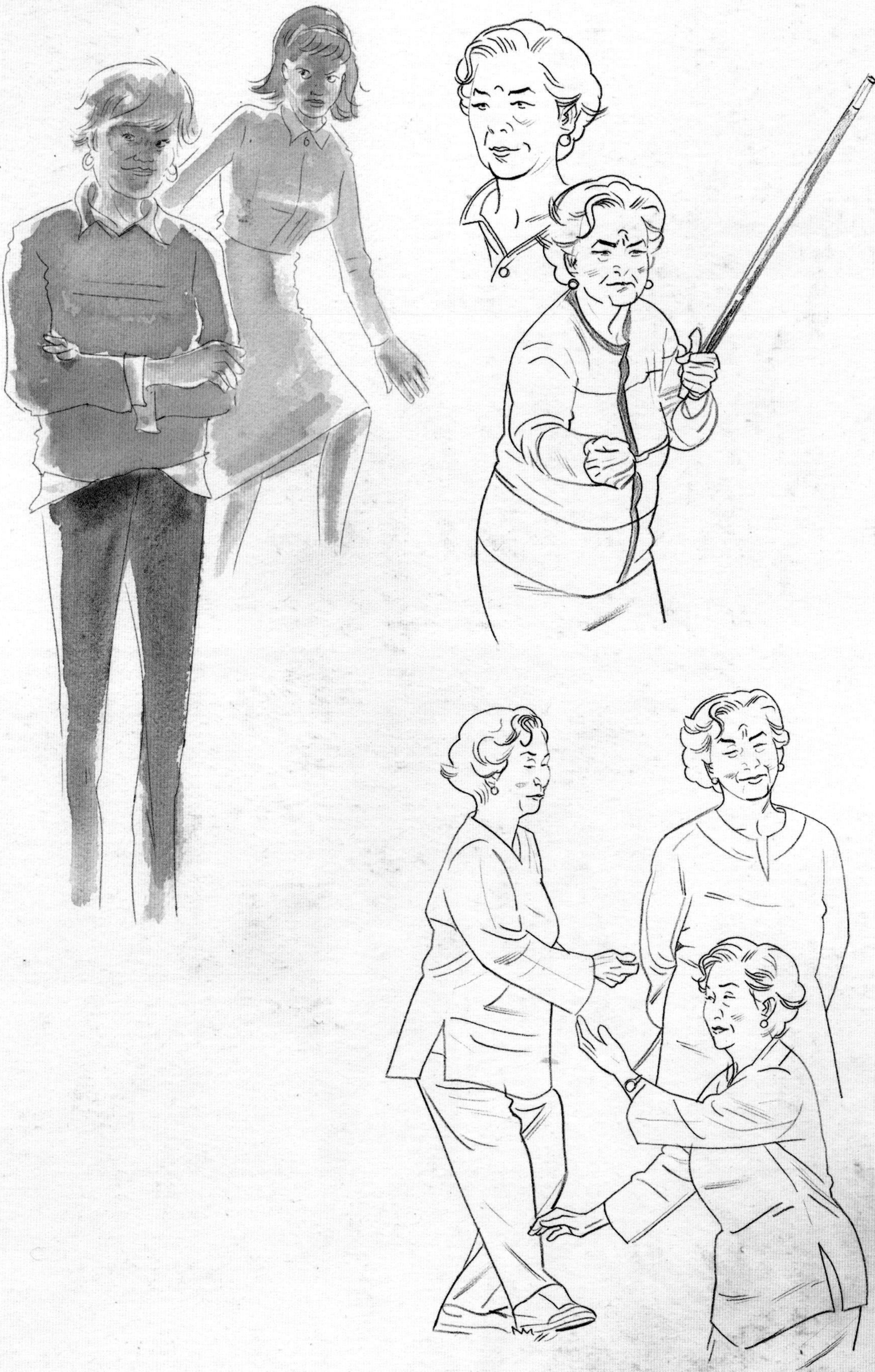

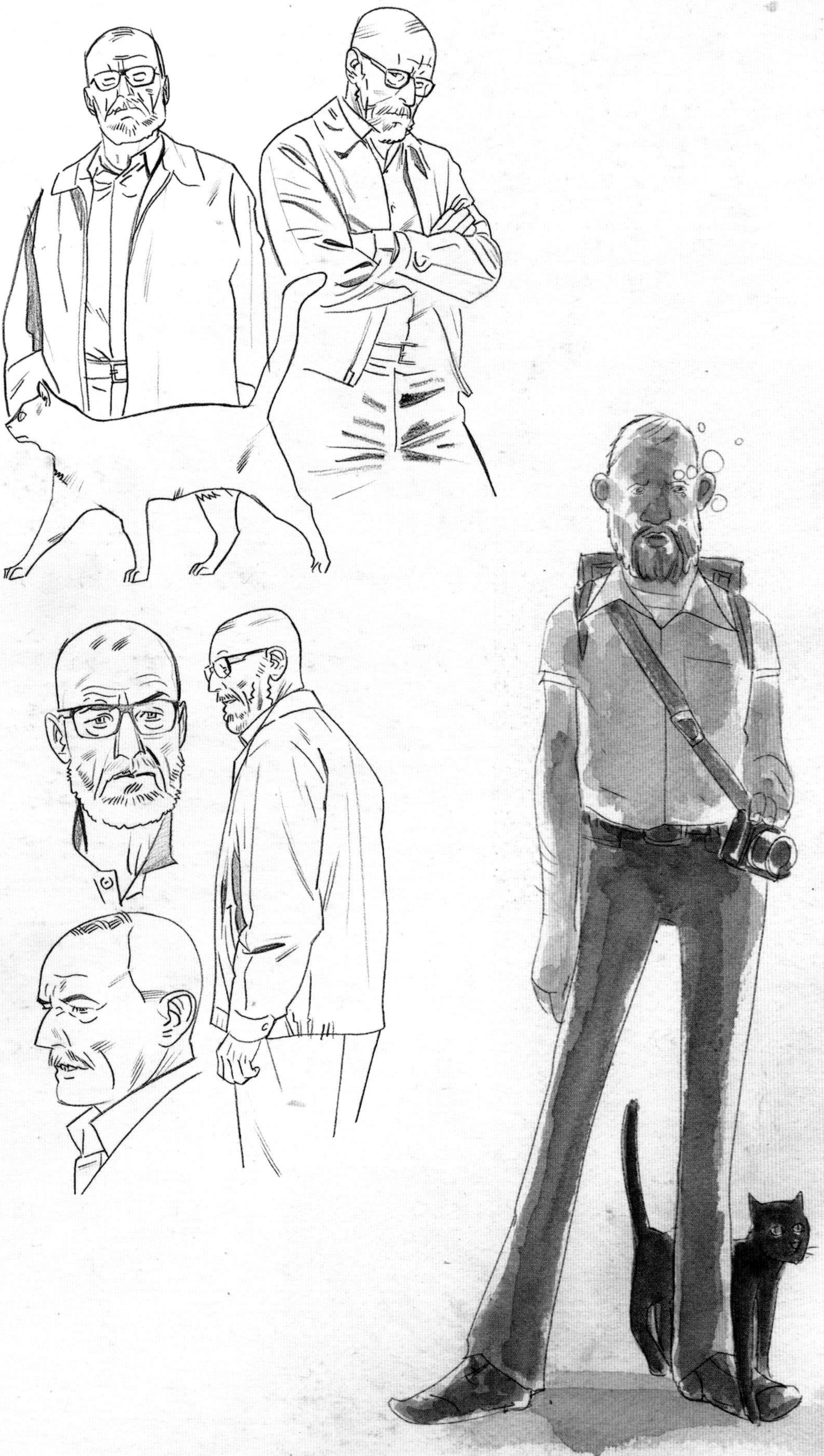

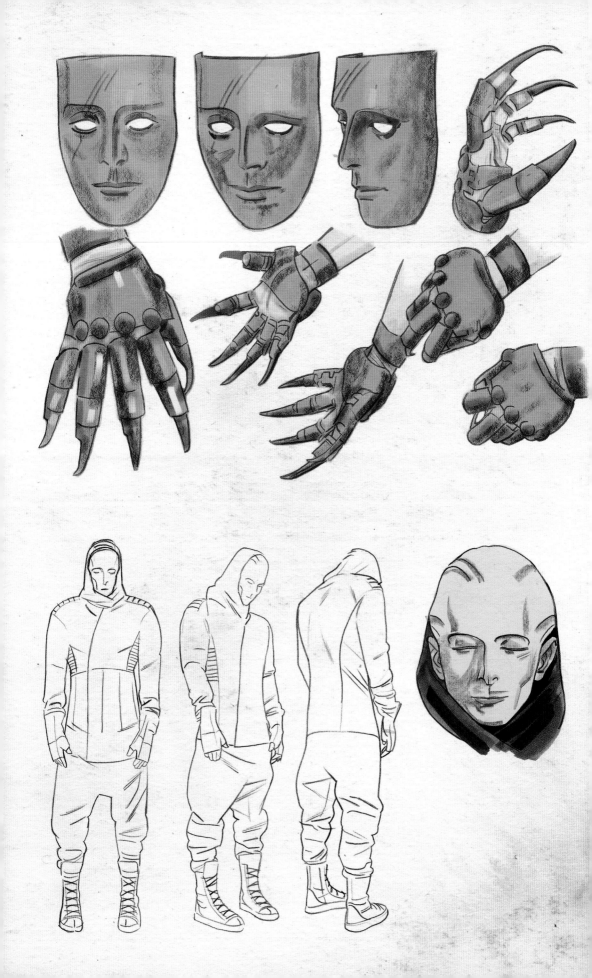

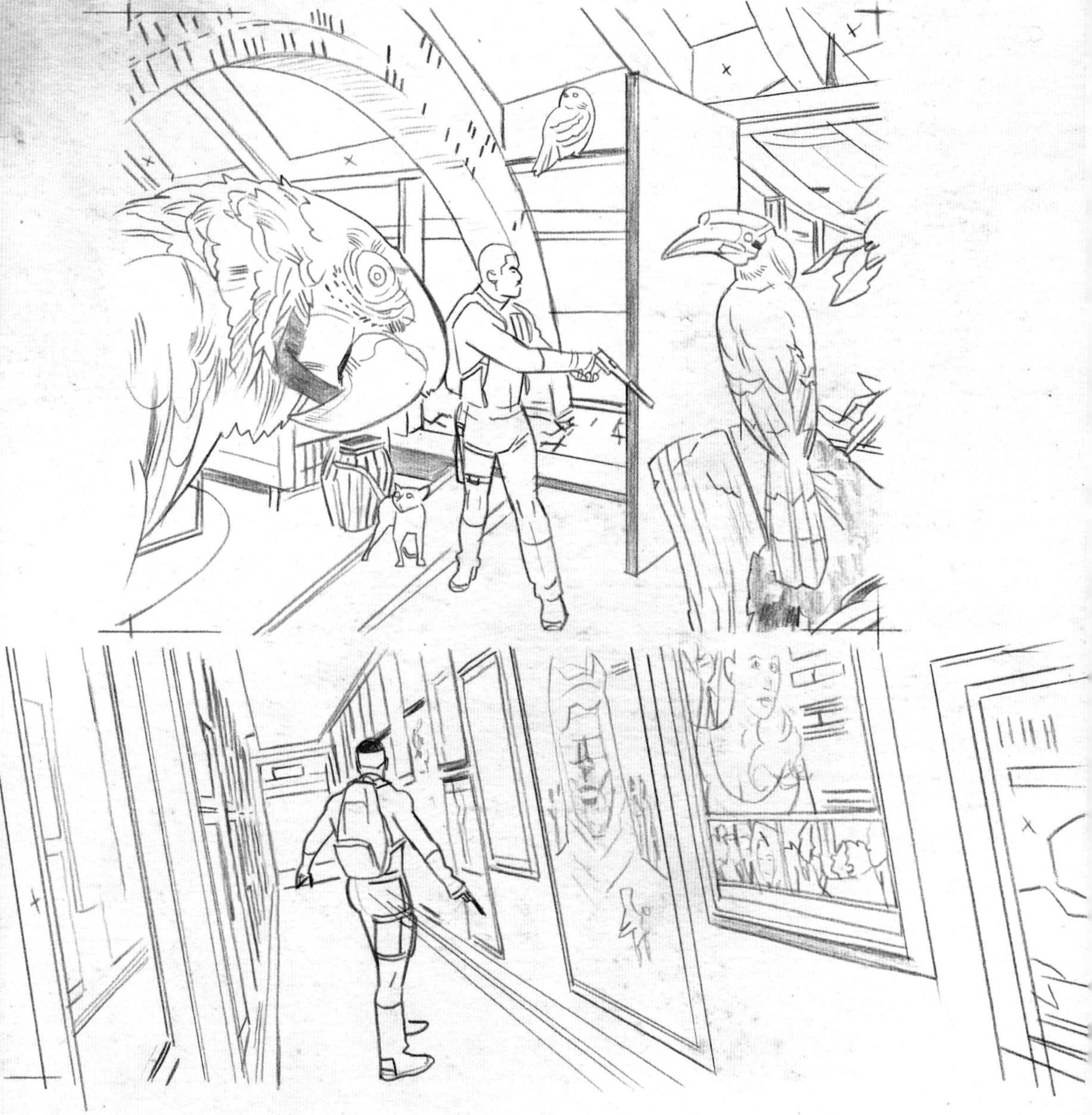

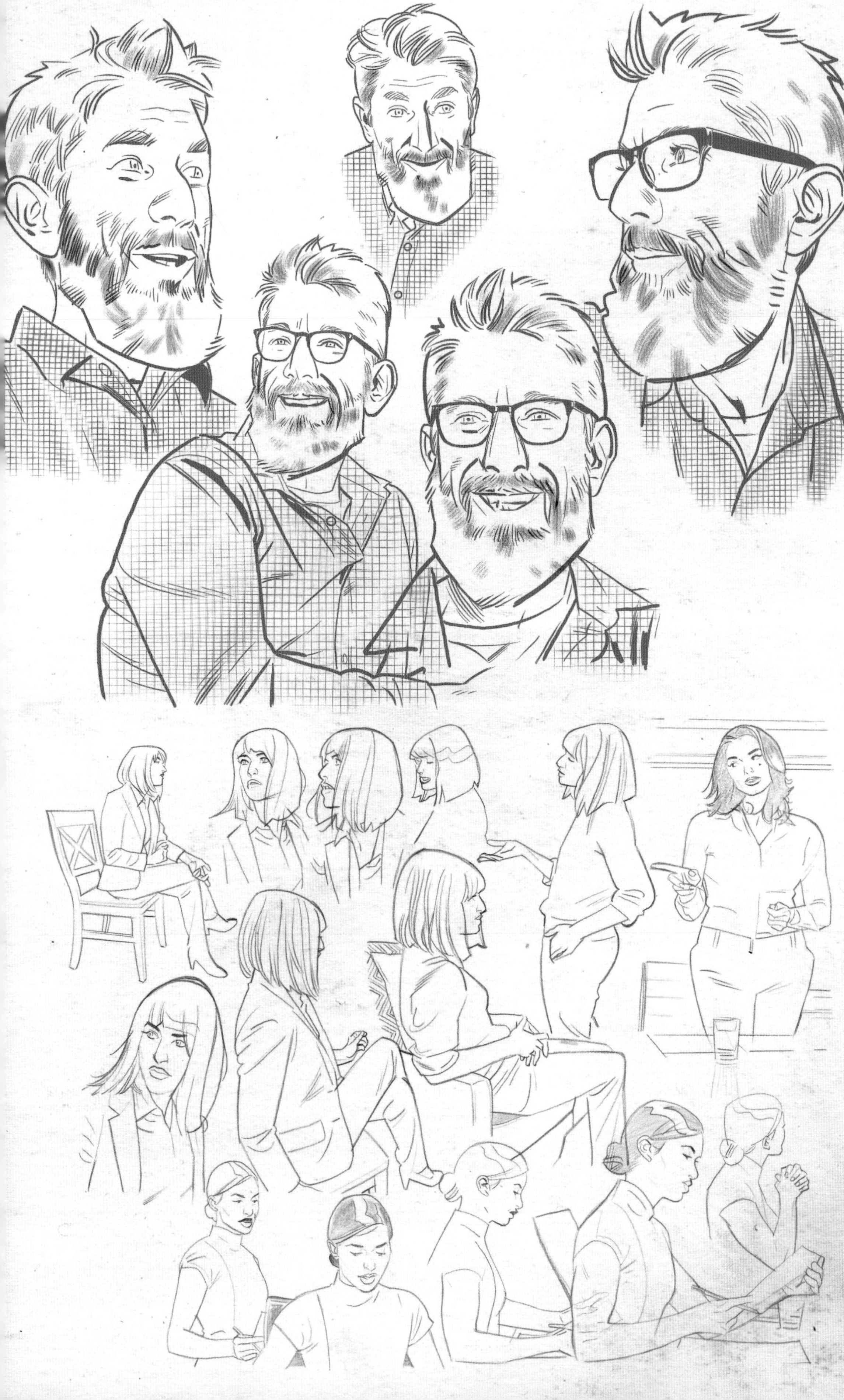